# ETHNICITY, POLITICS, and DEVELOPMENT

This book is volume 2
in the monograph series
of the
David M. Kennedy Center
for International Studies
at
Brigham Young University

# ETHNICITY, POLITICS, and DEVELOPMENT

edited by
DENNIS L THOMPSON
and DOV RONEN

LYNNE RIENNER PUBLISHERS • BOULDER, COLORADO

Published in the United States of America in 1986 by
Lynne Rienner Publishers, Inc.
948 North Street, Boulder, Colorado 80302

**Library of Congress Cataloging-in-Publication Data**

Ethnicity, politics, and development.

  Bibliography: p.
  Includes index.
  1. Ethnic groups—Political activity.  2. Developing
countries—Politics and government.  3. Economic
development.  I. Thompson, Dennis L.  II. Ronen, Dov.
JF1061.E85  1985     323.1'1     86-3228
ISBN 0-931477-57-3 (lib. bdg.)


Distributed outside of North and South America and Japan by
Frances Pinter (Publishers) Ltd, 25 Floral Street,
London WC2E 9DS England   UK ISBN 0-86187-595-8

Printed and bound in the United States of America


The paper used in this publication meets the minimum requirements
of the American National Standard for Permanence of Paper for
Printed Library Materials Z39.48-1984.

# Contents

# Tables and Figures

# Preface

The essays in this book grew out of a roundtable discussion by members of the International Political Science Association Research Committee on Politics and Ethnicity held at the University of Glasgow in Scotland, August 15–17, 1984. The conference theme was "Economic and Social Development in Multi-Ethnic States." From the papers presented there we chose a number that focused specifically on ethnicity and politics in developing states. They are presented here in revised form; their common thread is discussed in Dov Ronen's introductory chapter.

The following papers were also delivered at the conference. Some of them have appeared in print elsewhere, and others are still to be published.

Fred Riggs, University of Hawaii at Manoa (USA) "Empirical Analysis of Data—A Glossary"

Paul Brass, University of Washington (USA) "Ethnic Groups and the State"

James Kellas, University of Glasgow (U. K.) "Scotland: Political Aspects of Ethnicity"

Boguslaw Zaleski, University of Warsaw (Poland) "The Yugoslav Federative System"

Dennis L Thompson, Brigham Young University (USA) "Interface of Culture and Politics in Arid Lands"

J. A. Laponce, The University of British Columbia (Canada) "The French Language in Canada: The Regional Imperative"

John Robbins, University of Adelaide (Australia) "Pressures for Economic and Social-Cultural Development: The Case of Australia"

Jack Brand, University of Strathclyde (U. K.) "Governments' Reactions to Nationalism: Britain, France, Spain, and Belgium Compared"

Elena Florea, The Institute of Political Sciences (Romania) "Economic Development and the Solving of the National Problem: Romania's Experience"

The co-convenors of the conference were James Kellas, Dov Ronen (Harvard University), and Edward Bagramov (Soviet Academy of Sciences). John Trent (University of Ottawa) served as rapporteur.

This was the second roundtable of the Committee; each of those held in the past and planned for the future deals with a specific topic of politics and ethnicity.

Major funding in support of the Committee's activities is provided by the David M. Kennedy Center for International Studies at Brigham Young University. Additional support for this roundtable was provided by the University of Glasgow and the International Research and Exchanges Board. We appreciate their support as well as that of James Kellas, who hosted us in Scotland, Martha Olcott and John Trent, who helped organize the roundtable, Lynne Rienner, who has been so supportive and interested in publishing a portion of our findings, and Spencer Palmer of the David M. Kennedy Center, who has agreed for the Center to help underwrite the publication costs of this volume.

*Dennis L Thompson*
Secretary, IPSA Research Committee
on Politics and Ethnicity

# 1 Ethnicity, Politics, and Development: An Introduction

Dov Ronen

Understanding the relationship between ethnicity, politics, and development is fundamental to the study of change, not only in the so-called developing world but also in the so-called developed one.[1] However, the terms "ethnicity," "politics," and "development" are loosely defined. In previous years the terms "nationality," "national grouping," and "minority" have been used in rough reference to the same phenomenon to which the term "ethnicity" is applied. In the past, "progress" and, now especially, "modernization" have also been used for "development." What seems to have remained constant throughout the years is the concern for understanding the dynamics of change within constituted political entities. It seems that more often than not in the literature, "development" is presented as social change toward conformity with the legal entity and "ethnicity" (or its substitute terms) as an obstacle to that direction of change, which "politics" is to be used to overcome.

As most of the contributors to this volume have indicated, ethnicity is a matter of ascription. However, ethnicity is politicized into the ethnic factor when an ethnic group is in conflict with the political elite over such issues as the use of limited resources or the allocation of benefits—issues that are particularly intense in developing Third World countries, where the greater the stakes involved, the greater the ethnic factor with which the central government must deal.

The phenomenon of ethnicity and state relations is more complicated than this simple outline would indicate, however. As some of the chapters herein suggest, miscalculation of the ethnic factor or strict adherence to current social science theories concerning group identity can have serious consequences. According to John A. A. Ayoade, the Nigerian Constitution of the Second Republic failed due to the ethnic problem, despite provisions for including ethnic groups in the government, because the underlying assumptions concerning ethnicity were wrong. The framers of the Nigerian Constitution had erroneously assumed that: "(1) modernization eliminates ethnicity; (2) ethnicity is only a middle-class pathology; and (3) ethnicity paradoxically is an urban phenomenon or is symptomatic of cosmopolitanism." Likewise, group identity has been misunderstood by both Western and Soviet social scientists. As Martha Brill Olcott points out, Khomeini's Iran has challenged social scientific theory in both camps, for these "theories of nationalism and national consciousness are predicated on the existence of a secular society, and . . . maintain that once introduced secularism should be considered an irreversible phenomenon. . . . Both groups of scholars see religion as a form of false consciousness."

Some scholars have suggested alternative models to current theories regarding ethnicity and group identity. Robert J. Thompson and Joseph J. Rudolph advocate a comparative framework with which to study the relationship between ethnic conflict and public policy. They describe ethnicity as "a type of cultural segmentation that may also intersect class and territorial segmentation," and classify types of ethnicity according to the various intersections between ethnic, cultural, class, and territorial segmentation. The hegemonial exchange model proposed by Donald Rothchild describes ethnicity-state relations in Africa as "a form of state-facilitated coordination in which a somewhat autonomous central state actor and a number of considerably less autonomous ethnoregional interests engage, on the basis of commonly accepted procedural norms, rules, or understandings, in a process of mutual accommodations." The state must cooperate with those ethnic groups who hold the key to the government's continued election to power, whereas the ethnic groups negotiate for scarce resources which the government allocates. Rothchild cautions, however, that "hegemonial exchange is an expedient to be used during a transitional period . . . for collaboration to build more durable institutions and relationships." For, as Naomi Chazan observes, ". . . in situations of drastic economic fluctuation, the forms of ethnicity multiply and the social distance between them increases." Furthermore, "patterns of ethnicity in conditions of economic crisis may themselves be viewed as outcomes of the failure of development strategies and the particular types of state disintegration they set in motion."

Analysis of the relationship between the state and ethnicity often reflects contrasting viewpoints concerning the role of the state in creating or in dissolving an ethnic problem. While some scholars maintain that the state can resolve ethnic conflict, others, such as Michael Banton, argue that the state itself is the cause of ethnic conflict. As Banton states, ethnicity only becomes a political problem when "groups are crystallized in polarization because the political structure renders impossible the kind of bargaining that might otherwise modify the boundary between the communities."

The question that one might wish to raise here is whether a shared conceptual framework can be derived, which might lead to resolution of the confrontation between ethnicity and development. In such a context one must note that the term "ethnicity" has enjoyed a seemingly sudden resurgence in social science literature since the late 1960s and early 1970s. Interestingly enough, the resurgence of the concept, especially in the United States, probably came first in reaction to the emergence of ethnic movements, ethnic nationalism, in the industrialized world. Walker Connor's seminal articles focused on ethnonationalism in the industrialized Western hemisphere.[2] A volume edited by Milton Esman, published in 1977, was entirely devoted to an examination of "the reinvigoration of communal and ethnic solidarities and their emergence in recent years as important political movements in the industrialized and affluent societies of Western Europe and Canada."[3] Cynthia Enloe correctly points out that "ethnic variables seem much more critical in non-Western than in Western political development. [But] . . . this may be merely due to our own historical shortsightedness."[4] Even so, major sections and several cases in her book are devoted to an examination of the Western rather than the non-Western experience.

Ethnicity was of course not a new term, nor was the phenomenon new or unrecognized previously; it was merely labeled differently. Karl Deutsch's seminal work, *Nationalism and Social Communication: An Inquiry into the Foundations of Nationality,* first published in 1953, is devoted in its entirety to the study of ethnicity, although Deutsch uses the terms "nationality," "national diversity," and "differentiation" in lieu of "ethnicity." In the index of Charles Tilly's book on *The Formation of National States in Western Europe,* the term "ethnicity" is not listed. Nevertheless, sections of the book are devoted to, and others are concerned with, the issues of religious and cultural diversity.[5]

What may have contributed to the emergence (or more correctly, the reemergence) of the *term* "ethnicity" is that a familiar *phenomenon,* for which the new term was to be used, emerged in circumstances different from the circumstances that existed prior to the mid-1960s. This familiar phenomenon was a nationalistic awakening or movement. However, from the mid-1960s on, this phenomenon emerged in sovereign, independent, modern, even democratic, states, in "developed" as well as in "developing" countries, where national awakening was not a legitimate phenomenon as it had been prior to World War II when various nationalities were incorporated into the political framework of the modern state. Now there was the unexpected emergence of a phenomenon *within existing, internationally recognized, modern political entities.*

In addition, the phenomenon reemerged at a time when disruption of the functioning of modern states in the West and in the Western "camp" were very much evaluated within the context of East-West relations. Ethnicity was seen as a possible indication that Western ideology, policies, and developmental efforts were failing. As Milton Esman notes:

> Rapid economic growth, the spread of state-provided welfare services, and expanded educational opportunities have undermined the ideologies of class conflict and of religious authority that for three generations had oriented much of the political organization and activity in industrialized countries. Their loss of appeal has been reinforced by erosion of the once powerful ideologies of liberal individualism and state-associated nationalism, which together had illegitimized ethnic particularism and relegated it to the status of backwardness and even subversiveness. . . . This development represents not the end of ideology . . . but the emergence of a competing ideology.[6]

Ethnicity (ethnic groups or ethnic nationalism) tended to be viewed as a destabilizing, potentially revolutionary force that threatened to disintegrate states or at least to disrupt their smooth functioning. Ethnicity appeared no longer as a term for a folkloric, or a "primordial" phenomenon,[7] the manifestation of local tribal feelings, but as a term applied to a political force with which to be reckoned.

Prior to World War II, a process of national integration and consolidation was believed to have taken place in Western Europe (and today is believed to have occurred later in the non-Western world), a process described by theories of modernization, nation-building, and development. In these models the central terms were "mobilization," "political party formation," and "nationalities." Ethnicity was to be seen as a disruptive form of national awakening. Even more important, ethnicity appeared now to rival the nation, which was viewed as the legitimate entity. It may be instructive to quote from a prominent student of nationalism who writes:

> The core nationalist *doctrine* . . . is constructed from a few far-reaching propositions: 1. Humanity is naturally divided into nations; 2. Each nation has its peculiar character; 3. The source of all political power is the nation, the whole collectivity; 4. For freedom and self-realization, men must identify with a nation; 5. Nations can only be fulfilled in their own states; 6. Loyalty to the nation-state overrides other loyalties; 7. The primary condition of global freedom and harmony is the strengthening of the nation-state.[8]

In the rivalry between ethnicity and nation, the latter is posited by scholars and political actors to be the legitimate entity, if for no other reason than because the nation fulfills the sovereign state. Ethnicity, ethnic groups, ethnic loyalties, ethnic regions, and/or ethnic nationalisms compete, as it were, with a full-scale, recognized actor in the international scene; ethnicity, in whatever form, competes with an entity, the nation-state, which conceptually is an integral part of modernity. According to such a scheme, ethnicity emerges due to the failure of national integration; ethnicity appears as a disintegrative factor, as an obstacle to be overcome. Such a negative casting of ethnicity is reinforced by our perception of development and the relationship of ethnicity to it.

Development, political as well as economic, became a specific subject of study and an object of public policy after World War II. But again, as with ethnicity, the phenomenon later titled "development" existed long before the post–World War II period. The notion of development may be anchored, at least conceptually, in the notion of progress, which in turn was believed since the Enlightenment to be a natural attribute of man. Charles Tilly remarks: "The idea of social development following a standard path and springing from the very nature of societies (as Robert Nisbet has pointed out) pervaded the western social sciences from their nineteenth-century origins, and remained in their tissue into the twentieth century. Marx, Weber, and Durkheim were all developmentalists of sorts."[9]

It might be recalled, however, that the nineteenth-century and early twentieth-century process of development in Europe (where many, if not all, of the elements identified in the process of development were found, such as role differentiation, political party formation, social transformation, participation, legitimation of a system, and the like) also included the breaking up of political entities, from which new political entities emerged. The national awakening in mid-nineteenth-century Europe might be seen as the forerunner of the consolidation of Germany and of Italy. But similar national awakenings also led to the breakup of the Hapsburg Empire into many of its components. In Asia, too, a process of change (why not call it development?) that had led to the independence of India also led to the emergence of Pakistan and later of Bangladesh, each inhabited by religious and linguistic minorities, nationalities, or ethnicities. In the process of development born during decolonization, is the emergence of Pakistan and Bangladesh a negative change? The wider questions that may be posed here are these: In the relationship between ethnicity and development, is ethnicity necessarily an obstacle or a hindrance to be overcome by the politics of assimilation, integration, or incorporation into an existing body politic? Does ethnicity—not only as a label for national awakening but as an activated group identity in the midst of economic bargaining relations within the state—need to be neutralized as a legitimate body or to be reduced to its folkloric skeleton? Is ethnic identity disintegrative?

As we noted above, ethnicity emerged in Europe in the mid-1960s and was promptly studied and noted by some scholars as a disruptive force. However, if we look at the mid-1960s in the context of the post–World War II period, we might venture to say that it was not so much that disintegrative forces set in with the emergence of ethnicity and ethnic nationalism in the mid-1960s, but rather that the integrative forces that commenced after the war had diminished by that time. During the war, organized life was disrupted; populations scattered; refugees abounded; and towns and factories were destroyed. The Coal and Steel Community, the European Common Market, and the Marshall Plan in Western Europe not only contributed to the material build-up of Western Europe, but also enhanced national integration and consolidation. At the time, it was hoped that this would lead to an all-European integration. By the mid-1960s, the Marshall Plan ended with positive results; and as mass poverty was prevented, the dynamics of national and supranational integration, which were supposed to have been promoted by the E. E. C., slowed down. The Scots, Bretons, Flamands, and other European (and Canadian) nationalities became salient again. From the point of view of the state, government, and leaders, as well as from the point of view of social scientists concerned with the post–World War II process, ethnicity appeared to be a disintegrative force and an obstacle to the national unity that all favored as a goal of development. But the reemergence and the reassertion of ethnicity in the mid-1960s may also be seen as a reaffirmation of a long-existing ethnic identity *in* the process of positive development—as an *integral part* of development where the state (or at least certain aspects of it), not ethnicity, is an obstacle to development.

Since social mobility reduced the salience of a rigid class identity in Europe (beyond the traditional, enshrined class distinctions), and since modern class distinctions were not yet institutionalized in the Third World (especially not in sub-Saharan Africa), the always available ethnic identity presented itself as a convenient rallying point to be utilized as a political instrument for developmental gains. Ethnic identity by the mid-1960s had become an organizational form, a weapon, a tool, and/or a means for the attainment of goals, just as integrative national identity often was in the nineteenth and at the beginning of the twentieth centuries. Ethnicity therefore has appeared as a political phenomenon, which has been no more disintegrative than has political party formation.

A comparison between the emergence of ethnicity in Europe and in the Third World might show that, commonly, prospects for social mobility as well as for economic advancement by political means encourage ethnicity. Numerous studies of European ethnicity have shown that it is not poverty but prospects for advancement that enhance the utilization of ethnic identity. The case in the "developing world" has been similar.

Under colonial rule ethnicity was the concern of colonial rulers and of anthropologists. In the fight for the termination of colonial rule, ethnic identity was blurred behind or under the nationalist mantle in the colonized world. In the eyes of observers, India's "religious fanatics," not ethnic groups, caused trouble and threatened India's pending national unity. At the same time in Africa the dominant slogan in the mouths of English-speaking Africans was Pan-Africanism; in the French-speaking colonies, *negritude*. Tribalism was considered to be a remnant of the past; postindependence development called for national integration.

Nevertheless the fact remained that most of the newly independent states inherited their colonial boundaries, which enclosed what later came to be called subnational entities. This meant that many of these states often included within their boundaries a wide variety of peoples, with different cultural traditions and memories of hostile relations with other groups included within the same national boundaries. It might be useful to remember that in the two or more decades that followed independence, governments of these independent states were to create a national oneness. In order to do this, they had to provide a replacement for the ethnic oneness that existed within the various groups that composed the populations of the new states. Let us also recall that African and Asian countries became independent in the immediate post–World War II period, when ethnicity was not yet recognized as existing in Europe either. Thus the "developing" countries followed the model that then existed in Europe. Even when the Biafra secession threatened in 1967, it was referred to as a "secession attempt" that led to a "civil war," not (at least, not commonly) as "ethnic nationalism."

In the Third World, as in Europe, national integration has not failed, but the impact of the nationalist integration of the decolonization period (roughly paralleling postwar efforts to build up Europe) has slowed down and weakened. Long-existing ethnic identities could be put on the back burner for an indefinite period; but when political struggles started, the ethnic identity could be enlisted for political purposes.

One may pose an intriguing question. How is ethnicity fundamentally different from class consciousness, which Marx argues emerges in certain conditions and disappears in others? Does ethnicity, ethnic loyalty, and/or ethnic group identity differ from class consciousness because the former pertains to some "primordial" factors, while class identity does not? Was Shi'i Islam bound to emerge as a political force in Iran, or did it emerge in and because of certain conditions?

There are no easy answers to these questions. But let us consider that humanity is composed of some four-and-one-half billion human beings. It may be indisputably true that human beings are social animals and hence must interact with each other; it is perhaps equally indisputable that this social requirement may be satisfied by interaction with any amalgamation of human beings. There is a propensity to interact with human beings who speak the same language, share common religion and historic memories, and so forth—all of which are commonly considered to be the attributes of ethnicity. Such groups provide certain specifics needed in the circumstances of development, such as a sense of security, a need for familiarity, a sense of continuity, which the nation *intends* to provide within the framework of the state if and as development proceeds. If that is so, then ethnic-group identity is not a special identity. Security, continuity, and familiarity are special propensities or needs that the ethnic group provides in given conditions.

The implications of such conclusions may be far-reaching in practice. It may mean that in the process of development, ethnic identity is to be *encouraged* as an identity that provides, at least temporarily, the societal needs that eventually the state or the nation is to provide. Rather than viewing ethnicity as an obstacle, we might see it as a potentially useful factor in the process of development. If ethnicity is thus not disintegrative, or need not necessarily be seen as such, the question is how to incorporate it into a politically viable unit.

Ethnicity may be rendered a useful element in some cases by mere administrative decentralization and in some other cases by structural reorganization into a federal system where a modicum of political sovereignty is provided. Let us note that one of the more developed countries in the world, the one that often stands as a model to emulate, is Switzerland, which is a confederal system.

Crawford Young writes:

> The widespread conviction that triumphant anticolonial nationalism would eclipse cultural pluralism derived powerful reinforcement from the dominant paradigm of assimilation in the industrial world. Theories of political development and modernization which appeared in the 1950s virtually all rested on the premises, if only implicit, that the universe of industrial nation-states was a model of the future of the underdeveloped world. At that moment, observable reality in the northern hemisphere seemed to validate the integrative hypothesis.[10]

By the 1970s, the observable reality had changed. As Pierre van den Berghe put it in 1976, "Now everybody (or nearly so) is on an ethnic kick."[11]

The difficulty in studying the issues of ethnicity and of development is that both concepts are slippery. The definitions and boundaries of ethnicity are fluid,[12] and development is not a process that is easily given to objective study. Samuel Huntington remarked bemusingly some time ago: "The principle function that political development has in fact performed for political scientists is neither to aggregate nor to distinguish, but rather to legitimate. It has served as a way for political scientists to say, in effect: 'Hey, here are some things I consider valuable and desirable goals and important subjects of study.' "[13]

Development is a process of change, or at least pertains to change. It is not, or at least should not be held to be, synonymous with modernization. Hence, development is not a process of change toward a specific goal of modernity. Development, as Enloe remarks, "refers to change that takes place in stages."[14] In effect, development is a change toward goals at which government, leaders, or the state aims. In other words, development is a change that is seen as desirable by the state, and as such is a demand imposed on a given population. In the context of ethnicity and development, the demand may not necessarily be for assimilation or for integration, but nevertheless represents a direction of change posed by the state.

Crawford Young, after a superb and exhaustive analysis of ethnic pluralism, arrives at the conclusion that "there is simply no escape from the existing state system, as the political frame within which mankind must seek a better life. . . . The sensitive application of wisdom accumulated in the observation of the politics of cultural pluralism is not beyond the reach of statesmanship. There is, of course, no other choice."[15] Perhaps there is no choice. But recent history shows that "sensitive application of wisdom" and "statesmanship" are oftentimes rare commodities. Thus if there is no alternative to the state, there might be no alternative to ethnic conflicts or to resulting repression and bloodshed. Such a state of affairs may *oblige* us to focus on the state and to examine possibilities of various internal rearrangements within the state, especially in the Third World. Cynthia Enloe perceptively points out the dilemma: "The problem nagging at multi-ethnic, underdeveloped nations is this: underdevelopment in the modern era creates a need for centralized authority to offset communal fragmentation; yet centralization effective enough to control disintegrative forces requires resources beyond the reach of underdeveloped systems."[16] The options available in addition to the usually inherited politically centralized unitary system are numerous, and range from mere administrative decentralization to a full-fledged federal system. In between these two extremes there lie possibilities of regional juridical, cultural, or political autonomy, of proportional representation, of a rotating presidential system, of consociational arrangement, of a cantonal system, and the like. All, however, require a weakening of the central political power—in the recently dominant vocabulary of Africanists, the legitimation of the "soft state." Whether or not such legitimation is a realistic proposition should be the subject of further research. In any case, the possibility is that it is not so much ethnicity that poses the greatest challenge to development, but politics itself.

## NOTES

1. Among the many seminal works see Crawford Young, *The Politics of Cultural Pluralism* (Madison: University of Wisconsin Press, 1976); Cynthia Enloe, *Ethnic Conflict and Political Development* (Little, Brown and Co., 1973); Milton J. Esman, ed., *Ethnic Conflict in the Western World* (Ithaca, N. Y.: Cornell, 1977); Donald Rothchild and Victor A. Olorunsola, eds., *State Versus Ethnic Claims: African Policy Dilemmas* (Boulder, Colo.: Westview Press, 1983); Michael Hechter, *Internal Colonialism: The Celtic Fringe in British National Development, 1536–1966* (London: Routledge and Kegan Paul, 1975); W. H. Morris-Jones, ed., *The Politics of Separatism,* Institute of Commonwealth Studies, Collected Seminar Papers, no. 19 (London: University of London, 1976); Milton M. da Silva, "Modernization and Ethnic Conflict: The Case of the Basques," *Comparative Politics* 7, no. 2 (January 1975); Paul R. Brass and Pierre L. van den Berghe, "Ethnicity and Nationalism in World Perspective," *Ethnicity* 3 (1976); Michael Hechter and Margaret Levi, "The Comparative Analysis of Ethnoregional Movements," *Ethnic and Racial Studies* 2, no. 3 (July 1979); Anthony Birch, "Minority Nationalist Movements and Theories of Political Integration," *World Politics* 30, no. 3 (April 1978); and Dov Ronen, *The Quest for Self-Determination* (New Haven: Yale University, 1979).

2. Walker Connor, "Nation-Building or Nation-Destroying?" *World Politics* 24, no. 3 (April 1972); Walker Connor, "The Politics of Ethnonationalism," *Journal of International Affairs* 27, no. 1 (1973); see also the influential article by Arend Lijphart, "Consociational Democracy," *World Politics* 21 (January 1969).

3. Esman, *Ethnic Conflict,* p. 11.

4. Enloe, *Ethnic Conflict,* p. 12.

5. Charles Tilly, ed., *The Formation of Nation States in Western Europe* (Princeton, 1975); see especially pp. 77ff.

6. Esman, *Ethnic Conflict,* pp. 11–12.

7. Clifford Geertz, "The Integrative Revolution: Primordial Sentiments and Civil Politics in the New States," in Clifford Geertz, ed., *Old Societies and New States: The Quest for Modernity in Asia and Africa* (New York: The Free Press, 1963), p. 157.

8. Anthony D. Smith, *Theories of Nationalism* (Harper Torchbook, 1971), pp. 20–21.

9. Charles Tilly, "Western State-Making and Theories of Political Transformation," in Charles Tilly, ed., *Formation,* pp. 603–604. It should be noted, however, that Nisbet does not see the roots of the idea of progress in the Enlightenment period, but as going back to ancient Greece. See Robert Nisbet, *The Idea of Progress* (New York: Basic Books); for a contrary and more convincing view see J. B. Burry, *The Idea of Progress* (New York: Dover Publications, Inc., 1955; Macmillan, 1932).

10. C. Young, *Politics,* p. 7.

11. Pierre van den Berghe, "Ethnic Pluralism in Industrial Societies: A Special Case?" *Ethnicity* 3 (1976), p. 242.

12. C. Young, *Politics,* p. 11.

13. Samuel P. Huntington, "The Change to Change: Modernization, Development, and Politics," *Comparative Politics* 3, no. 3 (April 1971), p. 304; quoted in Enloe, *Ethnic Conflict,* p. 9.

14. Enloe, *Ethnic Conflict,* p. 9.

15. C. Young, *Politics,* pp. 527–528.

16. Enloe, *Ethnic Conflict,* p. 92.

# 2 Ethnic Bargaining

### Michael Banton

Ethnic groups do not persist because of some property of inertia in the social system or as a product of genetic processes favoring ethnic solidarity. Individuals who sometimes identify themselves ethnically, at other times identify themselves in terms of nationality, class, religion, occupation, and so on. If ethnic alignments persist, it is because ethnic divisions are maintained by the efforts of their members as part of a pattern of social interaction. As circumstances change, some minority identifications wither away while old ones are revived or new ones appear. Old coalitions break up and new ones are negotiated. Any view of ethnic politics is severely impaired if it cannot allow for the ways in which the size and character of ethnic minorities depend upon the transactions between them and the majority. In the study of these transactions a prominent place must be given to processes of bargaining.

## GLAZER'S LAW

To try to cast a new light upon these processes, I shall examine what I call Glazer's law. This states that a small group for which one issue is everything will overcome a large group for which the issue is only one among many. My wording goes beyond Nathan Glazer's own claims, for in the original text the passage states that a small group *may* overcome a large one, not that it *will*. It appears in the course of a discussion of the constraints upon the exercise of presidential power.[1] My contention is that in making this statement Glazer is relying upon a body of theory that he fails to make explicit; he may indeed be unaware of the ways in which the parts can make a whole.

Glazer writes of "a small group for which one issue is everything." The first task must be to explain the recruitment and organization of such a group. How is it that the members regard one issue as paramount? Cannot the majority deploy power to defeat such maneuvers? The search for answers

11

to this kind of question, and for an understanding of the conditions under which Glazer's law applies, leads into the theory of collective behavior.

In *The Logic of Collective Action,* Mancur Olson explained why rational self-interested individuals will not necessarily combine to advance their common interests. They will prefer to take a free ride, benefiting from the organizations established as a result of the altruism of others. Yet manufacturers do cooperate to fix prices, restrict production, and organize pressure groups. Trade unions often acquire great power, and class-based political parties are scarcely unusual. Olson's view of collective action as a by-product of organization to provide private benefit does not carry conviction as a sufficient explanation of organized activity. He himself acknowledges the ability of people to appreciate that if everyone tries to take a free ride no one gets a ride at all, and that therefore they may vote for a closed shop.[2] This illustrates the utility of the distinction between act-utilitarianism, in which individuals act so as to maximize their utility, and rule-utilitarianism, in which they formulate rules which, when enforced, enable them collectively to maximize their utility. A closed-shop rule prevents free-riding. Rule-utilitarianism resolves what Olson mistook for a paradox.[3] It opens a door to the study of collective behavior as comprehending both conscious goal-oriented conduct and habitual or unreflective activity.

Any set of rules creates captives. The free-rider has his complement in the person who is an unwilling rider, the captive traveler. This is the person who conforms to the behavior expected by fellow members of his group, even though he believes it contrary to his, and perhaps the group's, long-term interest. Politicians are frequently captives of their parties' decisions. They may believe some of these to be quite wrong, but they are restrained from rebelling because other features of the party program are more important to them. Potential rebels are often obliged by other members to profess their loyalty to the whole program in view of the importance of organizational unity. Politicians usually understand the constraints to which they are subject as party representatives, but electors are often less aware of the bonds by which they are bound. The person who does not realize that he is a captive is more securely captured than one who can identify his bonds. This is of great importance to the study of ethnic relations. Michael Hechter and his associates have formulated a theory of ethnic collective action working from the same standpoint as that which underlies my own recent work. In Hechter's view the most striking fact about any kind of collective action is its relative rarity, and the reasons he offers are Olson's.[4] They both presuppose act-utilitarianism and focus on conscious behavior. I am trying to utilize rule-utilitarianism and to comprehend behavior that is not necessarily consciously goal-oriented. My contention is that there is less ethnic collective action because there is so much ethnic collective behavior. Public good may in some circumstances be produced more effectively by the enforcement of rules which ethnic group members observe unconsciously.

## RATIONAL CHOICE THEORY

The theory that I have advanced can be expressed in five propositions. It presupposes (a) that individuals act so as to obtain maximum net advantage; and (b) that actions at one moment of time influence and restrict the alternatives between which individuals will have to choose on subsequent occasions. The theory then holds that

1. Individuals utilize physical and cultural differences in order to create groups and categories by the processes of inclusion and exclusion.
2. Ethnic groups result from inclusive and racial categories from exclusive processes.
3. When groups interact, processes of change affect their boundaries in ways determined by the form and intensity of competition; and, in particular, when people compete as individuals this tends to dissolve the boundaries that define the groups, whereas when they compete as groups this reinforces those boundaries.[5]

Since it is a theory of racial and ethnic relations it has to be a theory of the boundaries between groups, because unless the groups are bounded there cannot be relations between them. If it is to be applied to other problems, like racial discrimination in housing and employment, then, as I have shown, more particular propositions can be added to it.

The theory does not attempt to account for the differential resources available to particular groups at particular times; that I see as something to be considered from an historical standpoint. Nor does it comprehend the processes by which subjective preferences and evaluations of costs and benefits develop; one theory cannot do everything and it is best to proceed step by step. The theory deals with aggregate behavior; just as a retailer may know that if he spends so much on advertising he may expect to sell so many more of his products to particular categories of consumers, so he will not know whether, within such a category, it will be Mr. Brown or Mr. Smith who makes a purchase (that, too, has to be answered with the help of a different kind of theory). Finally, I acknowledge that there is often an element of tautology in explanations of the kind I am employing but insist that this does not mean that they can therefore be dismissed. Critics should seek to furnish better explanations.

I have called it a rational choice theory since it clearly belongs with other theories so designated, but this is a name and not the substance. The name causes confusion because the recent discussion of rationality has been so much concerned with whether particular actions are to be considered rational ways of relating means to ends that can only be inferred. This neglects the social dimension. It has been remarked many times that the more complex an organization, the stronger is the call for consistency between its constituent parts, though while old inconsistencies are steadily reduced new ones keep opening up, so that no organization is ever completely rational. This is the social process of rationalization that so impressed Max Weber. So seen, rationality is a characteristic both of individual conduct and of social organization. Individual decisions have to be related to social rules that have the effect of helping people collectively to maximize their utility. These rule-governed features of behavior are most easily detected by studying aggregate behavior.

Can existing practices in polyethnic states serve as viable models for social and economic development in the developing world? My answer is that the course of political development is one which extends the range of that which can be negotiated, increases the consistency of practice, and integrates ethnic politics with wider political relations. At some stages in this sequence ethnic affiliation is regarded as qualitatively distinct and gives rise to what we call ethnic conflict, but the long-term pressure is to increase its commensurability with other kinds of social differentiation. Any attempt to transfer lessons about ethnic policies from one kind of state to another kind must allow for the extent to which the systems permit ethnic bargaining and the parties are willing to engage in it. For the present purposes, three features of political organization are of central importance: (1) a constituency of supporters or potential supporters; (2) a set of shared priorities; (3) means for ensuring the commitment of supporters to these priorities. The three features will be considered in turn.

A sense of shared ethnicity creates a potential constituency. Ethnicity is a variety of that only partly understood species we call nationalism. This word is applied to many different kinds of organization and sentiment, but none of them can be understood without attending to the values round which relations are built. Nationalist movements share characteristics with revitalization movements, but since they do not fit within the original definition of the latter I prefer to use the broader expression "revaluation movements." The leaders of such movements seek to make their fellow constituents conscious of a shared attribute, one that is contingently associated with shared interests, and they persuade them that this attribute is more important than they had been inclined to acknowledge; they persuade them to put it higher in their list of preferences. The historical conditions in which this is possible have been illuminated by Ernest Gellner and Benedict Anderson. Like Elie Kedourie, Anderson stresses the part played by a small minority; he quotes a historian of Hungary as saying that "a nation is born when a few people decide that it should be."[6] But the exhortation and altruistic activity of those few people is not necessarily sufficient. Gellner has concluded that there is "one effective nationalism for every possible ten cases."[7] Similar considerations must apply to ethnic constituencies.

Ethnic differences do not cause conflicts, nor do two individuals come into conflict with one another simply because they differentiate themselves

ethnically. Conflict groups have to be communities, that is, groups differenti-
ated on several dimensions and with a sense of identification. Ethnicity is one
mode of identification. Group organization implies a set of priorities and sets
of this kind express what is distinctive about the groups. One place to study
them is in the law courts, for social development is marked by a process of
progressive rationalization as the law is used to define priorities for ever
more fields of activity. In the organization of political parties, electoral mani-
festos and conference decisions lay down priorities, while the leaders seek to
preserve some flexibility permitting them to modify their strategies to suit
prevailing circumstances. Since they want to appeal to as many supporters as
possible, they need this flexibility to attract people who share some of the
same priorities but dissent on particulars. These principles are most easily
observed with respect to collective action, but they are likely to apply just as
much with regard to collective behavior.

The decision of the members of a group to vote for a closed shop is a
form of commitment restricting their future freedom.[8] Such a rule, once
adopted, may be enforced legally or by more informal sanctions, including
exclusion from membership. Commitment will be the greater when there is
no alternative group with which a dissenter can identify. When communities
are locked in conflict, as in South Africa, Northern Ireland, or in the deep
south of the United States earlier in this century, and when the attributes used
as markers of group assignment are not easily changed, then the group is
enclosed by a hard boundary. Commitment has nevertheless to be maintained
by enforcement procedures which can entail heavy costs. As Frank Tannenbaum observed:

> Wherever we had slavery, we have a slave society, not merely for the blacks,
> but for the whites, not merely for the law, but for the family, not merely for
> the labor system, but for the culture—the total culture. Nothing
> escaped. . . .[9]

In such circumstances the parties see themselves as locked into a zero-sum
game; a gain by one side can only be at the expense of the other. The
observer may believe that the costs of enforcement exceed any benefits they
bring, and that if the boundary were removed the welfare of the total society
would increase. If this were the case, and the parties would agree to a change
in the rules, they might be able to play it as a positive-sum game. It is equally
possible however, and Lebanon might be seen as a case in point, for one of
the parties unilaterally to force a change in the rules that is not generally
accepted (e.g., to say "we will now compete by using guns and ammunition
donated by another state") and for the outcome to be a negative-sum game.

Effective enforcement procedures in situations of ethnic confrontation
oblige members of ethnic groups to play the ethnic game all the time and
prevent them from going off and starting their own individual games in which
they bargain with others according to the value which they individually place

upon ethnic attributes. Enforcement is likely to be stricter when the opportunities for individualistic strategies are greater. Enforcement will also be strict when a group's bargaining power rests upon an earlier constitutional settlement that has come under pressure for change, as has been the case for the province of Quebec within the Canadian system and for the Unionists in Northern Ireland since 1922. The constitution lays down the rules which govern ethnic bargaining and one party in the dispute claims that it is time to amend the rules; the other party refuses to mandate any bargaining agency because its members know that the outcome of new negotiations could only be a reduction in their group privileges.

In applying an approach like mine to the study of political behavior it is important to acknowledge that decisions are influenced by assessments of long-term as well as short-term advantage. A powerful group may direct resources towards a minority to reduce the likelihood of trouble in the future, and this may be seen as a form of tacit bargaining. Long-term assessments depend upon qualities of judgment which are often submerged by short-term considerations. For example, the Greek Cypriots were warned that a continuation of their sectional policies might lead to Turkish intervention in their island and they ignored those warnings. Group commitment to short-term perspectives is more easily enforced than commitment to long-term advantage as the informed observer assesses this. Hence the blind spots in the political vision of mobilized minorities.[10]

As has already been implied, game theory is another member of the family of theories to which my theory belongs. It is more difficult to draw upon game theory because political behavior has a complicating dimension. As new events and changing circumstances shake the political kaleidoscope, so new players appear and old ones vanish or lose their identities in new coalitions. The number of players is indeterminate and this promotes uncertainty. Reference to game theory is useful, however, because it brings a reminder that bargaining has to follow rules and that governments are the primary bodies for deciding and enforcing those rules. One of the functions of the state is to draw up the rules in such a way that bargaining results in a positive sum. Two simple examples of ways in which the federal government in the United States has broken up the white supremacy structure of the deep south spring to mind. It has constrained white commitment to sectional interests by pushing through superordinate federal legislation that changes priorities in the domain of public contacts. More recently it, or the bureaucracy of the Equal Opportunities Commission, has created new constituencies by establishing quotas for the employment of minority members. In this way it has changed the rules of the game and introduced new players.

The first question this raises is that of explaining what is distinctive about the recruitment and organization of the kind of small group Glazer had in mind. My response is threefold. Such a group has to be based upon the constituency within a larger society and is therefore a smaller, more easily organized unit than the one which it confronts. It mobilizes by a process that is now widely referred to as "consciousness raising"; this entails the cultivation of distinctive values, their elevation in a collective order of priority, and the institutionalization of measures both psychological and economic to ensure commitment to that order.

The second task is to explain why such a group should succeed when bargaining with a much larger one, especially since minorities so often perceive themselves to be powerless. Sometimes, of course, minorities *are* powerless, as Jews are in Muslim countries, for example. They are unable to escape from their ghettoes because the system to which they belong differs from that of the United States, which formed the framework for Glazer's observation. The most remarkable feature of the U. S. system is the separation of church and state, permitting minorities to claim equality without renouncing their faith. Jews in countries like Britain have obtained their objectives not by seeking to overcome the majority but by strategies that do not draw attention to themselves. Glazer's law seems to envisage the kind of minority which follows a high-profile strategy, one which, at the extreme, makes "nonnegotiable" demands, and which, because its members believe they have nothing to lose, will issue threats that put its own security in peril.

If such a minority succeeds, it is not because it is concerned about fewer issues than the majority but because it is able to concentrate its pressure. A new minority (such as was the women's movement to start with) has a particular advantage because it can press its claim before the majority has worked out how the required concession stands in relation to its priorities or what the implications of a concession may be. Thus the very features that distinguish a minority may also explain its power. The gains to be achieved by a successful strategy, however, depend upon the relation between minority and majority preferences. Groups trade with one another only when both parties benefit from the transactions. The successful bargainer is the one who allows the other party to make only just enough of a gain for the transaction to be worthwhile and enables his side to get not just its minimum but most of the difference that separates the two minimum positions. How big that difference is varies from one situation to another.

A third task remains. Sometimes one party does not wish to trade, even though observers are convinced that it is in their long-term interest to negotiate. How can such a party be brought to the bargaining table? One reason for such reluctance has already been mentioned. A stalemate can be maintained when one party fears a change of rules to its disadvantage, as has been the case in Canada and in the U. S. deep south and is still the case in Northern Ireland and South Africa. Another more generalized way of representing this situation is suggested by the studies of spheres of exchange in economic anthropology. Some small-scale economies would be destroyed if everything could be traded against everything else by referring to a common measuring rod of money. In our economy price relates demand to supply, but in a Pacific island with a limited ability to store produce from one season to another, a comprehensive pricing system could not alter the levels of demand and supply fast enough or regulate the effects of a natural disaster. The economy functions better if exchange is restricted. So is it in intergroup relations. Some people regard a change of religious, racial, or political identity as nonnegotiable. For them, such an identity cannot be valued on the same scale as the items about which they are prepared to bargain. An important feature of any culture is its demarcation of the goods that can be regarded as commodities.

## NORTHERN IRELAND

It may be worthwhile to look more closely at group relations in Northern Ireland to see if they can assist the better formulation of the theory or illuminate the conditions under which Glazer's law may be expected to hold. At the outset it should be noted that there are difficulties in identifying the parties to the Northern Ireland conflict and in finding suitable names for the main political blocs in the province, and that these very difficulties highlight important dimensions of the social structure. Most commentators label the blocs Protestant and Catholic, though Elliot Leyton has good grounds for preferring the labels Orange and Green, since they are used to designate political groups identifying themselves in religious terms.[11] It is national allegiances that lie at the heart of the conflict. Of course, there is more to it than this, since the actors' perceptions of the social scene are profoundly influenced by the beliefs about God's creation that they learn from their churches. The particular nature of these beliefs also has important implications, as in the Catholic commitment to parochial schools and the power of excommunication as a sanction. Protestants fear that they would lose some of their civil liberties were they to be absorbed into a Catholic state. But if the conflict is not properly religious, neither is to be called sectarian, since Protestantism and Catholicism are not sects. It is less objectionable to identify the distinction as one of religious confessions.

As Edward Moxon-Browne has recently demonstrated, there are many disagreements among Protestants and among Catholics. A substantial proportion of Protestants proclaim an allegiance to Ulster rather than Britain, while some Catholics prefer to call themselves British rather than Irish.[12] Several authors, too, have shown how these disagreements are exacerbated by distrust. Protestants distrust Protestants of different class, denomination, and political opinions. Many of them, even though they identify with Britain, cannot trust the government in London not to do a dirty deal with the one in Dublin. Some of the Catholics who look to Dublin distrust its government. In his 1978 survey of attitudes Moxon-Browne employed a sixfold division of respondents by socioeconomic status. He found 43.9 percent of Protestants and 32.5 percent of Catholics to be in the top three classes, but adds that since there are roughly twice as many Protestants as Catholics there are more poor Protestants in Northern Ireland than poor Catholics. The Protestant workers have wished to maintain a pattern of employment whereby Protestants are favored, so that there is little likelihood of the working class ever forcing a political realignment along class lines. At the same time there is resentment within each confessional group associated with class distinctions, and a fear among working-class people on each side that "their" middle class may desert them and collaborate with the middle class of the other side.

Since 1968 there have been many important changes to the political scene and yet "there has been an almost negligible change in the polarization between the two communities. . . . What we seem to have is a crystallised society, crystallised in polarization, but not torn apart by the strife."[13] It may be helpful to recapitulate the main events. In 1967 new players entered the game, the Northern Ireland Civil Rights Association in Belfast and the Derry Housing Action Committee, and by their agitation changed its character. A group of Protestants in the following year formed the New Ulster Movement and supported the conciliatory policies of a new premier, Terence O'Neill, but a series of riots caused the London government to bring in the army to preserve order. In 1979 the Irish Republican Army (IRA) split and the Provisional IRA seized the initiative. In the same year two new parties were formed. The Alliance sought to bridge the confessional divide, attracting support from both the Unionists and the Nationalists; and the Social Democratic Unionist Party was established to represent the hard-line Unionists. In 1972 direct rule from London was introduced as a temporary measure subject to annual renewal by the British Parliament. The British government was reluctant to involve itself more deeply in the affairs of Northern Ireland. It searched for a middle ground between the two main sections and changed the rules (e.g., by introducing proportional representation) to try to build up the center. It established a Northern Ireland Assembly and, using veiled threats and bluff, encouraged the formation of a new power-sharing Executive consisting of six Unionists, four Social Democratic and Labor Party (SDLP) and one Alliance party member. As part of the deal worked out at Sunningdale, there was to be a Council of Ireland acknowledging the "Irish dimension" to the problem, but the Irish premier failed to support this initiative at the critical time. On 1 January 1973, direct rule was suspended and the power transferred to the new executive. Most of the Unionist MPs then withdrew from the Assembly and, soon after a general election had brought the Labour Party back to office in London, the Ulster Workers' Council called a general strike which paralyzed the province and caused the collapse of the executive and the restoration of direct rule on 28 May. With the policy of his government in ruins, the British premier spoke insultingly of those who called themselves loyalists as "people who spend their lives sponging on Westminster and the British democracy and then systematically assault democratic methods."

Yet the search for compromise continued. In 1975 a constitutional convention was elected. Moxon-Browne reports that "in private contacts outside the formal Convention sessions, some kind of deal between the SDLP and the unionists looked close but, as always, the problem of 'selling' a deal to the rank and file proved insoluble."[14] Referring to the later initiative from Dublin, he remarks that the Protestants could not be "bought off."[15] "However peculiar or perverse the British identity of unionists may be to outsiders, its roots run too deep to be bargained for economically." The stalemate persists because so many people see direct rule as a "second best" in circumstances in which their first preference commands too little support to be the basis for a solution. The number of deaths attributable to the political strife is little more than half the number caused by road accidents, so people learn to cope with it. That may be so, but as an explanation it overlooks the ways in which intergroup attitudes are actively sustained by intragroup social relations. Reviewing a study of a predominantly Catholic community whose inhabitants confront a conflict for which they do not hold themselves in any way responsible, a social anthropologist at Queen's University, Belfast, observes:

> This seems to be the message of virtually all the rural community studies which have been carried out in Northern Ireland: all the communities seem to be reacting to sectarianism which they did not create. . . . Is it not time that the question of conflict was addressed by anthropologists? Bufwak recognizes that peace is fragile in Naghera; wherein lies the fragility? Fragility . . . must be discernible *within* communities.[16]

It is all too easy to offer *post hoc* interpretations of evidence, but my answer to this question would call upon the factors of constituency, priorities, and enforcement. Protestant and Catholic residents of a locality may put their ballot papers into the same box but in the more important sense they are separate constituencies. Few Unionists can attract Catholic support; few Nationalists, Protestant support. Only a change in the rules can modify this. Within the present electoral framework a change in the rules could be achieved by legislated social engineering that increased the costs of separate activity (like the Malaysian government's premium for joint ventures that bring together Malay and Chinese businessmen) but there is no electoral support for such innovations. A change in people's priorities might also be achieved by publicity about the long-term costs of failure to negotiate. A parallel can be drawn with campaigns to persuade cigarette smokers to give up smoking. Since smokers derive short-term pleasure from their habit, campaigners can either argue for an increase in the short-term costs through higher taxation or seek to persuade smokers that they are underestimating the long-term threat to their health. The latter course may succeed by bringing smokers to attach different priorities to their preferences. The explanations given by those who resist these campaigns bear comparison with the explanations offered by people unpersuaded by arguments for policies designed to reduce future ethnic conflicts, while the evident difficulties in reducing cigarette smoking teach a lesson about the difficulties in reducing intergroup prejudices.

Just as the shared habits of peer groups reinforce smoking behavior so they reinforce group attitudes. Much that people say about members of other groups can be interpreted as an expression of identification with the groups to which they themselves belong or seek to belong. There is a conservative bias built into the patterns of conversation in many such groups. Any topic likely to provoke from just one member a response that will spoil a sociable atmosphere is subjected to that member's veto, so that a change is possible only when there are weighty considerations on the other side. The concern for equable relations which characterizes rural communities becomes an enforcement process excluding from the agenda discussion of long-term problems and especially the possibility of concessions to outside critics. Were people rational actors they might work out how much future peace would be worth to them and what value they would place upon whatever they would have to sacrifice to this end. It looks as if the pattern of community life in Northern Ireland prevents such matters from appearing on the agenda and it is here that the fragility of the peace is to be discerned.


## CONCLUSION

Glazer's law envisages a small group that has mobilized to press its claims upon a majority that is preoccupied with other matters and is therefore willing to buy off the minority. In Northern Ireland both the Protestants and the Catholics are politically mobilized—and the same issue is the top priority for both groups. The religious division is threatened only by secularism, and that is something identified by both parties as a prime enemy. The religious beliefs of the two sections sustain their insistence that important issues are nonnegotiable. Few people on either side support population transfer or a revision of the border, so that both groups are locked into a union crystallized in polarity. The pressure to negotiate lies heaviest on the Protestants since it is they who are called upon to admit some Catholics into a power-sharing agreement, or into some set of institutions minimally accountable to a Council of Ireland that would ensure a greater measure of social justice and give the political order legitimacy in Catholic eyes. The Protestants feel that they cannot take risks since no new political arrangements will take the edge off the conflict between two religions, each claiming to be the true faith. They are captives of the prevailing system as much as the Catholics.

Were Northern Ireland not part of the United Kingdom, the armed Republican organizations might be able to force the unionists to the bargaining table because the costs of maintaining public order and security would be too great for the province to meet unaided. The Unionists can maintain their present stance towards power sharing only because the London government pays the bill for security. (The parallel case of the Falkland Islanders' attitudes towards relations with Argentina is, in some respects, even more striking.) The Unionists' antagonists benefit from funds and supplies from outside Ireland. Another reason why Glazer's law does not predict the outcome is therefore that the contending parties within the province belong in political groupings that are partly outside the province, so that they can share the costs with other parties.

The history of the last fifteen years also demonstrates that though Northern Ireland is only one issue among many for the governments in London and in Dublin, they too have been obliged to give it priority and neither of them has been able to change the rules of political behavior in the province sufficiently. In the 1949 Ireland Act the British government declared that "in no event will Northern Ireland or any part thereof cease to be part of His Majesty's dominions and of the United Kingdom without the consent of the parliament of Northern Ireland." It then undertook a commitment which limits its freedom today to act in a manner that it may consider to be in the best long-term interests of the people of the Province. The debacle of 1974 showed how severe a constraint that can be. Moreover, if the Irish government were, in negotiations with London, to agree to any new status for Northern Ireland short of joint sovereignty, it would lay itself open to damaging attack from its own opposition for having reneged on the long-standing aim of the united Ireland. It too has commitments.

Northern Ireland therefore provides a dramatic example of the difficulties of setting ethnic bargaining in motion when there are several parties to the conflict and when neither the costs of its continuance nor the benefits of a settlement can be shared proportionately. It is a reminder that negotiations have to be conducted by agents bound by rules to those whom they represent. These rules have other, perhaps unintended, consequences; they limit the opportunities for individuals to act as free-riders, but at the same time they take captives. Those who might be expected to negotiate a resolution of the conflict cannot bargain effectively because they are unable to commit their own rank and file to any solution of the kind that could be achieved in present circumstances.

Protestants and Catholics in Northern Ireland are not normally thought of as ethnic groups but they have the requisite attributes, being political communities with distinctive cultural features and attitudes reinforced over many generations. Their distinctiveness persists because of the pressures on individuals to identify themselves in this way rather than in accordance with other attributes. The dynamics of social relations within these communities are influenced by the relations between the communities and in turn they reinforce those relations. The groups are crystallized in polarization because the political structure renders impossible the kind of bargaining that might otherwise modify the boundary between the communities. Seen in these terms, Northern Ireland exemplifies a type of ethnic politics that has parallels in other continents.

## NOTES

1. Nathan Glazer, *Affirmative Discrimination: Ethnic Inequality and Public Policy,* 2d ed. (New York: Basic Books, 1975).

2. Mancur Olson, *The Logic of Collective Action: Public Goods and the Theory of Groups* (Cambridge: Harvard University Press, 1965).

3. Ibid., p. 86.

4. Michael Hechter, Debra Friedman, and Malka Appelbaum, "A Theory of Collective Action," *International Migration Review* 16 (1983):412–34.

5. Michael Banton, *Racial and Ethnic Competition* (Cambridge: Cambridge University Press, 1983), p. 104.

6. Benedict Anderson, *Imagined Communities: Reflections on the Origin and Spread of Nationalism* (London: Verso, 1983), p. 71.

7. Ernest Gellner, *Nations and Nationalism* (Oxford: Blackwell, 1983), p. 45.

8. It is described in a sparkling discussion by Jon Elster as a form of imperfect rationality in *Ulysses and the Sirens: Studies in Rationality and Irrationality* (Cambridge: Cambridge University Press, 1979), pp. 36–111.

9. Frank Tannenbaum, *Slave and Citizen: The Negro in the Americas* (New York: Knopf, 1946), p. 115.

10. For an analysis of the psychological processes, see Gabriel Mugny, *The Power of Minorities,* European Monographs in Social Psychology, no. 31 (London: Academic Press, 1982), pp. 4–11.

11. Elliot Leyton, *The One Blood: Kinship and Class in an Irish Village,* Newfoundland Social and Economic Studies, no. 15 (Newfoundland: Memorial University, 1975).

12. Edward Moxon-Browne, *Nation, Class and Creed in Northern Ireland* (Aldershot, England: Gower, 1983).

13. Ibid., p. 167.

14. Ibid., p. 49.

15. Ibid., p. 19.

16. Graham McFarlane, "Review of Mary S. Bufwak, Village Without Violence," *Man* 19 (1984):166–67.

## BIBLIOGRAPHY

Anderson, Benedict. *Imagined Communities: Reflections on the Origin and Spread of Nationalism.* London: Verso, 1983.

Banton, Michael. *Racial and Ethnic Competition.* Cambridge: Cambridge University Press, 1983.

_____. *Promoting Racial Harmony.* Cambridge: Cambridge University Press, 1984.

Elster, Jon. *Ulysses and the Sirens: Studies in Rationality and Irrationality.* Cambridge: Cambridge University Press, 1979.

Gellner, Ernest. *Nations and Nationalism.* Oxford: Blackwell, 1983.

Glazer, Nathan. *Affirmative Discrimination: Ethnic Inequality and Public Policy.* 2d (1978) ed. New York: Basic Books, 1975.

Hechter, Michael; Friedman, Debra; and Appelbaum, Malka. "A Theory of Collective Action." *International Migration Review* 16 (1983):412–34.

Leyton, Elliot. *The One Blood: Kinship and Class in an Irish Village.* Newfoundland Social and Economic Studies, no. 15. Newfoundland: Memorial University, 1975.

McFarlane, Graham. "Review of Mary S. Bufwak, Village without Violence." *Man* 19 (1984):166–67.

Moxon-Browne, Edward. *Nation, Class and Creed in Northern Ireland.* Aldershot, England: Gower, 1983.

Mugny, Gabriel. *The Power of Minorities.* European Monographs in Social Psychology, no. 31. London: Academic Press, 1982.

Olson, Mancur. *The Logic of Collective Action: Public Goods and the Theory of Groups.* Cambridge: Harvard University Press, 1965.

Tannenbaum, Frank. *Slave and Citizen: The Negro in the Americas.* New York: Knopf, 1946.

# 3 Ethnic Politics and Public Policy in Western Societies: A Framework for Comparative Analysis

Robert J. Thompson
Joseph R. Rudolph, Jr.

The literature pertaining to ethnic politics and conflict has represented one of the major growth areas in the publication industry during the past decade. Unfortunately, in too many instances this literature has developed in a compartmentalized manner, avoiding both broad, cross-country studies of ethnic conflict and comparative explorations of the various types of ethnic conflict to be found in political processes in the contemporary world. There are exceptions to this generalization, but they have been too few. Thus, although a number of excellent case studies of different ethnic conflicts are now available, comparisons have often been hindered by the almost implicit assumption of uniqueness underlying each individual study. Furthermore, where comparative studies exist, they have inevitably suffered from one or both of two defects. They have usually focused on only one source of ethnic conflict (most commonly, ethno-territorial conflict), and within this arena the tendency has been to segregate the study of conflict in the multinational polities of the developing world from its examination in the states of North America and Western Europe.

This compartmentalized approach to the study of ethnic conflict has had its advantages. Scholars have been able to generate a large number of solid analyses covering a broad range of ethnic conflict. Yet there is also something less than satisfying about this approach. Understanding what ethnicity is, and tracing it into the political process, requires also understanding what it is not, where its boundaries fall, and how its political impact differs, not only in terms of where it manifests itself but in terms of how and in what form it emerges in a political process. Conceptualization and case studies require the development of a broader framework for analysis, lest they lead to a process of conceptual reification—studies resting on the somewhat unsatisfying, unproven assumption of comparability or noncomparability of different types of ethnic conflict, policy demands, and governmental responses, or generalizations of an untested or nontestable nature.

We address this problem in the existing literature, not as the pure about to hurl stones at a lost generation of writers but as sinners who have contributed to both the literature and the problem. Nor do we now write as born-again analysts of ethno-politics, imbued with *the* solution to existing problems of analysis. Rather, we offer a preliminary attempt to introduce some order into the literature by suggesting a classificatory framework within which the comparative study of ethnic politics, and the relationships between different forms of ethnic conflict and public policy, may be considered. We also offer in this chapter a tentative evaluation of this model by applying it briefly to an examination of public policy and ethnic politics in the Western political systems where our research experience and substantive interests have been primarily directed. We will not comment specifically on the utility of this approach for comparing the various manifestations of ethnic conflict in the political processes of the developed and developing world, beyond observing that the reasons traditionally cited for compartmentalizing the study of politics in the two areas, while important, may be overstated in the area of ethno-politics. Thus, although it is true that the citizens of developing polities are usually less subject to cross-cutting cleavages, more frequently mobilized along lines of ethno-linguistic identity, and less sophisticated in their understanding of impersonal political processes than are their counterparts in the developed world, it is also true that in matters involving ethnic conflict emotions have run high in the political processes of the First and Third worlds alike. Similarly, by definition ethnic conflict involves a dimension of politics resting at least in part on such traditional bases for political association as culture, language, territory, and ethnicity rather than on class or functional interests, regardless of where it is found. It may be more surprising to political scientists to find ethno-territorial movements in the political processes of late twentieth century Belgium or the United Kingdom than in contemporary Nigeria or India; however, our surprise at the discovery does not mean that the movements cease to have much in common with one another as political events. Nor do western political systems seem to be handling the foreign-workers problem conspicuously differently than many developing states are handling it. The urge to scapegoat foreign workers in a political process and the urge to expel them from a political process seem to be very agile in leaping developmental boundaries. But here we are getting ahead of ourselves and straying beyond our goal of offering for consideration at this time only a framework for analysis, which we have found helpful in analyzing the different forms of ethnic conflict in the democratic states of the

First World. We leave it to future writers, and more immediately to the readers of this study and book, to judge the appropriateness of this model for the study of ethnic conflict elsewhere.

## PROBLEMS WITH THE CONCEPT OF ETHNICITY

As any analyst familiar with the topic of ethnic politics can readily attest, the quantity of studies currently being turned out is astonishing, especially considering the scarcity of such studies less than a generation ago. The concept of ethnicity that emerges from these studies is, unfortunately, a perplexing one; too frequently there is little agreement on what constitutes an ethnic group or an ethnic issue. Yet ethnicity has become an important intellectual concept, if the number of people writing on the topic can be taken as a measure of significance. It has also become an important focal point for the formulation of public policy in most societies, and even if there is little agreement about the meaning of the concept, it is recognized as being of importance and warrants classification.

It is not necessary for our purposes to review all of the various definitions of the concept of ethnicity that have been given; this has been done by a variety of researchers.[1] More important for our purposes are three interrelated problems, common to most of these definitions and hindering the concept's analytical utility. The first difficulty is the breadth associated with the concept. There is little consensus upon what types of distinctions should be regarded as ethnic in nature. Some analysts wish to include social distinctions based upon racial (or physiological) characteristics, religion, language, culture, historical traditions, nationality, or various aggregations of these factors. Others desire to see the concept used in a more restrictive manner, particularly separating out racial and nationality groupings.[2]

The difficulties with these approaches are obvious. The broad inclusive approach raises questions about analytical precision. It seems so inclusive that it is difficult to conceive of what is not, or cannot be, an ethnic characteristic. If that is the case, then the older concepts of race, nation, and so forth, may be more useful analytically. Furthermore, an all-inclusive approach to the concept makes it difficult to integrate the less recent research with the new, given an incomparability of terms. Yet the more exclusive approach is not without its problems. When the concept is used restrictively, to denote distinctions between such concepts as racial and ethnic groups, then one is forced to overlook the fact that the boundaries between the distinctions noted above have been intellectually and historically fuzzy. Seldom does any example of an ethnic group possess a clear set of these traits, particularly given the fact that the importance of group distinctiveness is derived from its ascriptive qualities. The usual pattern is for a group to possess an overlapping set of traits, such as language, religion, and culture, while sharing others with the rest of the society, with group distinctiveness becoming manifest only in various forms of social, economic, and political interaction. Likewise, the stereotypes and prejudices commonly associated with racial conflicts are not restricted to such cases, as the British, Irish, Poles, and Jews, among many others, can testify. Thus, neither approach provides the necessary clarity required for adequate comparison.

The second problem involving the concept of ethnicity pertains to the difficulty of comparing various types of ethnicity to one another. There is a tendency for analysts to deal almost exclusively with a single type of ethnic conflict and frequently a single case or related set of similar cases. Yet definitions of ethnicity clearly suggest a set of interrelationships between such types as indigenous native populations, immigrant groups, religious minorities, linguistic minorities, and nationalities. We need to know more precisely what sociological and political distinctions (if any) exist between these categories and how they interact with one another. Should, for example, indigenous native populations such as American Indians or Eskimos be considered, analytically, as being basically the same as recent immigrants? Where, how, and when does an immigrant group become part of the dominant population group or does it? How are ethnic groups and nationalities related? When does the pressure for the recognition of an ethnic group's distinctiveness become nationalism? Furthermore, are the forms of political actors (parties, pressure groups, etc.) representing these types in the policy-making process the same across categories? Are the policies formulated by governments in response to ethnicity comparable in design and impact across varying types? These questions suggest some of the possible interrelationships which need to be made more explicit if the concept of ethnicity is to be analytically fruitful. The concept will be of little use if analysts are not able to be clearer in distinguishing the interactions that exist among the concept's component categories.

A third problem related to the concept of ethnicity is its relationship to other forms of identification and conflict. Just as different types of ethnic conflict may overlap with one another, so, for example, do ethnic and social-class conflicts. Regional issues may also coincide with ethnic ones. But the literature as a whole is generally unclear concerning the importance of these intersections in stimulating political action. Likewise it is not clear whether the development of ethnic political movements is comparable to other types of movements. Do they experience a comparable process of development? Do public policy processes treat ethnic issues as a variety of and in the same manner as cultural issues, or socioeconomic issues? Are the same political and governmental actors involved? Are the same types of policy alternatives available to them or are ethnic issues less resolvable? Such questions indicate the significance of this difficulty. In order to understand ethnicity we must also comprehend the interrelationships between it and other forms of conflict and organization.

These three problems summarize the major complications present in the literature concerning ethnicity. They do not, however, warrant a rejection of the concept, which can serve a useful analytical purpose. Hence, it may be helpful to consider momentarily why these problems exist. To a large extent, they are related to the fact that analysts of ethnicity have been from unusually multidisciplinary backgrounds and are multidisciplinary in their approach. It is not at all uncommon for them to cite anthropologists, sociologists, historians, religious scholars, linguists, political scientists, and psychologists, as well as political activists and governmental leaders. Given this diversity of intellectual traditions, analytical perspectives, and research foci, it should not be surprising that there is little agreement over the content of ethnicity as a concept. Moreover, this degree of interchange is a healthy situation because it permits scholars to perceive the richness of the subject; however, it does not mean that we should not seek greater clarification.

## A FRAMEWORK FOR CONCEPTUALIZING ETHNICITY

The framework we suggest is designed to overcome some of the difficulties discussed in the preceding section. Ours is obviously not the first attempt to achieve this and, in fact, is heavily based upon an earlier effort by Aristides Zolberg.[3] In his 1976 International Political Science Association paper Zolberg criticized various conceptualizations on grounds similar to our critique of them. He then tried to isolate ethnicity as a form of social segmentation. Zolberg argued that societies tend to have three primary sets of segmentation: cultural, territorial, and class segmentation. He schematized ethnicity in the manner portrayed in Figure 3.1, and using this device he proceeded to discuss generally various types of ethnicity and the factors that tended to stimulate their political saliency. In doing so, Zolberg went on to note the dynamic nature of ethnic identities. Under some circumstances a group's ethnicity would have little or no political saliency; in others it would become significant. Moreover, the degree of saliency attached to ethnic identification could change, not only from setting to setting but over time as well.

Zolberg's scheme illustrates the essence of the concept of ethnicity as a category of cultural distinctions. It can, however, be extended. If the bases of segmentation are considered as different bases of identity and as types of public policy issues, then we can place examples of the different manifestations of ethnicity within the areas of intersection. This conceptualization in turn, can suggest interrelationships between both the categories of ethnicity and other forms of social organization. It can also provide a means of comparing the different policies adopted by governments to deal with such conflicts.

The heuristic value of this scheme can be demonstrated by elaborating

**Figure 3.1   Zolberg's Location of Ethnic Segmentation**

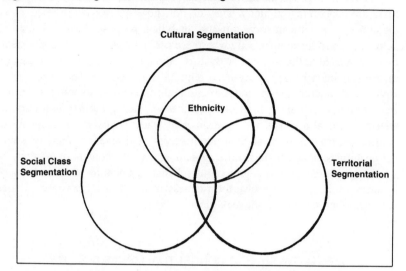

Source:   Aristides R. Zolberg, "Culture, Territory, Class: Ethnicity Demystified."
Paper presented at the International Political Science Association Congress,
Edinburgh, 16–21 August 1976. Reprinted with permission.

upon the nature of the various forms of segmentation and the kinds of issues
related to them. (See Figure 3.2.) To begin, cultural segmentation can be
accepted in a broad sense as segmentation based around normative values
associated with the religion, customs, ethical principles, and historical traditions of a population grouping. Closely linked to these is language. Generally, people sharing the foregoing traits also share a common tongue. It is
easy to conceive of issues arising within a society that are primarily cultural
in nature. These frequently involve such things as moral questions, educational policies, and religious practices. Such issues may arise without involving ethnic identities. Church-state relations in the West are a good example of
conflicts which have overlapped with ethnic identities in some societies but
have not done so in others.

The social-class sphere includes segmentation derived from socioeconomic conditions within the society, in terms of both the political and economic relationships associated with them. Issues typical of this form of
segmentation involve questions of income distribution and resource allocation between social classes. At the turn of the century, such issues as the
right to unionize and political suffrage for working classes were typical of
this sphere. These, in fact, serve as good examples of class conflicts which
tended not to coincide with ethnic identifications in many Western countries.

Territorial segmentation is derived from the locality of the population
grouping. These issues are frequently concerned with the organization and
administration of the government. Questions of changing formulae for legis-

**Figure 3.2 Examples of Segmentation and Related Political Issues**

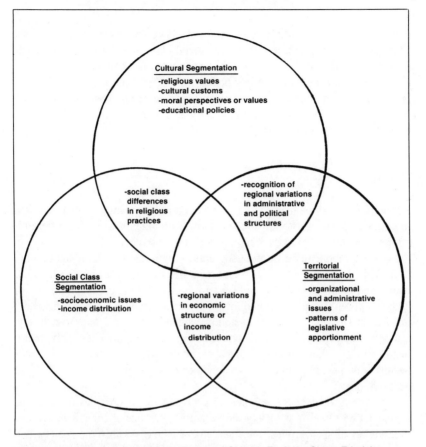

Source: Adapted from Aristides R. Zolberg, "Culture, Territory, Class: Ethnicity Demystified." Paper presented at the International Political Science Association Congress, Edinburgh, 16–21 August 1976. Reprinted with permission.

lative representation due to differential population growth, or increased investment for an economically underdeveloped region, can be considered as typical territorial issues. These issues, too, may or may not coincide with other forms of segmentation.

The intersections of these three forms of segmentation suggest a differing set of issues precisely because they involve overlapping identities which *may* reinforce one another. For example, the intersection between cultural and territorial segmentation might involve issues related to varying religious sects or practices in the different regions within a society. The intersection between cultural and social-class differentiation could involve issues linked to varying cultural perspectives of the different social classes in a system. On the other hand, it might reflect different languages or religious practices on the part of the separate social classes. Still other examples involving the intersection between cultural and class segmentation would include such minority conflicts as women's rights or the status of the elderly within society. Then there is the intersection between social class and territorial segmentation. One region of the society might be treated as if its citizens are of a lower class status or it may simply be less well-off economically because of a lack of resources. At any rate, a region might reflect a substantial variation from the social-class pattern of the society as a whole and issues could arise based around this aspect.

## Ethnicity

Ethnicity may now be located as a type of cultural segmentation that may also intersect class and territorial segmentation. The initial basis of this differentiation is usually linked to the perception that the members of the ethnic group possess a symbolically different geographic origin than the dominant population. This difference in origins may have been of a recent or an historical nature and is primarily important because it provides the perceptual basis for differentiation. The perception of distinctiveness may also involve differences in historical traditions, social customs, language, physical appearance, and religion, due primarily to variations in geographic origin. Ultimately, membership in an ethnic group is largely a matter of ascription. One belongs because one perceives oneself as a member of a group or because others so perceive one.

A variety of factors are potentially related to the complexity of ethnic segmentation found in a society. For example, the size of the ethnic groups, the number of such groups, their settlement patterns within the society, and the extent of overlapping or cross-cutting cleavages may each affect the nature of the society's ethnic segmentation. Furthermore, as ethnic identification is an ascribed trait its intensity, both for the individual and the society as a whole, may vary from time to time. This variance in the saliency of ethnic identity is, in turn, related to broader societal factors, such as socioeconomic change, the character of political organizations, or the policies adopted by the government that affect the ethnic groups in the society. It should also be clear that a society may concurrently experience several types of ethnic segmentation.

The basic types of ethnicity can be categorized by the various intersections between ethnic, cultural, class, and territorial segmentation. (See Figure 3.3.) The first type can be considered as *ethno-cultural differentiation*. This type would involve those aspects of differentiation based solely around cultural differences existing between the ethnic group and the dominant population, and/or among ethnic groups in the population. Examples of issues related to this type might involve the right to carry out various religious practices, or to wear symbolic clothing. Actual cases of this type could include the controversy in Britain over the refusal of some Sikhs to wear a

**Figure 3.3   The Location of Examples of Ethnic Segmentation**

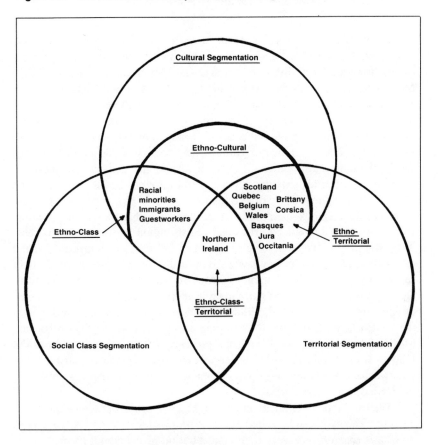

Source:   Adapted from Aristides R. Zolberg, "Culture, Territory, Class: Ethnicity Demystified." Paper presented at the International Political Science Association Congress, Edinburgh, 16–21 August 1976. Reprinted with permission.

helmet rather than their turban while riding a motorcycle, the refusal of several American Indian youths to cut their hair to meet the dress codes of the public schools, and the demands of Hispanic Americans for Spanish-English public schools in some sections of the United States. It could also include the relations between various ethnic groups, such as between Irish-Americans and Italian-Americans, differences that are essentially noneconomic and/or political in nature, although those dimensions may be present as well.

The second type of ethnicity may be characterized as *ethno-class segmentation*. This type is distinguished by a substantial difference in the social class status of the ethnic group from the rest of the society. Frequently the ethnic group will be, or will perceive itself to be, of a lower status because of the actions of the dominant population. This category commonly includes those ethnic groups with an identifiable geographic origin that differs from the society as a whole. Their presence in the society is due most often to their migration from other societies, whether by force or choice. We can further divide this type by noting that within a single society, such as the United States, racial minorities may be considered as analytically distinct from other migrant peoples who share the dominant population's basic physiological characteristics (primarily skin color), as may the "late-comer" guestworkers, who lack the status of citizenship. This division is not particularly precise, but it permits recognition of the society's conception of its own forms of ethnic segmentation. It also encourages the analyst to be aware of the basic similarities existing between these groups. Issues that would be typical of this category involve questions of the right of members of the ethnic group to change their social-class status, whether by greater economic participation or through governmental redistribution of society's resources. They would also likely involve the right to political participation and the elimination of discriminatory laws. Additionally, the primary institutions of the society might be called upon to safeguard the position of these disadvantaged groups, rather than to participate in their oppression. Actual examples of ethnicity of this type in the First World would include racial minorities in the United States and Britain, immigrant groups such as the Puerto Ricans, Mexican-Americans (even though the presence of Hispanic's in parts of the United States predates the American Revolution), Asians in Britain, the guestworkers of Western Europe, and many groups of American Indians in the United States and Canada.

The third type of ethnicity concerns the intersection between culture and territory. This type can be called *ethno-territorial segmentation*. Characteristic of this category is a very high concentration of the ethnic groups' members in a particular geographic area that is commonly perceived as their own. In Western Europe and Canada these are groups who, by one means or another, were incorporated into a larger political system. This usually occurred during the period of nation-state building or empire expansion of the dominant territory's population. As a result, the ethnic group frequently possesses a distinct set of historical and cultural customs, language, and religion. The actions of the larger territory's population may be perceived as an effort to dominate the ethnic group and possibly to destroy its distinctiveness. The governmental and political organizations may also be seen as tools of majority dominance. Issues typical of ethno-territorial segmentation concern the efforts of the ethnic group to maintain its culture and to obtain a fair share of the society's resources. These may be manifested in demands for political and governmental representation on a more equitable basis, such as has been the case in Scotland, Wales, Quebec, and the various regions in Spain.

Analysts who have studied examples of ethno-territorial conflict, in such areas as Quebec, Scotland, Wales, Belgium, and Spain (the Basques), have often had difficulty distinguishing between regionalism and nationalism. By further dividing the ethno-territorial category into ethno-regional and national groupings this problem can be alleviated. The distinction between an ethno-regional group and a nation can be made on the basis of both the intensity of the symbols central to the groups and the political demands normally generated by the respective ethno-territorial groups. Ethno-regional groups, for example, are those groupings such as the Bretons or Flemish in France, most of whom perceive themselves primarily as French regionalists, not as members of separate nationalities entitled to full self-government inside or outside the French state. For such actors, the symbols of France are generally stronger than those of the region, though the hold of the latter on the regional population may be by no means trivial (Brittany). In Scotland, on the other hand, an appreciable number of the region's people perceive themselves to be Scots primarily, and British only secondarily. For such people, the separate legal, educational, and religious institutions of Scotland represent important symbols of their national heritage and continued national existence, and under some circumstances may compete effectively with the system-wide symbols of the United Kingdom (Westminster, the "unwritten" British Constitution, etc.). In pursuing political goals, spokesmen for communities of the latter ilk will normally seek such primarily political objectives as independence, or governmental separation in the sense of creating their own political system distinct from that of the dominant territory. Such goals are distinctly nationalistic, as are the political movements pursuing them. Groups that see themselves as essentially ethno-territorial subnations in a broad national community, however, will be less motivated by the "urge for autonomy" and will more likely opt for lesser, reformist goals, such as economic assistance to struggling regional economies or the protection of a slipping regional tongue. To be sure, this distinction between nationalistic (often separatist) groups and reform-oriented ethno-regionalists is only a rough indicator of the differences to be found within the ethno-territorial category of ethnic conflict. It is obviously possible for a group to move from one category to the other (although this would appear to be a lengthy process), and within any ethnic group movement, there is seldom complete consensus on the goals of the movement at a particular point of time. It is the task of the analyst to ascertain the modal stance of the group being studied at a particular moment, and in the process of analyzing the character of any particular ethno-territorial movement, this (ethno-regional vs. national) distinction is a useful one to keep in mind, whatever explicit bases for the distinction an individual analyst may employ.

The final type of ethnic segmentation defies efforts to provide a succinct, descriptive label. This type concerns the intersection of highly salient ethnic, class, and territorial consciousness simultaneously, *ethno-class-territorial segmentation*. The resulting social stratification tends to disadvantage an ethnic group both in terms of distinctly lower social-class status and territorial segregation. Thus the issues typical of this category would tend to reflect a pattern of reinforcing cleavages rather than cross-cutting ones. Probably the best First World example of this type is the situation in Northern Ireland, where the numerical minority "Catholics" have been historically discriminated against politically and economically, while also having been forced into largely segregated living areas.

In summary, the consideration of these various types of ethnic segmentation can assist in the making of comparisons between examples of ethnic conflict and nonethnic issues. By locating the different subtypes in the areas of intersection between cultural, social-class, territorial, and ethnic segmentation, linkages with other related issues can be identified, as can cases that might otherwise go uncompared. This scheme is also helpful in suggesting some of the various factors that may be influential in affecting the saliency of different examples of ethnic conflict. Depending upon the type of ethnicity involved, one can envision the impact of socioeconomic change, cultural change, political organizations, or governmental policies in shifting the nature of the conflict over time from one intersection to another, or even into a nonethnic location. One should, thus, keep in mind the time-specific nature of the location of any case of ethnic conflict within this framework. The location depends upon assessing the primary features of the conflict during the time period under consideration. Recognition of this factor will also enhance our understanding that frequently regimes and ethnic groups differ in the direction in which they would each prefer to see the basic issues move, and that for some ethnic groups the political issues at stake may well fall within several intersections independently of one another.

## Ethnic Politics and Public Policy

The framework presented in the preceding pages is heuristically useful because it is suggestive of relationships of interest to political scientists and others concerned with the analysis of ethnic politics and public policy. However, in order to illustrate its utility further we need to examine systematically a variety of cases. The framework provides the means for categorizing conflicts; it is not sufficient by itself to identify the aspects that are important for comparing the interrelationship of ethnic politics and public policy. Consequently, these need to be elaborated separately, which we will do in the following sections on contextual developments and the salience of ethnic politics, the nature of the ethno-political demands, the nature of the policy responses to the demands, and the outcome or impact of the policy responses.

The cases chosen for preliminary comparison along these dimensions are as follows:

I.    Ethno-Territorial Conflicts
      A.  Belgium
      B.  Canada—Quebec

C.  France
D.  United Kingdom—Scotland
E.  Switzerland—Jura
II.  Ethno-Class Conflicts
A.  Belgium
B.  Canada
C.  France
D.  United Kingdom
E.  Switzerland
F.  West Germany
III.  Ethno-Class-Territorial Conflict
A.  United Kingdom—Northern Ireland
B.  Belgium—the Brussels-Brabant region

We have limited our consideration of these cases to the post–World War II era. Although this eliminates consideration of the antecedents of many conflicts, we think it captures an adequate time span for this preliminary study.

Furthermore, we should point out that we have chosen not to address two aspects of the framework at this time which would be necessary for its full evaluation. The examples of strictly ethno-cultural conflict that we have encountered have been largely confined to individual actions, though obviously representative of group concerns, and frequently involve legal proceedings. This category also includes examples of members of the dominant ethnic group reacting to policies designed for a minority ethnic group, e.g., white countersuits to affirmative action policies in the United States. As these examples would involve considerable discussion of legal doctrine, we have foregone including the ethno-cultural category in this phase of our study. Also for reasons of space, we have not developed the matter of the comparability of examples of ethnic issues and other political issues beyond a few suggestive remarks. With these general caveats in mind, we can draw some initial conclusions about our chosen examples of ethnic politics and their public policy connections.

## Contextual Developments and the Salience of Ethnic Politics

Among the most persistent problems encountered by scholars studying ethnic politics is the question of why these issues become politically salient. The diversity of variables of potential importance in explaining any single one, let alone several, is astounding. They can include changes in the economic status and conditions of a society's population groups, governmental policies affecting almost any aspect of social, economic, political, public, or private life, or even changes in the international system, to name but a few. Thus it is not surprising that there is little consensus as to their order of significance.

The one factor which does seem to be essential is the most obvious one, a sense of ethnic identification.[4] That identity need not always have been active. It may have been (or still be) relatively latent in comparison to other forms of social identification. This is, in particular, a feature of ethno-territorial conflict in Western Europe, which is one of the reasons that there is considerable disagreement over whether the present regional movements in France or the nationalists in Scotland reflect a resurgence of older identities or represent new ones in the process of formation, or even some combination of the two. Much of that argument depends on the analyst's perspective regarding the activation of the sense of identity, not its importance, and is thus misleading. For our purposes, whether the movement represents a resurgence of older identities or a development of a new regionalized one is less important than the fact that there be an ethnic self-identity factor present (active or latent) upon which to launch the regionalist or nationalist movement. It is this latter factor that is relevant, not only to the form the movement will take but also to the movement's potential for achieving a significant political impact. Recognition of this relevance focuses analytical attention on the factors that may make that sense of ethnic identity politically salient.

As indicated, a wide variety of structural, attitudinal, political, and environmental factors may be of importance in this process. Table 3.1 presents a summary of the more prominent factors that have been advanced as significant in the development of ethno-territorial and ethno-class-territorial movements. There is no particular need to review each of them here. It is sufficient for our purpose to note that most of these factors have been used by someone in explaining virtually every case of ethno-territorial politics that we have examined. Nor would we try to prioritize the importance of these elements, although we should also note that the evidence for explanations relying upon macro- or systems-level environmental changes in the economy to produce subsequent attitudinal changes, which in turn result in individuals possessing a heightened or lessened sense of identity, are currently tenuous. Based on the examination of our cases, we agree with Michael Hechter and Margaret Levi, and with Anthony Smith, that more emphasis needs to be placed on the role of elites, political organizations, and governments, since institutional actors are well placed to provide the linkage between empirically verifiable macro-level conditions and actual micro-level political behavior.[5] The actions of these entities are particularly important in determining the political content of the changing economic, social, and structural conditions for the ethnic groups.

In the area of ethno-class conflict, there tends to be a similar need for a sense of ethnic identity (and community) to exist amongst immigrants or foreign workers before their concerns become politically important as a result of their own actions. Otherwise, members of those analytical categories are dependent upon nonmembers to articulate their interests, and although this has occurred in almost every case, they have not been particularly successful.

**Table 3.1    Factors Influencing the Development of Ethno-Territorial Movements**

A.    Predisposing Factors

A sense of group identity incorporating a "we/they" differentiation from other members of the political system founded on perceived biological or cultural differences, socialization experiences, and/or a prior, separate political existence. A multinational setting and group awareness thereof. This element may be initially dormant.

B.    Causal Factors

Structural/Environmental Elements

1.    relative economic, cultural, or social deprivation vis à vis other groups in the state, aggravated by a modernization process which
    a.    heightens perceptions of regional differences by increasing communications inside the state
    b.    accentuates the growth of the center, aggrevating center/periphery relations by leaving outlying ethnies outside or on the edge of events at the center
    c.    attacks traditional life styles (such as the utility of the regional tongue in social mobility)
    d.    may result in a social welfare state in which benefits of modernization are unevenly distributed among the national groups present in a multinational state;

2.    relative economic superiority/advantage resulting from a sudden improvement of the group's regional economy vis à vis the center;

3.    the erosion or depoliticization of cross-cutting (nonethnic, nonterritorial) issues and cleavages, resulting in the relative increase in the importance of ethno-regional cleavages in a multinational state;

4.    repression of the group by the center;

5.    decline of overarching loyalties, including an erosion of state nationalism, which formerly made ethnic particularism appear illegitimate;

6.    the growth of postindustrial value systems, emphasizing political decentralization and regional populism; more broadly, the ideal of self-determination applied inwardly in multinational states;

7.    a decline in the global prestige of the multinational state; relatedly, a decline in its internal performance -- a loss of its aura of effectiveness in solving socioeconomic problems;

8.    the changing international setting, which formerly encouraged large state systems as a necessary path to political security;

9.  external models -- acheivement of regional self-government by communities in other democratic polities;

10. growing willingness of political leaders at center to entertain regional demands for increased political participation in decisionmaking.

### Attitudinal Changes/Changes in Political Culture

1.  anomie, derived from a sense of aleination from the impersonal, bureaucratic state, and resulting in a yearning to return to the ethnie;

2.  frustration within a potential leadership cadre, resulting from their increased access to higher education but limited career opportunities in peripheral regions or a state dominated by another, numerically superior or culturally "overvalued" ethnic group. A sense of ethnic discrimination;

3.  a renewed sense of ethno-regional identity resulting from the structural changes influencing the group's environment. A (re)discovery of ethnicity, and companion desire for nationalist objectives.

### Political Factors

1.  depoliticization of cross-cutting cleavages by system-wide political elites (see item 3 under Structural/ Environmental Elements);

2.  emergence of a skillful group of political leaders capable of mobilization the regional community on the basis of its sense of national identity in order to press communal demands within the established political order;

3.  incompetency of elites at center to deal with political issues confronting the state.

C.  **Factors Influencing Strength and Nature of Resulting Ethnonational Movements**

1.  size of individual groups; number of groups present in state; relationships to one another (e.g., degree of assimilation, internal colonialism, etc.);

2.  location of groups inside state (degree of remoteness from center defined geographically);

3.  range of cultural factors and type of cultural factors reinforcing sense of difference of group from others in state; relatedly, degree to which region was integrated into the state during prior nation-building periods;

4.    political situation within which group finds self --
      willingness of center regime to negotiate group demands;
      relatedly, pattern of prior domination (benign neglect,
      coercive rule, etc.).

Sources:   Milton Esman, ed., Ethnic Conflict in the Western
World (Ithaca:   Cornell University Press, 1977, especially
chapters by Walker Conner ("Ethnonationalism in the First
World"), Arend Lijphart ("Political Theories and the
Explanation of Ethnic Conflict in the Western World"), and
Esman ("Perspective on Ethnic Conflict in Industrial
Societies"); Aristide Zolberg, "Culture, Territory, Class:
Ethnicity Demystified," paper presented at the IPSA Congress,
Edinburgh, 1976; and Anthony Birch, "Minority Nationalist
Movements and Theories of Political Integration," World
Politics, 30, 3 (1978), pp. 325-334.   Used with permission.

The structural and political developments surveyed in our cases do not encourage a belief in the increased salience of immigrant and foreign-worker
identities.

On the other hand, the structural developments that have taken place in the
countries hosting these groups have activated the majority population's *ethnic*
(not class) reaction. A list of these developments includes: the rapid expansion
of postwar economies in Western Europe, which necessitated the addition of
outside workers to the domestic work force in numerous countries in order to
keep the economies expanding; the decline of France and Britain as imperial
powers, and the admission to their respective countries of large numbers of
sons and daughters from overseas colonies as the empires were terminated; the
gradual trend of the guestworkers becoming structurally permanent parts of
their host countries' economies and their tendency to send for their families to
join them; the resulting social conflict between host country nationals and the
foreign workers and their families coming from geographically and culturally
remote areas; and the economic downswing in most European states since
1968—and especially since 1979—which has resulted in an employment profile
no longer requiring large numbers of foreign workers and a heightening of
local reactions against their presence. The cases of ethno-class conflicts in our
sample indicate that structural and political developments appear to have a
considerably greater impact on the generation of ethnic demands from the
majority population than from the immigrant and foreign workers themselves.
The native majority already possesses a distinct identity and organizational
base around which to mobilize as well as the knowledge to utilize the techniques of political influence in their home counties.

## Ethno-Political Demands

There are three aspects of ethno-political demands of particular interest to our study. First, there is the content of political demands put forward by different ethnic groups. The second and third aspects, which will be considered jointly, are the range of actors involved in the demand process and the means by which the demands are conveyed, which together should provide considerable information about the nature of the ethno-political demands and how they may be received by the political system.

Ethno-territorial demands cover a wide range, though all require central government concessions to the ethno-territorial community. More specifically, they include the heavily output-oriented demands of regionalists seeking financial aid for teaching or promoting the ethnic language in the educational and communications outlets of their region, and the demand for additional economic assistance to the region's economy. They also include essentially nationalistic demands for some form of political autonomy, which may range from demands for guaranteed representation in central decision-making cartels to self-rule within an overall unitary framework, to federal autonomy for the region to—at the extreme—separatist or irredentist objectives. In none of the cases examined is there complete consensus over the content of the demands to be placed before political authorities. Each case exhibits a diverse range of factions with varying opinions about the goals to be pursued and how stridently they are to be pushed.

In contrast to ethno-territorial conflict, ethno-class conflicts involve two distinct types of issues and demands: those involving the conditions of the foreign workers or immigrants in the host country, and those involving the presence of these groups themselves. These are summarized below with some typical demands.

*Issues related to the status of foreigners*
- the need for more and better housing and health and educational facilities
- the need for language instruction and aid in integrating the workers and their families into the host country's society
- the need for civil rights protection
- the need for equal pay for equal work (compared to the nationals) and better union representation

*The foreigners as the issue*
- the presense of large numbers of foreigners threatens the country's unique character
- foreign workers depress the wages of all workers
- foreign workers represent a threat to the jobs of domestic workers

- consequently, more foreign workers should not be allowed into the country and those present should be encouraged to leave

Thus, the main distinction revolves around the question of the *legitimacy* of the presence of foreign workers in the host country. If their presence is legitimate, then they are entitled to certain rights and services. If not, then they are perceived to have no independent rights.

The issues involved in Northern Ireland, the prime example of ethno-class-territorial conflict, are a combination of those found in the two preceding categories. The main thrust of the Catholics' demands centers around guarantees regarding their political representation in any governmental system to be established, as well as some very specific improvements in their living and economic conditions. There are, however, also those who still desire unification with the Republic of Ireland. Those opposing the Catholics tend to adopt a mixture of demands in response. The more moderate Protestants appear to be willing to negotiate some form of power-sharing arrangement, basically an ethno-territorial approach. The more extreme ones seem to be more closely related to the more xenophobic of those opposing the presence of foreign workers in their respective countries, refusing to accommodate the Catholics in almost any way. For both groups the issue is ultimately one of legitimacy—of the legitimacy of the institutions to the Catholics and of the "legitimacy" of the Catholics to the Protestants.

Concerning the range of political actors involved in the conveyance of the policy demands, again some differences between our categories emerge quite clearly. Collectively, the ethno-territorial communities have utilized most conceivable means of influencing their respective political processes, the modes of action ranging from the organization of cultural association and regionalist/nationalist parties to the organization of direct action groups practicing civil disobedience confrontation politics (e.g., the Welsh Language Society) to the creation of clandestine groups employing overt violence aimed at the symbols of the central government (the French national banks and power installations targeted for bombing by Corsican and Breton terrorists) and even human targets (e.g., ETA militar's activities in Spain). Frequently, these actors also include factions or wings of broader, system-wide, political organizations, such as the Labour Party in Scotland or the Liberals from Quebec. Likewise, they may be sections or members of larger economically oriented bodies, such as regional unions or business associations. (In some cases, one level of government may even be an active conveyor of the ethno-territorial demands to other levels.)

The modes of expressing demands related to ethno-class issues parallel the division of demands noted earlier and are summarized in Table 3.2. Briefly, there are five potential sources of demands on behalf of the foreigners: the workers or immigrants themselves, interest groups within the host country, the countries of the workers' origin, the host country's govern-

**Table 3.2   Origins of the Ethno-Class Demands Concerning Foreign Workers**

Demands involving foreign workers may originate with:

1. the workers themselves, although this may be surprisingly infrequent given the factors working against the workers (and/or immigrants) organizing in pursuit of shared objectives;

2. domestic interest groups in the host country, such as those postindustrial groups concerned with the living conditions of all residents, or leftist parties and unions concerned with the solidarity of the working class movement (the workers themselves join unions only about half as frequently as host country nationals, membership ranging from about 10% of the foreign workers in France to 47% in Belgium);

3. the countries of the workers' origin, which may have encouraged their citizens to seek work abroad and have an interest in their welfare (specific conditions of employment may be the subject of bilateral agreements between the home and host countries involving the immigration of foreign workers);

4. the government of the host country, which may have a public interest in managing the inflow of foreign labor to a level commensurate with job availability or in easing their integration into the host country's population; and

5. transnational/supranational institutions, such as the European Community (which is concerned with the large numbers of legal foreign workers to be found in virtually all of its member states) and the Council of Europe (with its general concern for the migrant workers and their problems throughout Europe).

Demands involving the foreign workers as the issue may similarly be initiated by:

1. domestic nationals, reacting especially during periods of economic duress to the presence of large numbers of culturally different foreigners in their midst, either spontaneously or otherwise;

2. domestic interest groups, such as business associations and unions, concerned with the economic impact of foreign workers on the country's economic and wage/employment structure; and

3. the government of the host country, which may find it useful to coopt this issue for private reasons (e.g., regime maintenance, partisan reelection, etc.), as well as to preempt the issue to minimize social unrest.

ment, and transsystem institutions. When the foreign nationals themselves are the issue the demands come from three primary sources: domestic nationals, domestic interest groups, and the government of the host country. Contrary to the pattern exemplified by the ethno-territorial cases, the principal system-wide political parties appear to play little active role in the conveyance of these demands. They are, instead, the recipients of the demands, and are expected to act upon them in the legislative process.

Among these potential participants in ethno-class politics there is a considerable variance in the amount of their activity. It is understandable, but also paradoxical, that the groups most directly affected by the policy responses to the ethno-class demands, the foreign workers and immigrants (fw/i), appear to be the least active. In most instances, the fw/i have been composed of such a diverse mixture of nationalities, so mutually competitive in the host country's economy, and so mutually suspicious of one another in general, that even where they have possessed the requisite capability and political resources to form alliances, they have remained politically disorganized. Their ability to influence the political process has also suffered from their political disenfranchisement, especially since the opponents to their presence have been quite willing to use the leverage of the ballot box to effect their exodus. Thus, except where the fw/i have constituted nearly 100 percent of the workers in a particular sector, and have correspondingly possessed some economic leverage (as is true of the diverse lot of foreigners maintaining the Parisian subway system), or in those instances where their frustration with the state of their life has exploded in spontaneous public demonstrations, it is not so much that the fw/i groups have articulated their grievances as that political demands have been articulated on their behalf by concerned indigenous citizens in the host countries (e.g., demands concerned with the absence of any coherent settlement policy in the host countries, with the substandard conditions in which the fw/i live, etc.). In a sense these latter groups have emerged as European counterparts to the essentially white, middle-class founders of the NAACP in the United States, and like their American predecessors they have spoken for what is distinctly a minority viewpoint in their states. Aligned against them have been public opinion and interest groups such as the National Council of French Employers, which has argued that the number of foreign workers in France must be halved in a decade lest their employment be at the expense of French workers. Likewise, in Britain a political party, the National Front, has as one of its principal goals to send the foreigners packing. Finally, it should be noted that the demands of those fw/i leaders who have managed to articulate concerns on behalf of their groups have been essentially defensive in nature, that is, that they *not* be deported, dispossessed, or flagrantly discriminated against. Only secondarily have they pressed for specific civil or economic rights, and then usually in such a manner that they have rarely gained effectively the ear of government.

As would be expected given the overlap of cleavages present in the ethno-class-territorial case of Northern Ireland, virtually every conceivable participant and means of conveying demands can be found. Of particular note, though, are two participants who play a much greater role than is common in either of the other two categories considered: terrorist groups and the system-wide government. In the political setting of Northern Ireland, both the Protestants and Catholics have terrorist groups operating in the name of their respective cause. This tends to interject, almost by definition, an erratic and uncontrollable element into the policy process. It is, in part, in reaction to the terrorists that the British government has had to respond and in the process become an active participant in generating ethnically related political demands. Moreover, by emerging as a force between the two contending groups in Northern Ireland, the U. K. government has become not only the originator of such demands as better representation for the Catholics but also the focus of objections by both groups.

There is a final aspect that warrants brief consideration: the *lack of overlap* between the demands and participants concerned with ethno-class and ethno-territorial conflict, respectively. Aside from a few individuals, such as Enoch Powell, and the system-wide parties, there is almost no outstanding connection in Britain between the two types of conflict. This appears to be the most common pattern in our cases, with only one important exception: Quebec, where the ethno-territorial conflict has spilled over into immigration politics because of the French-Canadian's desire that non-English-speaking immigrants to Quebec learn the French language and have their children educated in French schools.

## The Nature of the Policy Responses to Ethno-Political Demands

There are two features of the policy responses to ethno-political demands that were of particular interest to us. Who receives the demands? And, how do they respond once the demands have been conveyed? Let us briefly consider these matters before we review—unfortunately with equal brevity—the comparative role of governmental institutions and some of the problems related to studying policy responses.[6]

With respect to ethno-territorial and ethno-class-territorial conflict, it appears that the central government and the system-wide political parties are almost invariably the recipients of the demands being generated. This is not unexpected as most of our cases are drawn from unitary political systems. Similarly, and again as would be anticipated, in the cases of Canada with its federal system and Switzerland with its confederal system, the provincial/cantonal level is equally—or even more—involved than the central government. A similar pattern emerges when one considers ethno-class conflicts over immigrants and foreigners in the host country; however, a broader range of recipients appear to be involved in issues related to the status of foreigners. Conflicts over the rights of immigrants, for example, frequently involve the legal system, unions, or employers more than high level governmental institutions or system-wide political parties, except where the latter choose to co-opt the fw/i issue.

How the recipients of the demands respond is a more difficult matter to summarize. With regard to ethno-territorial conflicts our cases indicate that a diverse set of policy responses have been utilized in Western societies. These, however, can be grouped into two broad (and largely self-evident) categories. Recipients of demands have either tried to accommodate the demands of ethno-territorial spokesmen by granting at least some concessions (essentially the reaction of Brussels to the demands of Belgium's ethno-linguistic communities, and the reaction of London through the mid-1970s to the demands of the ethno-regional organizations of Scotland and Wales), or they have responded with hostility to such demands (traditionally the official policy of the French government vis à vis the demands of regionalists, as well as the obvious response of the Protestant establishment in Ulster to the political demands of Northern Ireland's Catholics and to the proposal put forth by London in the 1970s that civilian rule be restored in Ulster within a committee system framework in which both communal groups would share power). On balance, the states in our study seem to have taken the pragmatic position that accommodation is preferable to conflict; at one point or another the central governments in Britain, Belgium, Spain, and even France (tacitly) have pursued this course of action—Paris offering Corsica in the middle 1970s increased economic aid in an effort to reduce support on Corsica for the island's various autonomy groups. Elsewhere, London proposed the power-sharing scheme as a means of extracting itself from politics in Northern Ireland and came close to creating assemblies in Wales and Scotland in an effort to placate ethno-territorial assertiveness in Britain's Celtic regions; decision makers in Brussels devoted an entire decade to trying to find an institutional arrangement for accommodating the tensions between their country's ethno-linquistic communities; and regionalization became an important step towards democratization for part of post-Franco Spain. Indeed, the only form of institutional accommodation that was systematically rejected by system-wide leaders in most states involved proposals to federalize fully their polity, federalism being equated with separatism by system-wide elites, and becoming the *bête noire* of political dialogues between ethno-territorial spokesmen and political leaders at the center.

In part, the nature of the response seems to be due to the degree of mobilization exemplified by the ethno-territorial and ethno-class-territorial groups and the economic importance of the region, as much as to the specific demands conveyed. Table 3.3 presents a general summary of these cases and the nature of the responses that have been forthcoming. As it indicates, and as would be expected, those regions with the greatest mobilization and of greater importance to the national economic systems have tended to receive the most favorable responses.

The issues generated by the presence of large numbers of foreign workers and immigrants in these countries have, comparatively, been approached with greater ambivalence by political leaders. Initially, the flow of foreign workers into France, West Germany, and Belgium, and to a degree the arrival of citizens from the "coloured commonwealth" in Britain, was greeted with a policy of "studied neglect." In the case of the foreign workers, the explicit operating assumption was that they were only temporary additions to the

**Table 3.3   Policy Responses in Ethno-Territorial and Ethno-Class-Territorial Cases**

| | Conflict | Mobilization and Regional Economic Importance | Response |
|---|---|---|---|
| I. | Regions asserting demands against the center;<br><br>Wales, Scotland, Flanders, Wallonia, Quebec | where region is important and mobilized; and | the central government has been willing to negotiate on the issue of regional autonomy. |
| II. | Regions asserting demands against the center;<br><br>Alsace, Brittany, Basque France, Corsica | but lacking in importance and/or a high level of mobilization; and | the government has been unwilling to negotiate (yielding a militant approach to the pursuit of ethno-territorial demands). |
| III. | Group within a region asserting demands against the regional government;<br><br>Jura Switzerland | and enjoying a high level of mobilization; and | eventually forcing the government to entertain accommodation as a tool of conflict resolution. |
| IV. | Northern Ireland as a class by itself given conflict also within region; | highly mobilized nature of relevant ethno-political communities<br><br>and<br><br>the geographical intermingling of the regional peoples, | unwillingness of one community to negotiate power sharing (by permanent majority with permanent minority) creating atmosphere of political violence<br><br>which precludes devolution of decision-making authority on a territorial basis as in Jura as a means for conflict resolution. |

domestic work force and would return to their home countries at some future time—an assumption that provided a convenient rationale for avoiding any policy designed to "settle" the guestworkers into the host countries. Later, as the permanency and number of foreign workers and immigrants became an issue in its own right on the public agendas of Britain and France, governments found it more difficult to retain a policy of passive neutrality, and the response in both countries tended towards an ambivalent combination of anti-discrimination statutes to end some of the more obvious forms of discrimination (which were enacted later in France than in Britain), even tighter controls on the admission of new outsiders, and finally, efforts designed to encourage the emigration of some of these people from the host countries. It has been easier to use these latter measures in France, given the greater legal vulnerability of most of its "temporary" foreign workers, than to take action against the immigrants who entered Britain as Commonwealth citizens or— for that matter—against the inflow of illegal immigrants from Mexico into the United States, given the generally delicate nature of U. S.-Mexican relations. Indeed, of the European cases, only in Belgium has the anti-fw/i policy had a low profile, and this state of affairs reflects Belgium's role in Europe and the nature of its foreign population at least as much as the tolerance of the Belgian people for outsiders. Until recently, the majority of Belgium's foreign workers have come from Italy and other countries of the European Community, exercising their legal right under the EC charter to move freely within the Community's member states. As the "Capital of the European Community" and home of its central executive institutions, Belgium has found it especially difficult to contravene the legal rights of these workers to enter its borders.

There may be another and more important reason why the foreign-worker issue has had less significance in Belgian than in French, Swiss, or West German politics: the fact that ethno-territorial politics dominated policymaking in Belgium throughout the 1970s and into the present decade. It may be that where ethno-territorial issues acquire and maintain saliency, they will tend to overshadow most other bases of ethnic conflict and keep other types of ethno-political demands off the public agenda. Such societal cleavages as those between foreign workers/immigrants and the citizens of a host country can threaten the public order, but ethno-territorial cleavages can threaten the physical unity of the state and accordingly command the full attention of the political process as long as the conflict emanating from them remains significant. This need not be an iron law—in some instances system-wide leaders may find it desirable to scapegoat foreign workers for domestic ills or even to deflect attention from indigenous communal conflict (e.g., Uganda's attack on its Indian entrepreneurs during Idi Amin's regime)—but it is probably a frequent rule of thumb in political processes simultaneously confronting significant manifestations of ethno-territorial and ethno-class conflict.

As for policy responses in the ethno-class-territorial case represented by northern Ireland, these have tended to be directed at keeping the two groups apart while trying to negotiate some form of power-sharing arrangement as a format for restoring civilian rule in Ulster. This has involved a series of British Cabinets in some complex negotiations without producing a particularly successful resolution. In the meantime, a considerable amount of the governmental effort must continue to focus on peacekeeping duties.

The special role of the governmental institutions in the patterns of response rapidly becomes obvious as one explores the conflicts. Examination of these cases indicates several differences between conflict types that are worth noting. In the area of ethno-territorial politics, the government of a country will most often find itself in the position of *responder* to the demands. Its position in the area of foreign-workers politics as the focus of demands of various types as well as from a variety of sources will, however, more often place the government in the position of acting as a political *mediator* or *broker*. Hence the frequently schizophrenic appearance of public policy in the fw/i area—the government concurrently pursuing policy designed to assure foreign nationals or immigrants of their civil rights while at the same time seeking to placate domestic public opinion by halting the inflow of additional foreigners and even trying to encourage many of those already present to return to their home countries. Moreover, insofar as private (partisan or regime maintenance) purposes may also influence a government's behavior in conflicts pitting foreign elements against the domestic population, a government is much more likely to assume the role of an *issue definer* or *policy initiator* in this area than in conflicts involving ethno-territorial demands for autonomy. One not inconsequential by-product of this tendency is that governmental policy concerned with (limiting) foreign labor may frequently run in advance of public opinion formation on the subject (Switzerland for example). On the other hand, the reluctance with which governments entertain demands for regional autonomy from groups deemed to have been integrated into the state often means that even when governments are willing to try to accommodate ethno-territorial demands, their responses will lag behind the demands being pressed by the mobilized ethno-territorial communities confronting them.

Finally, let us note some of the research problems of which we have become more aware. Foremost among these is the problem of measuring responsiveness. There are no particularly good standards for evaluating when the political system has been responsive to the demands made upon it. Frequently, there is a substantial time lag between the reception of demands and the making of a response. Even if the decision is to do nothing, considerable time may pass before the conveyers of the demand realize it. Moreover, there is the problem of comparing the significance of different responses. Within a single case some sense of relative importance can be attributed to each of the various responses that occur over time. Such a judgment is much more complicated to make, however, when one is comparing several cases. Lastly, it must be remembered that it is not easy to assess the motivations of decision-makers (or of anyone for that matter), which makes it difficult to determine exactly why the responses are made and what meaning they are intended to transmit. Bearing these problems in mind, we may now consider the impact that these responses have on ethnic conflicts.

## The Outcome or Impact of the Policy Responses

Examination of our sample cases indicates several types of impact that public policy responses may have on ethnic political demands and movements. The two most basic aspects likely to be affected are: (1) the nature of the movements and their mode of political participation and (2) the nature of subsequent demands. Our emphasis on these areas should immediately indicate that we are operating on a presumption that ethnic-laden issues normally defy permanent settlement. This should not be taken to mean that ethnic issues are by definition nonbargainable in nature. In fact, one of the remarkable aspects that our case studies have made clear is the high degree of bargainability characterizing many of these issues, particularly regarding matters of implementation. Political elites seem to have a rather considerable latitude of actions available to them in dealing with these questions, especially as long as the majority of the public remains unmobilized. But political settlements are never permanent. They are always subject to changing social, economic, and international conditions; consequently, they are always subject to renegotiation. It is only with the contrary presumption, that the current political status quo is the proper base for comparison, that these issues become unbargainable—a presumption that the contemporary presence of ethno-territorial movements in the Western world seriously questions (along with the argument that ethnic-political settlements are permanent).

The impact of policy responses on the nature of ethno-territorial conflicts has taken several directions. Generally, though, the key variable in determining the mode to be used for articulating demands has been the degree to which the existing regime has been willing to entertain and, at least in part, respond to ethno-territorial demands, especially requests for regional autonomy. Thus, in Britain, Canada, and Belgium, where political leaders were willing to negotiate with ethno-territorial spokesmen during most of the past decade, if not before, the principal means selected to express ethno-territorial demands were system-participatory, primarily the ethno-territorial parties which became strong participants in British, Canadian, and Belgian politics by the mid-1970s.

Conversely, where the relevant political leadership seemed to be insensitive to ethno-territorial demands, the tendency was for ethno-political organizations to develop as clandestine, system-challenging actors. The level of political violence employed tended to correlate (in our cases) with (a) the degree of insensitivity exhibited by the established leadership and (b) the number of overlapping cleavages encapsulated in the resultant political conflict between ethnic groups within the same region (such as in Northern Ireland), and between the ethno-territorial actors and the central authorities. Thus, ethno-territorial spokesmen for Alsacien Breton, and Corse demands have tended to be clandestine organizations, given the traditional unwillingness of French political leaders to negotiate officially with regional spokesmen. The level of political violence generated by these organizations, however, has remained relatively low despite France's history of political streetism and confrontation politics as a proven means of political change. This is primarily because the ethno-regionalists have seen themselves as part of an overarching French nation, and have accordingly pursued essentially "regionalist" demands for cultural autonomy (for Alsace) and regional home rule (for Brittany and Corsica) rather than, properly speaking, "nationalist" demands. In Northern Ireland, on the other hand, the combination of the multiple divisions separating the region's Catholic and Protestant communities, and the latter's hard-core opposition to the demands of the former, has produced a very high level of political violence, visibly represented by the IRA's terrorist squads, which the responses from London have had only limited success in abating.

As this consideration of impacts on the nature of ethno-territorial movements and their mode of participation in the political process suggests, policy responses are also likely to generate subsequent demands for additional action. The cases in our sample strongly suggest that responses based around institutional accommodation are likely to create a basis for new demands for further administrative or decision-making autonomy. Likewise, even primarily symbolic gestures may increase expectations and desires. Thus a seemingly favorable reception to ethno-territorial demands followed by little substantive action may increase the ante the next time around. Conversely, it might also deflect further interest for a substantial period of time. The introduction of violence into the conflict, however, only seems to further complicate the situation, because the violence itself becomes a focal point for demands and responses. That, in turn, seems to deflect governmental responses from the supposedly more basic issues of the conflict.

What seems to be more important for subsequent demands is the ability and willingness of elites from each perspective in the ethno-territorial conflict to reach some mutually agreeable rules of the game or patterns of interaction if an institutional arrangement is utilized. This need not result in a full-blown consociational resolution. It can be something which is far from that while still using consociational-like practices and principles of cooperation. If elites and political organizations are unable to reach some form of accommodation, then a policy of control or even suppression of the minority ethnic group appears likely, with the maintenance of the status quo being a form of control, although that response is apt either to eliminate demands temporarily or result in some new form of violence.

With respect to ethno-class conflict, the impact of public policies seems to depend on whether the status of the foreigners or their presence in the host country is the central question. The policy responses regarding the status of the foreign workers and immigrants do not appear to have had a major impact thus far on the nature of the movements generating such issues, perhaps because these issues have been too diffuse in character to achieve a noticeable impact. However, the policy responses have had an impact on subsequent demands of this type. Most commonly, these responses have been in the form of demands for legal protection, thus creating a basis for later action, especially by individuals.

Similarly, when the foreigners themselves are the issue, the policy responses do not appear to have much of an impact on the nature of the movements active from this perspective. If anything, the actions taken have deflected their growth a little. Moreover, compared to the importance of the policy responses to ethnic demands of this type, changing economic conditions seem to play a greater role in the generation of subsequent demands.

At this point a cautionary remark is in order. One should be on guard against assuming that ethnic conflicts result in continually more severe and system-threatening demands being generated. The recent failures of the home-rule style referendums in Quebec and in the United Kingdom serve as reminders that, at least in the short run, there may be ebbs and flows in the pattern of development for these issues. Moreover, these cases indicate that change is not entirely uni-directional, either for ethno-territorial conflicts or for ethno-class conflicts. As indicated, changes in economic conditions may affect conflicts involving the presence of foreigners in the country, lessening or increasing their severity depending on the economic changes. Similarly, there are pressures operating on governmental systems that seem to encourage further centralization of powers and responsibilities. For example, the increased emphasis being placed on economic planning in Western societies raises serious questions about the possibility and desirability of decentralizing some key categories of authority to ethno-national groups. Thus it is likely that accommodations may be made in some policy areas, while further centralization occurs in others.

## CONCLUSIONS

In this preliminary survey of ethnic conflicts and public policies we have obviously not answered all of the questions that we raised. Nor was that our purpose. We are still at the point of trying to develop efficient analytical categories to distinguish between and compare types of ethnic conflicts and to test them in an initial manner to see if these analytical devices warrant further consideration. Here, we have done this by comparing over a dozen cases across the policy process. Having completed this much of the project, we believe the classification scheme to be useful. Examining conflicts across the indicated categories has indicated a number of intriguing points of comparison and has simplified the investigation process. We are also still convinced of the need for more systematic data collection and for concepts that promote that goal in a comparative manner. Without these, theories with a comparative explanatory value are not likely to be developed. We hope that our effort encourages others to undertake such efforts as well.

There is no particular need to repeat the substantive conclusions that we have reached concerning the comparisons, but there are several matters that should be mentioned. One of these involves the real possibility of a changing arena for decision-making concerning ethnic conflicts in Europe. Should this take place it would obviously modify our earlier comments. At this time, most conflict takes place within and is "settled" by the policymaking process of the individual states. In the future, the policymaking process might become more complicated. The enlargement of the European Community, for example, to include Turkey, Portugal, and/or Spain, whose workers are now excludable by the members of the EC (who may not discriminate against their own work force), would concurrently add a dimension to the foreign-worker problem in each state of today's European Community (excepting Italy, the one net labor exporting state, and, to a lesser degree, Ireland), and force the EC itself to be more energetic in making foreign-worker policy binding on all members. A revitalized Regional Development Fund in Brussels might equally have the effect of drawing an appreciable number of regional demands for financial assistance from the EC by ethno-territorial communities inside EC member states. The point should not be belabored, but it is a potential future dimension of ethno-political conflict in Western Europe that should not go unacknowledged.

Additionally, there are some gaps in the research literature that warrant mentioning. Our study of these cases indicates that considerable work remains to be done in comparing the validity of different conceptualizations of what makes ethnicity politically salient and under what conditions. The tendency still persists for single-case studies to dominate the field. Second, more work needs to be done concerning ethno-political demands generated by the foreign workers and immigrants themselves. There is little discussion of their role in the policy process and this forces us to conclude tentatively that they have only a small role, but it is not a conclusion with which we are particularly comfortable. Third, more research is needed on the interrelationship between the various conflicts, the actors involved in them, and the means by which demands are conveyed. Information on these aspects would considerably improve our comparative understanding of the dynamics of these movements. Fourth, more work needs to be done on the patterns of interaction that political elites have with the various types of ethnic issues with which they must deal. This may involve only estimating their overall philosophic approach to ethnic issues, but it would improve our knowledge of the policy process. Fifth, our study suggests to us that better conceptualizations of the policy responses available to decision-makers are needed. Concepts such as consociationalism, federalism, repression, or oppression are inadequate to cover the range of responses exhibited. This is obviously a tall order of research, but improvements are needed if our understanding of these conflicts and their relationships to other forms of political identification and conflict is to be increased substantially.

And finally, to return full circle, what is the applicability to other settings of the framework for analysis which we have offered—especially non-Western societies? To repeat our point of departure, we have consciously limited our study to a relatively small number of democratic, Western societies because of both space considerations and our personal analytical experience. We believe, however, that it can be fruitfully used in other settings, including non-Western ones. In fact, the interaction between ethnic conflict and public policy may be even more significant in non-Western cases, given the more frequent overlapping of issues and the greater intensity that seems to characterize ethnic conflict in the Third World. This, in turn, implies that great attention needs to be placed on the role of political and governmental institutions in such polities, as well as on the greater range of options open to directive societies in responding to ethnic conflict than is customarily available to democratic societies, whose ethnic activists usually enjoy the right to organize politically and challenge the status quo. This area too is a topic to which we would like to devote future research, and invite others to join us, for addressing it may be the tallest order of all.

## NOTES

1. See Joseph B. Gittler, "Toward Defining an Ethnic Minority," *International Journal of Group Tensions* 7 (1977): 4–19; Donley T. Studlar, "Post-Industrial Society and Ethnicity" (Paper presented at the Annual Meeting of the International Studies Association, Los Angeles, 19–22 March 1980); and Jonathan H. Turner and Royce Singleton, Jr., "A Theory of Ethnic Oppression: Toward a Reintegration of Cultural and Structural Concepts in Ethnic Relations Theory," *Social Process* 56 (June 1978): 1001–18; and Joseph Rothchild, *Ethnopolitics* (New York: Columbia University Press, 1981).

2. We have consciously decided not to cite individual works typifying these problems as we think they are difficulties endemic to most of the field. This does not mean that there are not many fine pieces of work done in this field, even with these problems. There are, and many are cited in the accompanying bibliography.

3. Aristides R. Zolberg, "Culture, Territory, Class: Ethnicity Demystified" (Paper presented at the International Political Science Association Congress, Edinburgh, 16–21 August 1976).

4. Our work leads us to agree with the thrust of Milton J. Esman's statement that a wide variety of factors are involved, but "so compelling are the normative claims of *ethnic* self-determination that nowhere in contemporary Europe have regional grievances been successfully politicized except where they enjoy an ethnic base." "Perspectives on Ethnic Conflict in Industrial Societies," in *Ethnic Conflict in the Western World,* ed. Milton J. Esman (Ithaca, N. Y.: Cornell University Press, 1977), p. 377.

5. Michael Hechter and Margaret Levi, "The Comparative Analysis of Ethnoregional Movements," *Ethnic and Racial Studies* 2 (July 1979): 260–74; and Anthony D. Smith, "Towards a Theory of Ethnic Separatism," *Ethnic and Racial Studies* 2 (January 1979): 21–37.

6. For an expanded discussion of governmental response patterns to ethnoterritorial demands see Joseph R. Rudolph and Robert J. Thompson, "Ethnoterritorial Movements and the Policy Process: Accommodating Nationalist Demands in the Developed World," *Comparative Politics* 17 (April 1985): 291–311.

## BIBLIOGRAPHY

Adams, Adran. "Prisoners in Exile: Senegalese Workers in France." *Race and Class,* 16 (1974).

Alcock, Antony E.; Taylor, Brian K.; and Welton, John M., eds. *The Future of Cultural Minorities.* New York: St. Martin's Press, 1979.

Alexander, Alan. "Scottish Nationalism: Agenda Building, Electoral Process, and Political Culture." *Canadian Review of Studies in Nationalism* 7 (Fall 1980): 373–85.

Beer, William. "The Social Class of Ethnic Activists in Contemporary France." In *Ethnic Conflict in the Western World,* edited by Milton J. Esman, pp. 143–58. Ithaca, N. Y.: Cornell University Press, 1977.

_____. *The Unexpected Rebellion: Ethnic Activism in Contemporary France.* New York: New York University Press, 1980.

Bell, Wendell, and Freeman, Walter E., eds. *Ethnicity and Nation-Building.* Beverly Hills: Sage, 1974.

Bennoune, Mahfoud. "The Maghribin Migrant Workers in France." *Race and Ethnicity* 17 (1975).

Berger, Suzanne. "Bretons and Jacobins: Reflections on French Regional Ethnicity." In *Ethnic Conflict in the Western World,* edited by Milton J. Esman, pp. 159–78. Ithaca, N. Y.: Cornell University Press, 1977.

_____. *Peasants against Politics: Rural Organization in Brittany, 1911–1967.* Cambridge: Harvard University Press, 1972.

Beyer, Gunther. "The Benelux Countries: Belgium, The Netherlands, Luxemburg." In *The Politics of Migration Policies: The First World in the 1970s,* edited by Daniel Kubat, pp. 107–25. New York: Center for Migration Studies, 1979.

Birch, Anthony. "Minority Nationalist Movements and Theories of Political Integration." *World Politics* 30 (April 1978): 325–44.

_____. *Political Integration and Disintegration in the British Isles.* London: George Allen and Unwin, 1977.

Birrell, Derek. "A Government of Northern Ireland and The Obstacle of Power-Sharing." *The Political Quarterly* 52 (April–June 1981): 184–202.

Bochel, John; Denver, David; and Macartney, Allan, eds. *The Referendum Experience: Scotland 1979.* Aberdeen, Scotland: Aberdeen University Press, 1981.

Bogdanor, Vernon. *Devolution.* Oxford: Oxford University Press, 1979.

Bohring, W. R. *The Migration of Workers in the United Kingdom and the European Community.* Oxford: Oxford University Press, 1972.

Brand, Jack. *The National Movement in Scotland.* London: Routledge and Kegan Paul, 1978.

Brass, Paul R. "Ethnicity and Nationality Formation." *Ethnicity* 3 (September 1976): 224–41.

Brazeau, Jacques, and Cloutier, Edouard. "Interethnic Relations and the Language Issue in Contemporary Canada: A General Appraisal." In *Ethnic Conflict in the Western World*, edited by Milton J. Esman, pp. 204–27. Ithaca, N. Y.: Cornell University Press, 1977.

Castells, Manuel. "Immigrant Workers and Class Struggles in Advanced Capitalism: The Western European Experience." *Politics and Society* 5 (1975): 33–66.

Charlton, Sue Ellen M. "Comparing Ethnic Movements in France." Paper presented at the Annual Meeting of the Southwestern Social Science Association, Ft. Worth, Tex., 28–31 March 1979.

————. "Nationalism and Regionalism in France's *Occitanie.*" Paper presented at the European Studies Conference, Omaha, Neb., 12–14 October 1978.

Clarke, Susan E., and Obler, Jeffrey L., eds. *Urban Ethnic Conflict: A Comparative Perspective.* Chapel Hill, N. C.: Institute of Research in Social Science, University of North Carolina, 1976.

Connor, Walker, "Ethnonationalism in the First World: The Present in Historical Perspective." In *Ethnic Conflict in the Western World,* edited by Milton J. Esman, pp. 19–45. Ithaca, N. Y.: Cornell University Press, 1977.

————. "The Politics of Ethnonationalism." *The Journal of International Affairs* 28 (1973): 1–21.

————. "A nation is a nation, is a state, is an ethnic group, is a. . . ." *Ethnic and Racial Studies* 50 (October 1978): 377–400.

Covell, Maureen. "Agreeing to Disagree: Elite Bargaining and the Revision of the Belgian Constitution." *Canadian Journal of Political Science* 15 (September 1982): 451–69.

Dorman, James H. "Ethnic Groups and 'Ethnicity': Some Theoretical Considerations." *The Journal of Ethnic Studies* 7 (Winter 1980): 23–36.

Duchacek, Ivo D., ed. *Federalism and Ethnicity. Publius* 7 (Fall 1977): the entire issue is devoted to the topic.

Enloe, Cynthia. *Ethnic Conflict and Political Development.* Boston: Little, Brown and Company, 1973.

————. "Police and Military in Ulster: Peacekeeping or Peace-subverting Forces?" *Journal of Peace Research* 15 (1978): 243–58.

————. "State-Building and Ethnic Structures: Dependence on International Capitalist Penetration." In *Processes of the World System,* Vol. 3, edited by Terence K. Hopkins and Immanual Wallerstein, pp. 266–88. Political Economy of the World-System Annuals. Beverly Hills: Sage, 1980.

Esman, Milton J., ed. *Ethnic Conflict in the Western World.* Ithaca, N. Y.: Cornell University Press, 1977.

————. "The Management of Communal Conflict." *Public Policy* 21 (Winter 1973): 49–78.

————. "The Politics of Official Bilingualism in Canada." *Political Science Quarterly* 97 (Summer 1982): 233–53.

————. "Public Administration and the Struggle for Shares in Ethnically and Racially Plural Societies." Paper presented at the Annual Meeting of the American Political Science Association, New York, 31 August–3 September 1978.

————. "Scottish Nationalism, North Sea Oil, and the British Response." In *Ethnic Conflict in the Western World*, edited by Milton J. Esman, pp. 251–86. Ithaca, N. Y.: Cornell University press, 1977.

Evans, A. C. "Development of European Community Law Regarding the Trade Union and Related Rights of Migrant Workers." *The International and Comparative Law Quarterly* 28 (July 1979): 354–66.

Fenwick, Rudy. "Social Change and Ethnic Nationalism: A Historical Analysis of the Separatist Movement in Quebec." *Comparative Studies in Society and History* 23 (April 1981): 196–216.

Freeman, Gary P. *Immigrant Labor and Racial Conflict in Industrial Societies: The French and British Experience, 1945–1975.* Princeton: Princeton University Press, 1979.

————. "Immigrant Labor and Working-Class Politics: The French and British Experience." *Comparative Politics* 11 (October 1978): 24–41.

————. "The Political Economy of Immigration Policy: Labour Supply and Legitimacy." Paper presented at the Council for European Studies Conference for Europeanists, Washington, D. C., March 1979.

Gingras, F. P., and Nevitte, N. "Religion, Values, and Politics in Contemporary Quebec." Paper presented at the Annual Meeting of the American Political Science Association, New York, 1981.

Gittler, Joseph B. "Toward Defining an Ethnic Minority." *International Journal of Group Tensions* 7 (1977): 4–19.

Glazer, Nathan, and Moynihan, Daniel P., eds. *Ethnicity: Theory and Experience.* Cambridge: Harvard University Press, 1975.

Gourevitch, Peter Alexis. "The Reemergence of 'Peripheral Nationalism': Some comparative Speculations on the Spatial Distribution of Political Leadership and Economic Growth." *Comparative Study of Society and History* 21 (July 1979): 303–22.

Green, Leslie. "Rational Nationalists." *Political Studies* 30 (June 1982): 236–46.

Grove, John D. "A Cross-National Examination of Cross-Cutting and Reinforcing Cultural Cleavages." *International Journal of Comparative Sociology* 17 (September–December 1977): 217–27.

Hanham, H. J. *Scottish Nationalism.* Cambridge: Harvard University Press, 1969.

Hayward, Jack. "Institutionalized Inequality within an Indivisible Republic: Brittany and France." Paper presented at the International Political Science Association Congress, Edinburgh, Scotland, 16–21 August 1976.

Hechter, Michael. *Internal Colonialism: The Celtic Fringe in British National Development, 1536–1966.* Berkeley: University of California Press, 1975.

Hechter, Michael, and Levi, Margaret. "The Comparative Analysis of Ethnoregional Movements." *Ethnic and Racial Studies* 2 (July 1979): 260–74.

Heisler, Martin, ed. "Ethnic Conflict in the World Today." *The Annals* 433 (September 1977): the entire issue is devoted to the topic.

Hoffman-Nowotny, Hans Joachim, and Killias, Martin. "Switzerland." In *International Labor Migration in Europe,* edited by Ronald E. Krane, pp. 45–62. New York: Praeger, 1979.

Horowitz, Donald. "Patterns of Ethnic Separatism." *Comparative Studies in Society and History* 23 (April 1981): 165–95.

Hughes, Christopher. *Switzerland.* New York: Praeger, 1975.

Jacob, James. "Ethnic Mobilization and the Pursuit of Post-Industrial Values." *The Tocqueville Review* 2 (Spring–Summer 1980): 52–85.

Jones, Barry, and Keating, Michael. "The Resolution of Internal Conflicts and External Pressures: The Labour Party's Devolution Policy." *Government and Opposition* 17 (Summer 1982): 279–92.

Jones, Barry, and Wilford, Rick. "Further Considerations on the Referendum: The Evidence of the Welsh Vote on Devolution." *Political Studies* 30 (March 1982): 16–27.

Kahrs, Karl H. "Foreign Workers in the Industrial Societies of East and West Europe." Paper presented at the Annual Meeting of the American Political Science Association, New York, September 1978.

Kasfir, Nelson. "Explaining Ethnic Political Participation." *World Politics* 31 (April 1979): 365–88.

Kauppi, Mark V. "The Decline of the Scottish National Party, 1977–81: Political and Organizational Factors." *Ethnic and Racial Studies* 5 (July 1982): 326–48.

Keyes, Charles F. "Towards a New Formulation of the Concept of Ethnic Group." *Ethnicity* 3 (September 1976): 202–13.

Koelstra, Rein W., and Simon, Gildas. "France." In *International Labor Migration in Europe,* edited by Ronald E. Krane, pp. 133–43. New York: Praeger, 1979.

Kofman, Eleonore. "Differential Modernisation, Social Conflicts and Ethnoregionalism in Corsica." *Ethnic and Racial Studies* 5 (July 1982): 299–312.

Krane, Ronald E., ed. *International Labor Migration in Europe.* New York: Praeger, 1979.

Krejci, Jaroslav, and Velinsky, V. *Ethnic and Political Nations in Europe.* New York: St. Martin's Press, 1981.

Kubat, Daniel. "Canada." In *The Politics of Migration Policies,* edited by Daniel Kubat, pp. 19–36. New York: Center for Migration Studies, 1979.

_____, ed. *The Politics of Migration Policies.* New York: Center for Migration Studies, 1979.

Levy, Roger. "The Non-mobilization of a Thesis: A Reply to Mughan and McAllister." *Ethnic and Racial Studies* 5 (July 1982): 366–77.

Lijphart, Arend. "Political Theories and the Explanation of Ethnic Conflict in the Western World: Falsified Predictions and Plausible Postdictions." In *Ethnic Conflict in the Western World,* edited by Milton J. Esman, pp. 46–64. Ithaca, N. Y.: Cornell University Press, 1977.

_____. *Democracy in Plural Societies.* New Haven: Yale University Press, 1977.

_____. "Religious vs. Linguistic vs. Class Voting: The 'Crucial Experiment' of

Comparing Belgium, Canada, South Africa, and Switzerland." *American Political Science Review* 73 (June 1979): 442–58.

Loh, Wallace D. "Nationalist Attitudes in Quebec and Belgium." *Journal of Conflict Resolution* 19 (1975): 217–49.

Lubin, M. "System Maintenance in Quebec: The Parti Quebecois." Paper presented at the Annual Meeting of the Northeastern Political Science Association, New Haven, Conn., 1980.

Lustgarden, Laurence. "The Grounds of Discrimination Under the Race Relations Act of 1976 in the United Kingdom." *The International and Comparative Law Quarterly* 28 (April 1979): 221–40.

Lustick, Ian. "Stability in Deeply Divided Societies: Consociationalism versus Control." *World Politics* 31 (April 1979): 325–44.

Madgwick, Peter, and Rose, Richard, eds. *The Territorial Dimension in United Kingdom Politics*. London: Macmillan, 1982.

Markovits, Andrei S., and Kazainov, Samantha. "Class Conflict, Capitalism, and Social Democracy: The Case of Migrant Workers in the Federal Republic of Germany." *Comparative Politics* 10 (April 1978): 373–91.

Matasar, Ann B. "Ethnic and Religious Factors in the Swiss Reaction to Their Foreign Worker Problem: A Look at the Schwarzenbach Initiative." Paper presented at the Annual Meeting of the American Political Science Association, Chicago, August 1974.

McKay, James. "An Exploratory Synthesis of Primordial and Mobilizationalist Approaches to Ethnic Phenomena." *Ethnic and Racial Studies* 5 (October 1982): 395–420.

McRoberts, Kenneth. "Internal Colonialism: The Case of Quebec." *Ethnic and Racial Studies* 2 (July 1979): 293–318.

Mehrlander, Ursula. "Federal Republic of Germany." In *The Politics of Migration Policies*, edited by Daniel Kubar, pp. 145–62. New York: Center for Migration Studies, 1979.

Miles, R., and Phizacklea, A. "Class, Race, Ethnicity and Political Action." *Political Studies* 25 (December 1977): 491–507.

Miller, W. L. "What Was the Profit in Following the Crowd?: The Effectiveness of Party Strategies on Immigration and Devolution." *British Journal of Political Science* 10 (January 1980): 15–38.

Moulier, Yann, and Tapinos, Georges. "France." In *The Politics of Migration Policies*, edited by Daniel Kubat, pp. 127–43. New York: Center for Migration Studies, 1979.

Mughan, Anthony. "Accommodation or Defusion in the Management of Linguistic Conflict in Belgium?" *Political Studies* 31 (September 1983): 434–51.

————. "Modernization and Ethnic Conflict in Belgium." *Political Studies* 27 (March 1979): 21–37.

Mughan, Anthony, and McAllister, Ian. "The Mobilization of the Ethnic Vote: A Thesis With Some Scottish and Welsh Evidence." *Ethnic and Racial Studies* 4 (April 1981): 189–204.

Osmond, John. *Creative Conflict: The Politics of Welsh Devolution*. London: Gomer Press and Routledge and Kegan Paul, 1977.

Rabushka, Alvin, and Shepsle, Kenneth A. *Politics in Plural Societies*. Columbus, Ohio: Charles E. Merrill, 1972.

Ragin, Charles E. "Ethnic Political Mobilization: The Welsh Case." *American Sociological Review* 44 (1979): 619–35.

Rayside, David M. "The Impact of the Linguistic Cleavage on the 'Governing' Parties of Belgium and Canada." *Canadian Journal of Political Science* 11 (March 1978): 61–97.

Rees, Tom. "The United Kingdom." In *The Politics of Migration Policies,* edited by Daniel Kubat, pp. 67–91. New York: Center for Migration Studies, 1979.

Reimann, Horst, and Reimann, Helga. "Federal Republic of Germany." In *International Labor Migration in Europe,* edited by Ronald E. Krane, pp. 62–87. New York: Praeger, 1979.

Rist, Ray C. *The Guestworkers in Germany: Prospect for Pluralism.* New York: Praeger, 1978.

_____. "Migration and Marginality: Guestworkers in Germany and France." *Daedalus* 108 (Spring 1979): 95–108.

Rokkan, Stein, and Urwin, Derek W., eds. *The Politics of Territorial Identity: Studies in European Regionalism.* Beverly Hills: Sage, 1982.

Ronen, Dov. *The Quest for Self-Determination.* New Haven: Yale University Press, 1979.

Rose, Richard. *Governing Without Consensus: An Irish Perspective.* Boston: Beacon Press, 1971.

_____. *The United Kingdom as a Multinational State.* Survey Research Centre Occasional paper, no. 6. Glasgow, Scotland: University of Strathclyde, 1970.

Ross, Jeffrey A., and Cottrell, Ann Baker. *The Mobilization of collective identity: Comparative Perspectives.* Edited by Robert St. Cyr and Philip Rawkins. Lanham, Md.: University Press of America, 1980.

Rothchild, Joseph. *Ethnopolitics.* New York: Columbia University Press, 1981.

Rudolph, Joseph R. "Ethnic Sub-States and the Emergent Politics of Tri-level Interaction in Western Europe." *Western Political Quarterly* 3 (December 1977): 537–57.

_____. "Ethnonational Parties and Political Change: The Belgian and British Experience." *Polity* 9 (Summer 1977): 401–27.

_____. "Ethno-Regionalism in Contemporary Western Europe: The Politics of Accommodation." *Canadian Review of Studies in Nationalism* 8 (1981): 323–41.

Rudolph, Joseph R., and Thompson, Robert J. "Ethno-territorial Movements and the Policy Process: Accommodating Nationalist Demands in the Developed World." *Comparative Politics* 17 (April 1985): 291–311.

Safran, William. "The French Left and Ethnic Pluralism." Paper presented at the Annual Meeting of the Western Political Science Association, Seattle, 24–26 March 1983.

Savard, Jean-Guy, and Vigneault, Richard, eds. *Les états multilingues: problèmes et solutions/Multilingual Political Systems: Problems and Solutions.* Quebec City: Les Presses de L'Université Laval, 1975.

Savigear, P. "Corsica 1975: Politics and Violence." *World Today* 31 (November 1975): 462–68.

Schmitt, David E. "Ethnic Conflict in Northern Ireland: International Aspects of Conflict Management." In *Ethnic Conflict in the Western World,* edited by Milton

J. Esman, pp. 228–50. Ithaca, N. Y.: Cornell University Press, 1977.

Schmitter, Barbara E. "Immigrant Minorities in West Germany: Some Theoretical Concerns." *Ethnic and Racial Studies* 6 (July 1983): 308–19.

Smiley, Donald V. "French-English Relations in Canada and Consociational Democracy." In *Ethnic Conflict in the Western World,* edited by Milton J. Esman, pp. 179–204. Ithaca, N. Y.: Cornell University Press, 1977.

Smith, Anthony D. *The Ethnic Revival.* Cambridge: Cambridge University Press, 1981.

————. *Theories of Nationalism.* New York: Harper and Row, 1971.

————. "Towards a Theory of Ethnic Separatism." *Ethnic and Racial Studies* 2 (January 1979): 21–37.

Steiner, Jurg, and Obler, Jeffrey. "Does the Consociational Theory Really Hold for Switzerland?" In *Ethnic Conflict in the Western World,* edited by Milton J. Esman, pp. 324–42. Ithaca, N. Y.: Cornell University Press, 1977.

Studlar, Donley T. "Ethnicity and the Policy Process in Western Europe." Paper presented at the Annual Meeting of the Southern Political Science Association, New Orleans, 3–5 November 1977.

————. "Great Britain." In *International Labor Migration in Europe,* edited by Ronald E. Krane, pp. 88–117. New York: Praeger, 1979.

————. "Policy Voting in Britain: The Colored Immigration Issue in the 1964, 1966, and 1970 General Elections." *American Political Science Review* 72 (March 1978): 46–64.

————. "Post-Industrial Society and Ethnicity." Paper presented at the Annual Meeting of the International Studies Association, Los Angeles, 19–22 March 1980.

————. "Elite Responsiveness or Elite Autonomy: British Immigration Policy Reconsidered." *Ethnic and Racial Studies* 3 (April 1980): 207–23.

Thompson, Robert J. "Political Change in Scotland: The Rise of Scottish Nationalism and the Devolution Issue." Ph. D. dissertation, University of Oklahoma, 1979.

————. "The Scottish National Party: A Study of Its Bases of Support, 1949–1978." *Historicus* 1 (1978): 44–81.

Thompson, Robert J., and Cediel, Maria. "Comparative Analysis of Ethnonational Referendums: The Cases of the U. K., Canada, and Spain." Paper presented at the Annual Meeting of the Midwest Political Science Association, Cincinnati, 1981.

Tinker, Hugh, ed. *The Banyan Tree.* Oxford: Oxford University Press, 1977.

Turner, Jonathan H., and Singleton, Royce, Jr. "A Theory of Ethnic Oppression: Toward a Reintegration of Cultural and Structural concepts in Ethnic Relations Theory." *Social Forces* 56 (June 1978): 1001–18.

Warmenhoven, Henri J. "The Swiss Dilemma: Foreign Labor Problems in Light of *Ueberfremdung.*" Paper presented at the European Studies Conference, Omaha, Neb., October 1976.

Webb, Keith. *The Growth of Nationalism in Scotland.* Glasgow, Scotland: The Molendinar Press, 1977.

Weinstein, Brian. "Language Strategists: Redefining Political Frontiers on the Basis of Linguistic Choices." *World Politics* 31 (April 1979): 345–64.

Williams, Colin. *National Separatism.* Cardiff, England: University Press, 1981.

_____. "Social Mobilization and Nationalism in Multicultural Societies." *Ethnic and Racial Studies* 5 (July 1982): 349–65.

Wilson, Frank. "French-Canadian Separatism." *The Western Political Quarterly* 20 (March 1967): 116–31.

Wirsing, Robert. "Cultural Minorities: Is the World Ready to Protect Them?" *Canadian Review of Studies in Nationalism* 7 (Fall 1980): 220–43.

Yannopoulos, G. N. "Mediterranean Labour in an Era of Slow Community Growth." *World Today* 35 (December 1979).

Young, Crawford. *The Politics of Cultural Pluralism.* Madison: The University of Wisconsin Press, 1976.

Zolberg, Aristides R. "Culture, Territory, Class: Ethnicity Demystified." Paper presented at the International Political Science Association Congress, Edinburgh, Scotland, 16–21 August 1976.

_____. "The Making of Flemings and Walloons: Belgium: 1830–1914." *Journal of Interdisciplinary History* 5 (Autumn 1974): 179–235.

_____. "Splitting the Difference: Federalization Without Federalism in Belgium." In *Ethnic Conflict in the Western World,* edited by Milton J. Esman, pp. 103–40. Ithaca, N. Y.: Cornell University Press, 1977.

# 4 Hegemonial Exchange: An Alternative Model for Managing Conflict in Middle Africa

Donald Rothchild

*"Mutual adjustment among leaders . . . is inevitable
even in a highly authoritarian system."*
Charles E. Lindblom[1]

The relations between the state and ethnic groupings in middle Africa are far more complex than the oft-used control-consociational democracy dichotomy might suggest. No doubt this dichotomy is valuable in explaining the most representative examples of subjection or of power-sharing, for example in hegemonic (hierarchically structured) South Africa and in polyarchical Nigeria under the 1979 federal constitution, respectively. Its utility seems more circumscribed when the many African states ranged between these polar points must be accounted for. Hence, unless more precise conceptual tools are developed, social scientists will likely find it difficult to analyze state-ethnic (or the subregional aggregates of such groups, henceforth referred to as ethnoregional) relationships, or to make policy recommendations on facilitating constructive conflict by altering their terms of interaction.

The control model, which involves a broad network of state restrictions or the threat of such restrictions upon the actions of ethnic groups in order to modify their social behavior, is most likely to be observed in situations where intergroup conflict is intense and brokerage institutions are ineffectual. In this Hobbesian world of group against group, such brokerage mechanisms as the multiethnic party or the coalition of ethnic-based parties are dissolved, and interparty communication and cooperation are obstructed and often entirely disappear.[2] Under such circumstances, the dominant political class, appropriately or not, defends systematic state coercion as a means of compensating for a lack of societal consensus.[3]

Certainly mechanisms of formal political dominance (which I have disaggregated elsewhere into subjection, isolation, avoidance, and displacement)[4] are plainly in evidence on the middle-African scene. This is hardly surprising in light of the prevailing scarcity of distributable resources and the intensity of the struggle among groups for favored allocations. In such environments, the state may be "soft" (that is, low on legitimacy and lacking in the capacity to implement public policies effectively throughout its realm),[5] and even biased in favor of dominant class or ethnic interests. Yet, largely because of its fiscal ascendancy, the state represents a valued prize to be sought after, not only because of its recruitment and allocative activities, but also because of its ability to influence (if not set) the terms and costs of intergroup relations.[6] In brief, then, the state is an influential but not exclusive element in the decision-making process. It exercises a degree of autonomous authority, but, due to its limited bureaucratic reach and competence, it is by no means the sole autonomous actor in the community.

This results in a fluid context in which dominant state-party elites must, of necessity, conciliate and bargain with the other class and ethnic interests in society. Describing how a weak state-party elite at the center avoids a confrontation with powerful interests at the periphery, Goran Hyden writes: "The softness of the state emerges because leaders do not control the rural masses through ownership of existing means of production. As a result, they have been able to obtain their loyalty only through purchase, that is, they have been forced to give away benefits to the masses without necessarily getting anything in return to strengthen the system they rule."[7] One could reasonably contend, without doing damage to Hyden's basic argument, that leaders have given away public goods in exchange for political stability. But what is clear is that the soft state gives rise to spiraling ethnic claims,[8] and a dynamic of state-ethnic exchanges materializes which gives and takes in accordance with the power and capabilities of the various political actors.

In light of this reality, it is essential to focus upon the networks of reciprocities and the "rhythm of ethnic political interchanges," and not upon such abstract European formulations as "command" or "totalitarianism."[9] The soft African state, lacking the force and sophisticated machinery of modern tyrannies, more often than not fits poorly with classical control models for regulating relations in multiethnic societies.[10]

The consociational democracy model, regarded by some analysts as the realizable liberal alternative to control in multiethnic societies, also seems artificial, even inappropriate, under Third World conditions. Where a consociational arrangement is said to be operating, conflict among segments and their various political parties is recognized; even so, some overarching social norms and values are shared by the groups, making it possible for a cartel of elites to act cooperatively and to mediate disputes between rival interests. Elite cooperation, rather than destabilizing competition, is the cornerstone of a decision process geared to overcoming divergent interests and achieving "positive-sum" outcomes. Hence to reduce the divisive effects of open political conflict in socially and culturally fragmented societies, the majority-rule principle is replaced by an inclusive norm which emphasizes the participation of the political leaders of all main segments in a "grand coalition."[11] To further ensure that all segments will be guaranteed a significant autonomy to regulate their own internal affairs, central government power is limited by the application of a mutual veto rule and by the principle of proportionality in recruitment and public allocations. Consociationalism reconciles freely expressed partisan activities with effective elite cooperation in the day-to-day conduct of public business—a combination that can only succeed where the general public is deferential toward its various representatives.

In a unique effort to engineer such an arrangement on the African continent, a commission appointed by Chief Gatsha Buthelezi in South Africa proposed the integration of his Zulu homeland of KwaZulu with the White-run Natal provincial administration. The commission sought to form a single political entity in which all groups would share political power. At the outset, the executive would consist of equal White and Black segments, with representation for the Indian and Coloured communities; the legislative assembly would be elected by universal adult suffrage on a proportional representation basis. "At a later stage," the commission noted optimistically, "the group associations would be found to have changed toward common political and economic interests and by agreement the groups represented on the executive could be varied under an amended consociational agreement."[12] As might have been anticipated, the Botha government, recoiling from proposals to institutionalize ethnic power-sharing, rejected the Buthelezi commission recommendations immediately. In light of this rejection, further movement toward a compromise along the lines of consociational democracy would only seem likely where Blacks and Whites alike come to regard such an arrangement as mutually beneficial. This could possibly occur when the currently dominant Whites perceive the costs of the status quo to be unbearable and the repressed majority views a negotiated compromise as in its interests, temporarily at least, because of the economic costs arising from exaggerated White fears.[13]

Though consociational arrangements might have meaning in certain small, unified, and relatively affluent Western democracies (Belgium, Austria, and, until recently, the Netherlands),[14] the model has not proved easily transferable to postcolonial Africa. The explanations for this are many and varied. Conditions in postcolonial Africa contrary to those required for consociational democracy include the following:

1. Whereas consociationalism builds a political arrangement upon accepted social cleavages, many new African states, uncertain as to their unity and identity, stress the legitimacy of community-wide values and purposes as against contending sub-unit claims. In doing so, they seek to foster national

unity both by weakening ethnic linkages and by creating common ties, remembrances, and values. Public policies which abolish chieftaincy (Guinea),
deny the right to organize ethnically based associations (Kenya, Zaire) and
political parties (Ghana), ban state-creation movements (Nigeria's Federal
Military Government, 31 December 1983), or sponsor single-party and no-
party systems are, in part, efforts to overcome what are perceived to be
adverse effects of ethnic fragmentation.

2. The intensity of interethnic competition in contemporary Africa is
largely explained by the overriding economic scarcities in that area. In contrast to West Europe in the 1970s and 1980s, most African states, heavily
impacted by the world recession and the fall in world commodity prices, have
become mired in a situation of low economic growth, increasing population
pressures, and widening income gaps. The resulting frustrations and resentments have contributed to military interventions and populism (Rawlings'
Ghana), and are hardly propitious circumstances for an experiment with a
liberal political system based on restraint and deference, such as consociationalism.

3. Though many African states are indeed small in size—a favorable
condition in the eyes of consociational theorists because it means greater
face-to-face interaction—some of the most prominent candidates for a consociational arrangement (Nigeria, Sudan, and Zaire) seem sufficiently large
and divided to represent experiments in pan-Africanism, with all the diversity and fragmentation this entails.

4. Similar to their West European counterparts, African ethnic groups
are likely to represent anything but homogeneous bargaining partners. Not
only are many of Africa's ethnoregional units heterogeneous in character but
its ethnic groups are divided by personality clashes, class interests, and
schisms based on clan and region. In Kenya, for example, the political rivalries among Muranga, Nyeri and Kiambu in predominantly Kikuyu Central
Province may prove just as intense and significant as those at the top among
the Kikuyu, Luo, Luhya, Kalenjin, and others. Hence ethnic bargaining in
African circumstances is complicated, and inevitably places a heavy burden
upon leaders: they must actively negotiate a common position within the
panethnic group before entering into exchanges with the spokesmen of other
ethnic interests at the center. This two-step process not only complicates the
operation of a consociational arrangement, it also increases the likelihood,
always present to some degree, of governmental *immobilisme*. [15]

5. Most prominent among the characteristics of consociational democracy is the cooperation of elites in an enduring coalition. [16] During the anticolonial struggle, African elites did display a considerable willingness to
cooperate for the common good, submerging their differences to present a
united front against the continuance of imperial rule. In succeeding years, as
independence came and went, cooperation sometimes turned quickly into
competition within the dominant political elite over the securing of political

power and the goods of modernity. Informal understandings and norms of relationship worked out among elite notables proved transitional features of particular countries' situations, not always transferable to new leaderships in periods of succession (Cameroun, Kenya). The result has been to make reciprocity among rural group interests more tentative and ad hoc than anticipated by consociational theorists. And where members of the dominant elite have been inflexible in the face of changing conditions, such as the demographic shifts of Lebanon, the maintenance of a consociational arrangement proved impossible.[17]

6. In an authoritarian context, where the single-party bureaucracy at the center often places its imprimatur on local candidates for political office, there is no guarantee that the true spokesmen for ethnic interests will emerge as the ones to participate in the decision process. The result, in the African context, can be an elite coalition in which some members reflect the opinions of their constituents inadequately or even falsely. Noting the manipulation of the Luo and other opposition constituencies by the Kenyatta regime in Kenya in the 1960s, Dirk Berg-Schlosser concluded that "the present attempt at a grand coalition, even though it represents a fairly wide balance of forces, thus cannot be considered to have incorporated all strands of opinion or potential sources of opposition in Kenya's wider and quite dynamic society."[18]

In addition to recognizing these unfavorable conditions for consociationalism in Africa, it is also important to note an undesirable consequence that might follow from the introduction of such an arrangement. The implementation of a consociational arrangement could, by making ethnicity the basis for participation in political life, have the effect of increasing the polarization of the society. "Because consociational democracy recognizes the legitimacy and constructive functions of the segments and because it encourages and subsidizes their separate organizations," Arend Lijphart observes, "it is in the nature of consociationalism to make a plural society more plural, at least in the beginning."[19] Rather than fostering a national consciousness—a critical objective in the eyes of the new African elite—consociationalism would focus upon the ethnic unit, thereby treating group affiliations and interests as primary.[20] The possible dangers of political mobilization on the basis of ethnic affiliation are quite apparent to various observers. Thus Brian Barry, writing about relations between the English- and French-speaking communities of Canada, comments appropriately on the hazards of "deliberately" creating the conditions that will enable the conflict to be resolved through a consociational solution.[21] Clearly, given the intense emotionalism of an ethnically divided society, the risks entailed in promoting group-based political participation, even of a nonadversarial sort, should not be discounted lightly.

In sum, while both the control and consociational models offer useful insights into Africa's interethnic relations, they fail to catch the complexity of actual encounters between the state and ethnic groups. What is needed, then, is a more realistic assessment of the impact of political institutions on social behavior. This necessitates greater attention to the overlap between formal institutions and informal practices, or, in the case at hand, between the use of hegemonial and exchange decision mechanisms to regulate social behavior. In order to probe the overlaps occurring in group interactions on the African scene, I first put forth an alternative decision model, which I will designate as "hegemonial exchange." After describing the types of state-ethnic encounters which have occurred under a hegemonial exchange system in middle Africa, I examine the reciprocal motives that state and ethnoregional actors have for entering into political exchanges within a hegemonial context. From there, I turn to the perceptions of group conflict—essentialist, pragmatic, and reciprocative—which shape the nature of group conflict and, most significant for our purposes, facilitate or impede the process of political exchange. In the concluding sections, I comment briefly on the policy implications and trade-offs arising from the use of a hegemonial exchange approach under middle-African circumstances.

## THE HEGEMONIAL EXCHANGE MODEL

In the scarcity-prone and soft-state conditions of contemporary middle Africa, neither hegemonic control nor direct and open political exchange accurately describes the dynamics of the state-ethnic relations occurring in most of these countries. If interethnic conflict has for the most part remained manageable, this can hardly be explained by the state's capabilities to coerce compliance or by the political actors' observance of the explicit rules governing exchange. To be sure, direct bargaining and a regularized process of political exchanges did exist around the time of independence in Zambia, Kenya, Zimbabwe and elsewhere; however, because of domestic and international pressures and elite impatience with the constraints upon decision-making, the formal rules on reciprocity hammered out with the departing colonial powers proved difficult to sustain. Hence African elites, with little choice but to adapt the forms by which reciprocal interactions might be conducted, shifted from a process of direct and formal to tacit and informal exchanges. With that shift, informal rules of tension management, described by one author as a "semicodified set of procedures," came quickly to prevail.[22] In these new postcolonial circumstances, it is the ongoing stream of these informal state-ethnic exchanges (and not the open and more formalized bargaining process of a consociational arrangement) that determines stable and effective (although frequently unequal) intergroup relations.

Within the parameters of the single- or no-party arrangement, state and ethnoregional actors enter into exchanges involving different spheres of value—what can be depicted as "multiplex exchanges."[23] In these situations, central state leaders quite typically give some measure of status, autonomous power, representation, or economic resources in exchange for the ethnoregional unit's support of and compliance with the state's regulations. Normally the process is implicit and understood; only rarely is it a matter of separate and openly contracted agreements. As Warren Ilchman and Norman Uphoff note: "In practice, exchanges seldom occur in isolated, explicit, or barter situations. Rather resources are usually exchanged as flows, with changes made at one time affecting subsequent flows."[24] Thus state-ethnic exchanges are an ongoing process of relations and involve a variety of linkages among political actors, quite commonly with economic values being exchanges for such political values as compliance and support. What seem critical to the coherency or regularity of these state-sector relationships are the strength of moral links tying the different actors together and the predictability of these flows.

Neither the hegemonial nor the exchange model of conflict regulation, then, appears likely to materialize in pure form under contemporary middle-African conditions. Postcolonial middle-African governments, anxious to consolidate their hold over the bureaucratic apparatus as well as the society at large, shunned classical, Eurocentric formulas of statecraft, and sought, in their own ways, to restructure conflict along controlled yet cooperative lines. This restructuring often entailed a reduced scope for open manifestations of vertical as well as horizontal intergroup conflict and a redefining or abolishing of what the new leaders perceived as irksome restraints upon their ability to govern, most notably inherited institutions such as federalism, *majimbo* (regionalism), multipartyism, bicameralism, and entrenched constitutional safeguards, especially those concerning amendments. The results included new restrictions on the interactions among groups and the emergence of one-party or no-party systems. Such systems were largely built upon those colonially transmitted institutions which enhanced the dominant position of the state-party elite, especially persons in leading positions in the executive, bureaucracy, military, and police. Meanwhile those institutions such as legal oppositions, constitutional guarantees, and autonomous and competing centers of power perceived by the new ruling elites as impeding their ability to govern were limited, terminated, or transformed.[25]

Yet the reduced scope for antagonistic conflict resulting from these measures hardly brought an end to ethnoregional rivalries. Even in Guinea, where Sékou Touré's Parti Démocratique de Guinée abolished the institution of chieftaincy and the ethnic-based party committees, party officials had to take special care, in the early years at least, to blunt the force of ethnic particularism by means of ethnic balancing.[26] Under these circumstances and similar ones elsewhere, the party system was likened to a "machine," and described as "not a dogma but an expedient."[27]

Within these partially closed systems, intergroup conflict and exchange persists—as evidenced by continuing factional power struggles and, on the output side, by the application of proportional principles (*Proporz*) to such issue areas as coalition formation, elite recruitment, and fiscal allocations. To arrive at these allocations, a process of political exchange may occur among party cadres or between state and ethnoregional spokesmen at the top of the political system, according to the procedures for quiet diplomacy defined by each state. And this exchange process is by no means limited to the central political arena, for the ethnoregional intermediaries must enter into further exchanges at the constituency level with ethnic kinsmen and other identity groups alike. Hence, in contrast to the classical models of hegemonic and consociational conflict management, the middle-African situation often subtly reconciles the twin thrusts of political transaction and party or governmental control. It allows, even encourages, agreement on political exchange outcomes while containing, and thereby attempting to avoid, the zero-sum antagonisms which might well lead to the undermining of the frail political order. To characterize this untidy but expedient process, it seems useful to set forth a new analytical model, one more appropriate to the informality of current African realities. To this end, I propose to characterize this linking of the two thrusts of control and political exchange under the rubric of *hegemonial exchange*.

As an ideal type, hegemonial exchange is a form of state-facilitated coordination in which a somewhat autonomous central-state actor and a number of considerably less autonomous ethnoregional interests engage, on the basis of commonly accepted procedural norms, rules, or understandings, in a process of mutual accommodations.[28] It is not a pure case of centrally determined coordination (i.e., control) because the middle-African state is "soft" and lacks the capacity to impose unilaterally its coordinating decisions on ethnoregional spokesmen or constituents. It is also not a pure case of direct negotiations among ethnoregional spokesmen combining in a freely elected coalition of elites (i.e., consociation) because open, partisan competition in elections is prohibited. Instead, hegemonial exchange brings together some devices from control—in particular, the single- or no-party system and encapsulated decision-making—with some devices from consociation—mainly, the securing of state-ethnoregional and interethnic exchange and reciprocity by means of quiet behind-the-scenes negotiations and the application of the proportionality principle. What materializes is a procedure for managing conflict best described as hegemonial or coercive exchange which may, so long as the contending actors maintain their relative power bases intact, promote conciliatory behavior and interdependence among disparate state and ethnoregional interests, under conditions of overarching scarcity and international dependency.

Envisaged for heuristic purposes in diagrammatic fashion, this relationship between core and periphery is depicted in Figure 4.1. In the context of a single-or no-party system, continuous state-ethnic exchanges, or what Richard Cyert and James March describe as "informal bargaining," (defined as "bargaining between groups in which conflict of interest is implicit") takes

**Figure 4.1    State-Ethno-Regional Interchanges and Brokerage**

—    **International Environment**
**State as Organizing Principles**

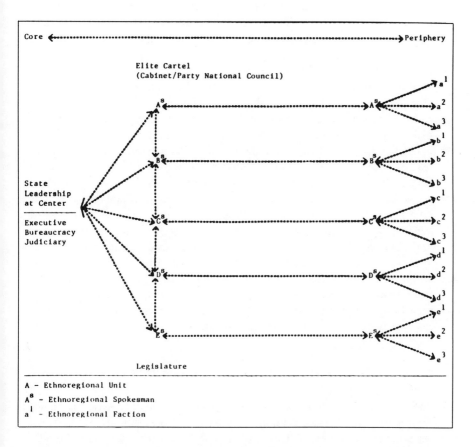

Core ⟵·············································································⟶ Periphery

Elite Cartel
(Cabinet/Party National Council)

State
Leadership
at Center

Executive
Bureaucracy
Judiciary

Legislature

A – Ethnoregional Unit
A[B] – Ethnoregional Spokesman
a[1] – Ethnoregional Faction

place at the center between key state actors and spokesmen for ethnoregional interests.[29] Ethnoregional intermediaries, themselves members of the dominant political class as well as spokesmen for subnational interests,[30] must engage both in simultaneous negotiations in two political arenas—with diverse ethnoregional factions at the periphery and with the central leadership in the cabinet or party national council—and in face-to-face relations with members of the executive and bureaucracy. Further interchanges with the spokesmen for other ethnic interests may take place when the elite cartel assembles or at sessions of the national legislature.[31] In terms of the regularity of these exchanges, the styles and preferences of the state leader or leaders and of the ethnoregional intermediaries are critical to the persistence—and hence the enduring nature—of these relationships. Where the state leadership makes effective use of its elite cartel or its dyadic exchanges to facilitate mutual accommodations, and where ethnoregional spokesmen also are prepared to act in accordance with the state's prevailing norms and values and to direct group demands along recognized lines, constructive conflict may materialize. The partially autonomous state and the subregional actors will then be encountering one another in conformity with state guidelines.[32] In fact, such a conflict-resolving outcome seems most likely to occur when both core and periphery actors shape their political behavior so as to advance the mutual interests of the dominant political class of which both are a part. This identification with dominant class interests, however, may weaken the exchange process if it undermines the subregional intermediary's perceived ties to his local constituency base, causing a burgeoning of candidates with claims to local legitimacy. As Nelson Kasfir notes, the central government could then find itself in a situation where it "is actively looking for local leaders with whom to bargain but cannot find anyone likely to be effective because the local groups are too fragmented." Although such a situation gives central authorities great leverage, it has the disadvantage, as Kasfir points out, that bargains struck could come unstruck.[33] Hence, a process of hegemonially controlled reciprocity can only be expected to settle conflict amicably on a long-term basis where both state leaders and ethnoregional spokesmen interact in accordance with the state's organizing principles, while maintaining minimal legitimacy among their diverse publics. The transfer of state resources in the process of hegemonial exchange must be seen to benefit ethnoregional clients as well as patrons if the political relationship is to gain broad acceptance over time.

## HEGEMONIAL EXCHANGE PRACTICES

The evidence on hegemonial exchange practices in middle Africa is highly fragmentary and varied, running from ad hoc dyadic transactions between state and ethnic representatives at the top of the hierarchy to a more broadly encompassing network of exchanges within an informal grand coalition of elites. The practices of political exchange are so various, in military- and civilian-led regimes alike, that the critical question is less the reality of interchanges than the legitimacy accorded them by the state.

For instance, the military governor or commissioner of a subregion may differ little in his operational mode or his closeness to his constituents' demands from his civilian counterpart.[34] This was brought home in a forceful manner to me in an April 1976 interview in Tamale with the regional commissioner of the Northern Region of Ghana. I found little to distinguish in his description of efforts to negotiate directly with the Minister of Finance and appropriate ministry officials in Accra on behalf of his region from what might have been expected of a civilian broker for ethnoregional interests. Nigeria's military governors, the sole official points of contact with the Supreme Military Council and the Federal Executive Council during the Ironsi regime in 1966, were careful to recognize the higher authority of the head of the National Military Government and the Supreme Commander of the Armed Forces and to adopt a national perspective, so far as possible, on policy matters; nevertheless, they did not remain long in office before coming to advocate subregional interests at the center. Robin Luckham notes: "Although none of the Military Governors had entirely abandoned the antipolitical image . . . they began to conceive of themselves as administrators and leaders concerned with the interests of their regions as a whole, in much the same way that they had previously identified with the national interest."[35] He goes on to illustrate this as follows:

> Colonel Adebayo's first speeches on appointment as Military Governor of the West in July 1966 keep reiterating the theme of the need for unity among the Yorubas. In August 1966, he chose Chief Awolowo after his release from prison as "Leader of the Yorubas" because he wanted "one man to talk instead of 10.5 million" and he thus started to think in terms of Yoruba irridentism. We begin to find Lt. Colonel Ejoor, the Governor of the Mid-West, complaining that his region had been "neglected by the Federal Government in the establishment of industries to absorb some of the unemployment. Yet the Region has contributed her full share to the building up of the country."[36]

In postrevolutionary Ethiopia provincial commissioners appointed by the Dergue, more often than not originally hailing from the area over which they now exercise authority, act as ethnoregional buffers, making demands upon the center for public goods.[37] And in neighboring Sudan, the man who served as president of the High Executive Council for the Southern Region during part of the 1981–82 period, Major General Gasmallah Rassas, behaved in a manner similar to that of his civilian predecessors and successor: he traveled to Khartoum, sometimes accompanied by the regional minister of finance, education, or health, to negotiate with President Gaafar Nimeiry or the appropriate ministers for increased public allocations on behalf of his constituents.[38] In brief, then, hegemonial exchange practices, often unrecognized and lacking in legitimacy, are by no means restricted to regimes led by civilians, or for that matter, to regimes which are non-Marxist in orientation.

Civilian-led regimes, which exhibit various forms of dyadic or coalitional "bonds between individuals of unequal power and socioeconomic status,"[39] differ considerably as to the legitimacy they accord these political relationships, but the reality of these dyadic linkages is apparent. The four civilian presidents or acting presidents of the High Executive Council of the Sudan's Southern Region from the time of the signing of the Addis Ababa agreement in 1972 to the redivision of the south in 1983 (Abel Alier, 1972–78; Joseph Lagu, 1978–80; Peter Gatkouth, 1980–81; and Joseph Tombura, 1982–83) all performed a similar function of representing ethnoregional interests at the center. This process of interest articulation at the center was facilitated for Alier by his also serving as Sudan's vice-president, a post also held by Lagu, the former Anya-Nya leader, during Tombura's tenure in office at the subregional level. Thus, the Nimeiry-led state came to play a critical role of mediating among group interests. "Without the extravagant use of patronage and coordination of parochial interests by Nimeiry through his network of protégés and informers in the national sphere and supporters in the foreign sphere," observed Dunstan Wai, "the Nimeiry regime would probably have collapsed by now."[40]

Dyadic political linkages between state leaders and ethnoregional buffers were also evident in Uganda in the 1960s and in Zambia in the 1960s and 1970s, but without in either case the state president's imprimatur. In Uganda, the decentralized nature of political parties and the continued strong influence of ethnic and religious politics in the voting process encouraged subregional politicians and administrators as well as members of parliament to look to their district power bases for political survival.[41] As a result, they tended to emerge as the champions of communal interests in their relations with the center. Acholi politicians, for example, "rarely operated in isolation from the central government"; rather they forged close links with central government ministries, seeking financial backing for projects in their area.[42] "Not a few representatives to Uganda's National Assembly," states Fred Burke, "are inclined to regard themselves (and, just as important, are regarded by their fellow tribesmen) as district-tribal ambassadors."[43] As ethnoregional brokers, these subregional intermediaries at the center were expected to engage in reciprocal relations with government officials, trading compliance and support for public goods to be distributed by the state. The primary measure of their success as brokers was their ability to extract resources from the state, a task made easier for those fortunate enough to gain entry to the inner sanctums of government itself. Those opposition MPs who appeared to be isolated from the main dispensers of patronage often found themselves subjected to pressure by visiting delegations of local notables; these local personalities were intent upon getting their representative to cross the aisle, and thereby to become linked with the party controlling the public purse strings.

The trend to single-party rule made little difference in the perceived rules of this game. A. Milton Obote, the master negotiator (in his early career at least), compensated for the softness of the Uganda state by entering into political exchanges with ethnoregional spokesmen—either MPs or district secretaries-general—as well as all important and politically strategic interest groups. As far as the ethnoregional exchanges were concerned, the outcomes were varied: the Acholi received fiscal allocations, the Sebei movement was granted a separate district, the Buganda-based Kabaka Yekka movement was, for a time, included as a coalition partner with the Uganda Peoples Congress, and so forth.[44] Whether in two- or single-party situations, the process of center-periphery relations was necessarily similar in that it involved an ingredient of political exchange, although the terms and outcomes of these exchanges varied according to the time and place. Yet the process of state-ethnoregional exchange did not gain long-term validity in Obote's eyes. As he outlined his "move to the left" in 1970, Obote spoke frankly about the dynamics of political exchange that had dominated Uganda politics in the 1960s, and then went on to outline a multiethnic electoral procedure he proposed to put into effect for the years ahead. Although the future he envisaged was cut short by the Amin coup, his description of the ethnic bargaining process gives an insight into his perceptions:

> The pull of the tribal force, however, has blinded some leaders to the extent that they cannot see developments in their own areas, but continue to act in such a manner that if they had their way developments could perhaps only take place in their own tribal areas and nowhere else. . . . To reduce it to its crudest form, the pull of the tribal force does not accept Uganda as one country . . . does not accept the National Assembly as a national institution but as an assembly of peace conference delegates and tribal diplomatic and legislative functionaries, and looks at the Government of Uganda as a body of umpires or referees in some curious game of "Tribal Development Monopoly."[45]

In brief, Obote now deemed a system of ongoing exchange relationships threatening to the political stability and developmental requirements of the country. Quite probably, he would have continued to engage in quiet quid pro quos with ethnoregional spokesmen even after his reforms had been enacted, but an open system of reciprocal relations was regarded as offensive in the new, more radical politics he envisaged for the 1970s.

In Zambia, dyadic state-ethnoregional linkages were also apparent in postindependence times, but, as in the case of Obote's Uganda, they again failed to secure official presidential blessing. Kenneth Kaunda has engaged in hegemonial exchange practices in both party and governmental affairs from the time of independence to the present. The national council of the United National Independence party had regional members "who in actual fact, represent[ed] their respective districts."[46] And, in governmental affairs, the cabinet, as described by Richard Hall, was "always . . . delicately balanced between the tribal poles of the Bemba and four Lozi in the Cabinet, however the portfolios were distributed. When two ministers, Mundia and Nalilungwe, were told to resign in January 1966 for acquiring shares in companies receiving government loans, they both happened to be Lozi. They were both replaced by Lozi. The balance was maintained."[47] Interesting, in terms of our concern here with political exchange, is the fact that the move toward a legally established one-party state in 1972 did not imply an end to the use of the proportional principle in making cabinet appointments in the subsequent 1973–1977 period. Thus, despite the defection of some Bemba MPs in 1971, the allocation of cabinet posts to Bemba-speakers remained steady in the years that followed.[48] It is also pertinent that the political decline and death in 1980 of the Bemba's acknowledged political spokesman, former Vice-president Simon Kapwepwe, did not leave this people, with roots in Copperbelt and Luapula as well as Northern Province, without a spokesman for communal interests. Not long after Kapwepwe's death, a new northern "strongman" emerged and gained widespread acceptance—Frederick Chiluba, the head of the Zambian Confederation of Trades Unions.[49]

Nevertheless, as was also the case in the Uganda experience discussed above, Kaunda recognized the reality of communal politics in Zambia but refused to accord any legitimacy to the political role of the ethnoregional intermediary. In party affairs, Kaunda rejected the Chuula Commission's recommendation that the United National Independence Party (UNIP) Central Committee be composed of sixteen members, two elected from each province.[50] On the question of representation in the cabinet, he was emphatic in rejecting any link to patronage ties. "From now on," Kaunda declared in 1972, "there is no such thing as a tribal leader with a provincial political base in my Government and who claims to be the champion of his province or be its spokesman in Cabinet or outside."[51] Finally, in a speech to a district governors' workshop in Lusaka, the president, decrying the fact that some governors had been drawn into tribal and sectional politics, told his audience that "instead of leading, you were misleading; instead of providing effective administrative machinery, you spent your time disorganising the efforts for unity and development; instead of implementing the Government policy and programmes, you became obstacles."[52] In brief, the ethnoregional patron was regarded as a "destructive" reality in the Zambian scene; this person would have to be weeded out for the sake of national unity, stability, and development. Thus the expedience of proportional behavior existed side by side with the rhetorical rejection of existing exchange practices.

So far we have described state-ethnoregional exchanges as a logical outgrowth of two factors: governmental control of scarce resources, and electoral systems organized along ethnoregional lines which perpetuate patron-client ties. While this interchange led to ambivalent behavior in Zambia and in Uganda under Obote (i.e., dyadic exchanges occurred though they were held in disfavor by high officials), elsewhere in countries more explicitly pragmatic in their political cultures, it has led to a somewhat more publicly countenanced process of political exchange among elites. Over time such acceptance has brought a widening of exchange practices, most notably in the case of Jomo Kenyatta's Kenya, to a point where an informal grand coalition—even a rudimentary elite cartel along "consociational" lines—may be said to have temporarily emerged. In such coalitional relationships a system of continuous interactions, where certain rules of the game for the handling of the authoritative actions of the state are understood and acquiesced in, can be said to have developed among top members of the state-ethnoregional elite. Thus—despite the evident constraints of external dependency, of economic scarcity, and of social pluralism, what Lijphart calls the "politics of accommodation" can be seen to exist in specific hegemonially organized African states. In these situations, flows of exchanges are processed by an elite political class which, like what is called a "regime" at the international level, regulates issue-areas in accordance with the norms, rules, and procedures agreed to by key state and ethnoregional actors.[53] To be sure, the effects of these interchanges may prove highly uneven for different actors; yet this does not in itself preclude stable political relationships, so long as all major parties perceive themselves to be benefiting at least minimally from the ongoing negotiations.

Where a grand coalition operates and regulates state-sectional exchanges, an acceptance, even a kind of legitimacy, is accorded to ethnoregional participants in the political process. In this encapsulated one-party coalition situation, state leaders make a conscious adjustment to the reality of ethnoregional identities, stressing the need to include all interests in the decision-making process.[54] Their effort to bring ethnic-based factions into the ruling coalition is an attempt to maintain the political system by means of cooptation. The expedient nature of this recognition is apparent in the secrecy that generally surrounds the state's relationship with ethnoregional intermediaries; yet, in contrast to the disapproval of the broker's role expressed by Obote and Kaunda, state leaders are careful in a hegemonial coalition situation to coopt and neutralize their potential challengers, not to deny their legitimacy in public.

Two variations of the hegemonial coalition will suffice for our discussion. In the Ivory Coast, especially in the 1960s and early 1970s, where the rules of the game involve an "acknowledge[ment]," but not a public display, of ethnic politics, President Félix Houphouët-Boigny has "tried to achieve some ethnic balance in his cabinets in order to mollify the resentment of Baoule dominance."[55] Although the supremacy of the *Parti Démocratique de Côte d'Ivoire* (PDCI) remains evident, Houphouët-Boigny is careful to demobilize potential ethnoregional challengers by coopting these local intermediaries into the ruling grand coalition at the center.[56] It is apparent that members of the National Assembly continue to draw from constituencies organized in a number of cases along ethnoregional lines. Aristide Zolberg describes the already familiar pattern of ethnoregional intermediation, as found in the Ivory Coast, as follows: "Viewing themselves as ambassadors of their region and of their ethnic group to the center, or as the spokesmen for the organization to which they belong, the *députés* are concerned mainly with gaining access to the ministers in order to secure tangible benefits for their constituents. Regardless of his specific duties as a member of the executive, each minister is also a kind of superrepresentative who keeps in touch with the country through his clientele of deputies."[57] Rather than challenging the validity of these ethnoregional appeals, Houphouët-Boigny has prudently provided for their incorporation into what Zolberg calls "a one-party coalition, a heterogeneous monolith."[58] All major ethnic groups are represented in the cabinet, and on a basis roughly proportional to their positions in the

National Assembly. Playing a key role by dominating and if necessary mediating between the different factions making up the cabinet coalition, Houphouët-Boigny has been able to build a political structure that ensures his political survival at least for the time being.[59] However, given his advanced age (he turned 80 in October 1985), the current political arrangement obviously will not endure; this creates the prospect of new political tensions during the transition period. In this period, as Richard Stryker stresses, "the potential for conflict in the Ivory Coast is certainly very great, particularly along ethnic and generational [and I would add class] lines."[60] An indication of the seriousness of these tensions emerged following the 1980 National Assembly elections, when Houphouët-Boigny felt it necessary to call a meeting of PDCI officials to reconcile the bitter differences that had surfaced between successful and unsuccessful candidates. Hence the Ivory Coast's hegemonial exchange system, which combines central governmental-party control with some proportionality in the distribution of political positions and fiscal resources, is about to undergo a critical test. Unless the various party interests can reach agreement on a "consensus candidate" who is prepared to inject new vigor into the hegemonial grand coalition, the political stability which has long been a hallmark of this ethnically heterogeneous society may be threatened.[61]

Finally, in Kenya a one-party grand coalition of ethnoregional notables gained considerable regime acceptance during the Kenyatta years. A process of hegemonially facilitated political exchange became customary practice, resulting, to the extent that all main actors were included, in relatively stable rules of interaction. On the hegemonic side, President Kenyatta exercised broad administrative control, ruling through the bureaucracy rather than the party; in the rural areas, the president's direct point of contact was via the agency of the provincial administration, whose personnel in the field were directly accountable to his office.[62] In addition, with the major exception of the militant populist interlude associated with Oginga Odinga's Kenya People's Union (KPU) from 1966 to 1969, Kenya was a de facto one-party state after 1964, when the ruling Kenya African National Union (KANU) absorbed its smaller and more conservative postindependence rival, the Kenya African Democratic Union.

However, KANU proved to be anything but a tightly organized and centrally disciplined party throughout the Kenyatta period.[63] With the central party organization exercising only loose control over affairs at the branch level, ethnoregional party notables were able to build strong bases of power in their constituencies and then, as in the case of such prominent ethnoregional champions as Ronald Ngala and Paul Ngei, to negotiate over the nature of their participation in the ruling cabinet coalition at the center. KANU, described by Carl Rosberg as resting upon "a coalition of key ethnic groups,"[64] thus united the single-party principle with elements of political exchange and mediation from the top of the hierarchy. "The political system," states Robert Jackson,

> is basically characterized by competition and bargaining between a number of ethnic groups and more modern interest associations on the one hand, and government on the other. . . . Government itself is highly plural, with bargaining and competition occurring among Cabinet members acting on behalf of supporting groups and between the ministries themselves.[65]

But if Kenyatta pragmatically engaged in an ongoing process of exchange relationships with the champions of ethnoregional interests (though notable exceptions here were Odinga and his compatriots, non-Luo as well as Luo, following KPU's formation), his successor, President Daniel arap Moi, a Tugan from western Kenya, appears less inclined to expend his political resources in this manner. The consequence has been damage to the networks of interpersonal linkages built up by Mzee (the old wise man) Kenyatta over the years. In the initial period following his accession to power in 1978, Moi moved cautiously, maintaining the Kenyatta constitution and cabinet intact. The dominant Kikuyu, with 21 percent of the total population, were still disproportionately represented in the cabinet, with some thirty percent of the posts in 1979; in addition, a Kikuyu, Mwai Kibaki, was appointed vice-president.[66] The selection in 1980 of a Luo cabinet minister closely associated with Oginga Odinga to replace another who had been defeated in a by-election was viewed at the time as a conciliatory gesture on Moi's part.[67]

Nevertheless, by 1982 it had become apparent that Moi had in fact distanced himself somewhat from the hegemonial exchange practices of his predecessor—and with highly destabilizing consequences. Pointing to the reduced center-periphery linkages as an underlying explanation for the rising tensions in Kenyan political life in 1982, one correspondent notes:

> Within two years President Moi had demonstrated that he intended to control Kenya through his own proteges rather than by alliances with the acknowledged popular leaders of the various key areas so Oginga Odinga, still preeminent in Luoland in Western Kenya, was prevented from standing in the 1979 election. Others such as Masinde Muliro and Jean Marie Seroney in the Rift Valley and Paul Ngei in Kambaland were soon acknowledged in Kenya's highly politicised society to be on the outside of the ruling group. Even the Vice-President, Mwai Kibaki, the current Kikuyu leader, was increasingly distanced from power.[68]

Thus Moi's preference for working closely with political associates drawn from the party but without a solid ethnoregional base of support weakened the linkages between center and periphery, thereby cracking the glue which had held the political system together during the Kenyatta reign. The result was political brittleness at a time of economic stagnation and rising political tensions: public restlessness, governmental repression, and, most unsettling, an attempted coup by a large section of the air force with the sympathy, if not the support, of other interests in the society.

The following year was to see a furtherance of the process of consolidation of power in Moi's hands. With the isolation and ousting of the former constitutional affairs minister, Charles Njonjo, from KANU, Moi called a new general election. Although the voter turnout was low, all but five cabinet ministers were reelected, and Moi appointed all but three of these to the new cabinet. Significantly, the formerly overrepresented Kikuyus were cut back in a somewhat smaller cabinet, but only to a roughly proportional 19 percent. The first impression of the new cabinet, remarked a correspondent in the *Weekly Review,* was that of a "well balanced" body—"one that takes care of the political interests of various geographic areas and at the same time appears to be chosen with an eye to dealing with the kinds of pressures the government in particular, and the country in general, are likely to face."[69] If the structure of understandings and working relationships so carefully put together by Kenyatta no longer had full legitimacy in official eyes, Moi, in his efforts to consolidate power, was nonetheless careful to take account of the need for ethnic proportionality and a broadened inclusiveness.

## RECIPROCAL MOTIVATIONS

What motivates state authorities, particularly those in one- or no-party situations, to expend precious political and economic capital to gain ethnoregional compliance and support? In most cases, central-state elites look upon the procedures of continuous negotiations with subregional intermediaries as a burdensome decisional cost, one to be reduced, preferably avoided, whenever possible. Hence the conclusion seems inescapable: *central-state elites regard political exchanges with such subregional spokesmen as a political necessity.* In contrast to the tight subordination of ethnoregional units "to the central bureaucratic power," as required by theorists on state corporatism,[70] the middle-African state has little alternative but to enter into political exchanges with the periphery. This is due to its all too apparent inability to impose its regulations. In middle Africa, as Hyden notes, "the 'civic public realm' lacks the legitimacy enjoyed by the 'primordial public realm' and thus there is a tendency to enhance the latter by taking from the former."[71] The effect is to place limits on the reach of the state; or, to quote Hyden again, "those who control the state do not necessarily control society."[72] Though "tough tactics" might have been tempting to Uganda's President Obote in his dealings with Buganda after his return to power, he lacked the military capability to ensure the country's peace and stability. Not only did his ethnically divided army have to deal with three guerrilla movements, but he had to cope with a fragmented political situation as well: "The country [was] effectively ruled by a group of warlords trying to control their own areas," as one observer commented.[73] Hence meaningful rehabilitation in Uganda required attention first to the political variable—the encouraging of political legitimacy through recognition of the limits of state coercive power and through allowing an element of reciprocity in the interchanges between the state and ethnoregional interests. Certainly the Uganda government's skills in reconciling obstinate sectors—offering benefits to competing elites "to induce grants of authority from them"[74]—were not to be underestimated; the army commander in the field reportedly displayed considerable diplomatic dexterity in his successful efforts in mid-1982 to work out differences with recalcitrant elements in the Northwest Region. Such bargaining skills *become* a necessity whenever the soft state *must*, because of its inability to impose unilateral terms, come to an understanding with semiautonomous actors in the periphery. From the state's standpoint, then, the cost of ethnicity is the need to bargain with the spokesmen for ethnic group interests.

While seeking by means of accommodation to avoid mutual damage, the dominant state elite never loses sight of what it views as its second imperative: the enclosure, and thereby the control, of social conflict, especially the antagonistic ethnic and class rivalries sometimes arising from open, partisan confrontations. The single- or no-party mechanism, although it recognizably does not eliminate the communal bases of political support, is valued nonetheless by this dominant elite for its presumed ability to reduce some of the most destructive effects of these direct encounters.[75] In its capacity to redirect group spokesmen away from hostile relations in a public arena and, hopefully, toward quiet transactions in a controlled setting, the single- or no-party mechanism is seen as a useful institutional channel for promoting political unity and stability.[76] Kenyatta's move to proscribe the Kenya People's Union and to detain Oginga Odinga and the main KPU leadership in 1969 was an effort to end open displays of disunity and to return to the de facto one-party system. Nevertheless, KANU remained divided along personal and ethnic lines,[77] and the reality of an ethnic grand coalition at the top was never altered: not only did Luo MPs continue to play an active role in governmental affairs in the period after KPU's proscription, but following the release of the detainees and their decision to rejoin KANU in the 1970s, some former KPU members gradually came to participate in public affairs again. Similarly, Prime Minister Robert Mugabe's steps to consolidate the power of his Zimbabwe African National Union (ZANU) in a one-party state can be interpreted as an effort to keep ethnoregional tensions manageable in an independent Zimbabwe. Not only did Mugabe appear anxious over the political threat arising from the autonomous power of Joshua Nkomo's Zimbabwe African People's Union (ZAPU), with its base among the Ndebele people, but these feelings of unease were heightened by ZANU fears of South African interference or manipulation of the country's ethnoregional differences and of the possibility of Ndebele initiatives to establish an independent state in Matabeleland.[78] In this respect, Nkomo's decisions to oppose a ZANU-ZAPU merger and to refuse the post of president were viewed in certain quarters as a preference for autonomous ZAPU power over working as part of a coalition of elites in a one-party situation. Nevertheless, Mugabe's attack on ZAPU political autonomy must be distinguished from his general pragmatism when dealing with the Ndebele minority and at least a segment of their twenty parliamentary representatives, whom he sought to bring within the framework of a strengthened ZANU.

From the standpoint of the state elite, then, what is attractive about a hegemonial system is its usefulness in extending central control over the country. Political exchange is reconciled with this hegemonial thrust as a matter of expediency. In terms of conflict relations under soft-state conditions, the degree of central state control over the periphery affects the nature of ethnoregional political demands (in particular, claims to political autonomy, i.e., Southern Sudan, Buganda, Biafra, Katanga), as well as the state-party elite's need to respond in a conciliatory manner. Moreover, it makes a great deal of difference in terms of antagonistic or conciliatory outcomes whether or not the central thrust of a regime strategy allows for a significant level of state-ethnic reciprocity. The differences are seen in the intensity of conflict and, therefore, the scope for political exchange (see Table 4.1).[79] The strategies of "avoidance," "buffering," "protection," and "redistribution" described in Table 4.1 are certainly quite compatible with hegemonial structures, yet they allow considerable possibilities for political exchange. Hence the dominant elite's choices among these mechanisms for regulating intergroup relations are critical in terms of group tensions and the possibilities for constructive interactions. Certainly the ability of state-party elites to respond in a conciliatory manner to the claims of the periphery is conditioned by circumstances and is therefore likely to vary significantly according to particular time-place situations. Consequently the performance of each state elite can appropriately be evaluated in terms of its skill in determining the most effective mix of political coercion and exchange to achieve its policy objectives—both short- and long-term.

But what motivates ethnoregional actors to enter into political exchange relations with state authorities at the center, that is, to give up some values of noncompliance and nonsupport to gain other values of political and economic participation and capacity? Clearly the international state system precludes ethnoregional secession, "freezing" the existing state units "in their inherited colonial jurisdictions and blocking any post-independence movements toward self-determination."[80] Hence, to the extent that ethnoregional spokesmen want the goods of modernity, they have little option but to operate within the confines of the state and to press their demands upon state authorities. Since the ethnoregional spokesman has no other major alternative supplier available, he (or she) has an incentive to trade compliance and support for the state's economic and social resources.

**Table 4.1 The Relationship Between Strategies of Conflict Regulation and Level of State-Ethnic Reciprocity**

| Strategy | Central Thrust of Strategy | Intensity of Conflict | Level of Reciprocity | Application of Strategy |
|---|---|---|---|---|
| 1. Subjection | Mechanisms of coercion applied throughout political system to maintain a structure of inequality | high | low | South Africa Burundi Uganda (Amin) |
| 2. Isolation | Conflict regulated by separating contending groups into distinct political systems | high | low | Katanga Biafra Eritrea Chad (1980-82) Angola (UNITA) |
| 3. Cultural Assimilation | State interpenetrates and absorbs politically weaker identities into a dominant core culture | high | low | Sudan Liberia (1847-1980) Ethiopia |
| 4. Avoidance | Decision-makers insulated from ethnic demands in order to restrain direct conflict | high/medium | low/medium | single-party no-party proscribe tribal parties, associations |
| 5. Displacement | Population transferred to alter nature of the group encounter | high/medium | low/medium | South Africa Algeria (colonial) Uganda (Asians) |
| 6. Buffering | Organization of rules for social interaction by third parties—state or international actor | medium | medium/high | Ivory Coast Cameroun Sudan (1972) |
| 7. Protection | Concessions of legal and constitutional guarantees to ethnic minorities | medium | medium/high | Kenya Zimbabwe Nigeria |
| 8. Redistribution | Reallocation of interethnic opportunities by means of redistribution programs | low/medium | medium/high | Zambia Tanzania Ghana Kenya Nigeria |
| 9. Sharing | Regularized and direct reciprocity through coordinated participation in the decisional process | low/medium | high | Nigeria Botswana |

Source: Victor A. Olorunsola and Donald Rothchild, eds. State Versus Ethnic Claims (Boulder, Colorado: Westview Press, 1983). Used with permission.

Lacking in readily available vehicles for communicating their felt needs and demands to the center, rural peoples not surprisingly fasten upon ties of ethnicity and membership in formal ethnoregional units as mechanisms of mobilization and linkage. As a consequence, the ethnoregional broker frequently comes to play an important political role—aggregating rural demands and, as a member of the dominant political class, gaining access to central state decision-makers. The influence of this linking process on the hegemonial exchange system may well be integrative. Effective connections usually involve reciprocity among state-ethnoregional leaders at the top of the hierarchy (or hierarchies), producing learned relationships, mutual expectations, and understandings which promote political stability. As John Lonsdale notes:

> Tribe has been the most economically available constituency for mobilizing pressure for access. Indeed, the growth and crystallization of tribes has been recognized as one of the most vigorous and creative social processes in modern Africa. Moreover, tribalism, far from being (as was once supposed) an index of African states' fragility, may well be an indication of their strength. . . . Stronger, richer areas, the ones that count, will use assertive tribalism to gain state access; it is the weaker ones which tend to mobilize retreatist ethnicity to resist state power in its alliance with capital. Tribalism may as much strengthen states as weaken them.[81]

The upshot is a two-directional flow of demands and responses within the framework of the single- or no-party state. Although both state and ethnoregional actors make, resist, and at times avoid demands, amicable settlement is facilitated in a number of instances by a recognition of mutual need. In practice, middle-African state leaders often make concessions to gain compliance and support in the periphery; their ethnoregional counterparts, determined to secure the distributable benefits sought by their constituents, give a measure of their support in exchange for public allocations. Under certain worst-case situations, these adjustments may prove insufficient and the two elite segments may find themselves "locked into a vicious circle of increasing violence."[82] One way out of this situation is for the state to secure sufficient control over resources to make ethnoregional opposition to state authority highly costly (e.g., Cameroun).[83] Another way, often more suitable under the "soft-state" conditions of contemporary middle Africa, is for the "representatives of hierarchies" to coordinate their interests by means of political exchange.[84] Where middle-African elites pursue the latter procedure, the course is likely to prove integrative, for it frequently leads to predictable interactions between ethnoregional interests. Nevertheless, these gains in managing conflict may be offset in part by delays and difficulties in arriving at decisions and by misallocations of scarce resources arising from the need to purchase compliance. Regarding the political marketplace, Goran Hyden notes: "Many of the deals that are entered into are expensive, at least as seen from the perspective of the capitalist or socialist modes of production."[85] However, high as the costs of such political exchanges may prove in the formulation and execution of rational policy choices, they often pale by comparison with the likely costs of violence, and the negative memories and "imprisoning myths" that follow from such encounters.[86]

## RECIPROCAL PERCEPTIONS AND COGNITIVE APPRAISALS

Even if the motivations for state-ethnic exchange are in place, a state mediated reciprocity among ethnic interests is not guaranteed. Also critical to the multitiered exchange process in middle Africa, or anywhere else for that matter, is that the various conflicting ethnic and state actors form expedient, and preferably favorable, perceptions and cognitive evaluations of one another. Such expedient or favorable evaluations facilitate the decision by all sides to enter into exchanges. As used here, perception applies to the processes by which state and ethnic leaders gain information, accurate or inaccurate, about their social environment, while cognition relates to the processes of evaluating this information and, in particular, estimating the intentions of competing group actors.[87] The central issue we must assess is whether, in the middle-African context, reciprocal perceptions and cognitive appraisals have worked to obstruct the operation of a hegemonial exchange model. Clearly a coalition of ethnic elites cannot work effectively if the various ethnic buffers regard one another's intentions in the worst possible light.

Perception and cognition are necessarily selective. They may be affected by collective insecurities, economic, social, and political interests, ideologies, religious and ethical systems, and a variety of communal experiences and remembrances, all of which influence the aspects of the other side's behavior to be scrutinized and emphasized.[88] In time, images emerge and gain a widespread acceptance that may or may not be based on fact. Certainly, it is important to recognize at the outset that the perceptions and cognitive appraisals of elites and ethnic masses do not necessarily coincide. There are frequent instances where ethnic leaders, who come into greater contact with counterparts from other ethnic groups than do their constituents, have taken more pragmatic views of their opponents' intentions. Nevertheless, because these ethnic leaders must necessarily enter into political exchanges with their ethnic supporters, they remain limited in their freedom to negotiate with rival leaders at the top of the hierarchy.

The perceptions that ethnic groups have about one another can be grouped, for heuristic purposes, under three categories:[89]

1. *An essentialist perception.* Where ethnic leaders and groups view others as fundamentally threatening to their physical, cultural, or social survival, they tend to regard any compromises on their part as weakening their position. Since it is assumed that rival B (and any coalition partners) intend to harm A and will take advantage of any relaxation of A's defensive stance, B

is regarded by A as untrustworthy under any circumstances whatever. In line with this assessment, ethnic group B's word is considered to be lacking in credibility; therefore, it is taken for granted that B will twist any exchange concessions to A's disadvantage. Group A views signs of weakness on its part as likely to be misunderstood by its adversary. Conciliation will become the basis for new demands by B, requiring A to make greater outlays of political resources at a later date to reestablish the status quo between opposing interests within the state. As a result, A considers "realistic" only those approaches which are based on a perception of B's "unchanging resolve" to overwhelm A's unity and integrity and on a determination on A's part to maintain sufficient autonomous power to prevent any undermining of its position.

Since independence, middle Africa has experienced a wide range of essentialist views regarding interethnic relations. This is explained partly by the expectations that actors have of their adversary's behavior and partly by the intensity that politicized ethnicity engenders under conditions of severe economic scarcity. In the most extreme cases, such outlooks contributed to instances of "selective genocide" around the time of formal decolonization. Thus interacting and escalating ethnic and class fears in Zanzibar, Burundi, and Rwanda culminated in violent attacks upon defenseless communities, or sections of communities, in particular those that are labeled by one author as the "political intelligentsia."[90] In these three cases, a privileged minority, in control of state institutions and determined to preserve colonially inherited patterns of social stratification, perceived itself as pitted against an underprivileged "ethclass" majority dedicated to bringing about a radical restructuring of the distribution of social opportunities.[91]

The common thread running through these highly intense encounters was a reciprocity of fear and aggressive behavior, which grew precipitously whenever the stereotypic images of other groups were supported to any extent by actual events. In Rwanda, the rather unstructured Hutu uprisings of November 1959 and the Tutsi reprisals which followed substantiated the most negative assessments each ethnic group made about the other's intentions. Quoting G. Kayibanda's statement that between these two communities in Rwanda "there is no intercourse and no sympathy, [they] are ignorant of each other's habits, thoughts and feelings as if they were dwellers of different zones, or inhabitants of different planets," René Lemarchand stresses the polarization of expectations following the uprising and "the all-pervasive climate of fear and suspicion which gripped the country at the approach of the [1960] elections."[92] These events in Rwanda also exacerbated latent fears in neighboring Burundi where, according to Ambassador Thomas Melady, an "either-or mentality of dominating or being eliminated" became prevalent in the Hutu and Tutsi mind-sets.[93] Michael Lofchie describes Zanzibar's African nationalism as a reaction to the perceived "threat of Arab domination posed by the ZNP," and, in a different type of context with different consequences, former Biafran army commander, Major General Alexander Madiebo, appraised the intentions of the Northern officers as the "exterminat[ion]" of "a whole tribe."[94] Other instances of essentialist thinking on interethnic relations—in the Sudan, Ethiopia, Uganda, and elsewhere—could be cited, but these seem sufficient to illustrate the existence of insecure and hostile perceptions contributing to highly destructive conflict outcomes. Where group appraisals of an adversary's intentions predispose actors toward zero-sum expectations, a positively reinforcing hegemonial exchange relationship becomes extremely difficult to initiate and sustain. As I will indicate below, in certain situations a change of perceptions may not be beyond the realm of possibility; but, more commonly, essentialist thinking sets *en train* a cognitive process leading to interactions marked by fear and antagonism.

2. *A pragmatic perception.* Although the pragmatists appraise their relations with other actors warily, they tend to assess their rivals' intentions in broader and less threatening terms. They harbor no illusions about a basic conflict of interest with other groups; however, because A perceives B as seeking to maximize the opportunities of its own group members and not to harm A directly, some scope is available for the state to utilize existing rules and informal understandings to facilitate positive-sum outcomes, in certain limited areas at least. Hence the pragmatist reconciles a sense of distinct group interests in a scarcity-prone environment with a willingness to enter, albeit cautiously, into political exchanges with other communal intermediaries on specific issues. In doing so, the pragmatist distinguishes between his desire to distance himself socially from B and his preparedness, opportunistically, to serve his own group's interests by making conciliatory overtures. Provided that state leaders encourage conciliatory behavior and that ethnic leaders retain their credibility—mainly by fulfilling prior agreements under adverse as well as propitious circumstances—a basis may be made for rival leaders to enter into political exchange relationships, even to become part of a coalition of ethnoregional notables within a one-party context.

The costs of conciliatory behavior toward other ethnic groups on specific issues have in fact proved acceptable in a large number of cases in middle Africa. If ethnic units and their brokers have at times acted competitively and gained preferential treatment, they have, as pragmatists, done this in the spirit of self-maximization, not in an effort to destroy an adversary. Within the controlled context of a hegemonial state order, unacknowledged conciliatoriness on issues of public policy has become commonplace. To the extent that the various ethnic interests share moral and functional linkages, they are likely to be encouraged to reach accords on matters of mutual concern at least. The results of this pragmatism can be seen in such "markets of exchange" as political coalition; elite recruitment; resource allocation; and political, social, and cultural group rights and protections. In these issue-areas, moderate assessments of rivals' intentions have opened the way to effective hegemonial exchange relationships, for the costs of withdrawal are perceived as greater than those of interaction. Hence a focus upon the tangible and narrow issues that legitimately divide ethnic interests (instead of on those that raise collective consciousness about a generalized and unremitting "threat") appears crucial to the political exchange process.

3. *A reciprocative perspective.* Assuming that interethnic relations can be made less threatening through conciliatory moves by the main actors in a conflict situation, those adopting a conflict-reducing "reciprocative" perspective seek to transform the structure of relations to achieve mutual interests. Again the state can be expected to play a useful mediatory role, encouraging A to attempt to lower the costs of B's accommodation by taking the initiative and signaling its intention to pursue a conciliatory stance. In doing so, A seeks to encourage B to choose the path of mutual concessions, holding out the prospect of generally greater benefits through the avoidance of mutual damages. Group A seeks to "influence" B's behavior by offering B "palatable" choices, rather than a series of threats of increasing magnitude.[95] Group A does not assume B to be locked into a hostile way of thinking concerning the conflict at hand; consequently, it is in a position to envisage an opening which might be utilized to promote positively reinforcing behavior on all sides. Those engaging in this process of mutual adjustment may begin where the pragmatist often leaves off—that is, by entering into political exchanges over specific issues; however, a reciprocator's intention, too, is distinguishable from that of a pragmatist in that he seeks to establish a general basis for developing trust through a process of ongoing accommodations on the part of the parties to the conflict.[96] Commenting on the logic of inviting reciprocation from a rival actor, Robert Jervis observes:

> If the other undertakes an exchange in which he gives the actor more than he needs to and/or receives less than he has the power to exact, the actor is likely to conclude that the other has a positive stake in his well-being. He may believe that the other cares about him for intrinsic reasons . . . or that the other is guided by instrumental calculations. . . . In either case, the actor will infer that the other's behavior did not depend on conditions that are likely to change quickly and so he will expect friendly behavior from the other in the future.[97]

Acting in a conciliatory manner encourages a conciliatory response and, if repeated over time, sets the grounds for long-term mutual expectations of collaborative behavior.

Although the process of utilizing "exchange obligations" to promote cooperative behavior seems logical and appealing,[98] African state elites have only been able to make intermittent use of such an approach in managing their conflicts. This is hardly surprising in light of the circumstances that have confronted the African state since independence. A combination of economic scarcity, frail and overextended state institutions, and external dependency is commonplace, and where these contextual factors coincide with intense ethnic and class antagonisms, moral and material support for redistributional programs (i.e., those which go beyond proportionality and represent an extraproportional commitment of political, economic, or social resources by the relatively advantaged to the relatively disadvantaged) becomes difficult to mobilize.

Yet even in the face of such difficult environmental circumstances, African political parties and leaders in most middle-African states have continued to speak of their obligation to pursue policies of corrective equity.[99] Some of the most important among the various initiatives implemented toward this end are fiscal redistributions, quotas in scholarship grants and in the recruitment of personnel to public service positions, the siting of industries in the less advantaged areas, ethnic and racial preferences in the distribution of contracts, and special training and capital-assistance programs. It seems sufficient for our purposes here to limit our discussion to the critical issue of allocating public resources among the ethnoregional units on a redistributional basis.

If redistribution has for the most part been effective in terms of ensuring equity among the races in civil service and political appointments in the postindependence period, it has been less impressive in passing a more significant test with long-term implications: namely, the allocation of resources among domestic African ethnic and class groups. To take the example of Ghana, successive regimes have shifted somewhat in their domestic class and international economic alignments, but not on their pledges to expand agricultural productivity and to equalize subregional disparities. From Nkrumah to Rawlings, Ghanaian administrations have emphasized the values of self-reliance and subregional reallocation, seeking thereby to promote social integration and economic development as well as "to create conditions," as the Busia administration put it, "that would make the economic and social standards in the various regions of the country . . . reasonably equal."[100] Leaders in Zambia, Kenya, Cameroun, Tanzania, Nigeria, Sudan, and other states have given similar assurances of their intentions to equalize subregional opportunities in their countries.

Yet if the constraints of the environment were not sufficient, resistance on the part of the relatively advantaged class and ethnoregional interests to significant programs of corrective equity have placed decided limits on the implementation of such policies.[101] To be sure, redistribution does occur, but it is sporadic. For example, General I. K. Acheampong in Ghana, for all the mismanagement and corruption that marked his regime, did seek to extend his support base northward through budgetary policies aimed at redressing subregional inequities with respect to per capita capital fund expenditures for secondary schools in 1975–76; however in other areas, such as current fund expenditures on primary and middle education and capital fund expenditures on teacher training, the record was mixed, being strictly proportional or even quite nonproportional in nature.[102] In the case of Tanzania, Alan Amey and

David Leonard concluded, on the basis of a statistical breakdown of estimated government and parastatal expenditures by subregion during the 1969–70 to 1974–75 period, that "the evidence demonstrates that Tanzania is moving toward greater spatial equality in its government expenditures." Even though absolute inequalities in governmental expenditures remained generally constant, relative inequalities declined by 30 percent—from a relative deviation of 1.31 in 1969 on per capita distributions of development funds to the subregions to 0.91 in 1974.[103] Recently published data from Nigeria and Kenya also indicate an increasing tendency to use the proportional (and, in some instances, the extraproportional) principle. The index of variation decreased with respect to Nigeria's road programs during the period from 1975–76 to 1979–80 from 1.18 to 0.48, while that country's health programs showed a decline in the index of variation from .70 to .51. In Kenya, during the 1974–75 to 1982–83 period, the hospital programs index decreased from 1.01 to .89 and the education programs from .53 to .45.[104] In light of current economic scarcities in these countries, such efforts to put reallocative programs into effect are likely to be perceived positively by the articulate public in the less advantaged areas.

Clearly all three perceptions—the essentialist, the pragmatic, and the reciprocative—exist side by side in contemporary middle Africa. If the effect of the essentialist outlook is to complicate political exchange greatly, the impact of the pragmatic and reciprocative mind-sets is more positive, enabling moral linkages to endure among state and ethnic actors. The persistence of such moral linkages paves the way for possible exchange relationships in pluralistic societies.

Three additional points seem pertinent at this juncture. First, although it may seem logical to contend that conciliatory gestures are likely to encourage like-minded responses from rival intermediaries and lead to an ongoing process of reciprocations over the long term, this is not to maintain that redistributive policies necessarily bring about a reduction in interethnic conflict, in the short term at least. In fact, in situations of resource scarcity, such as prevail in most of Africa, reallocative programs can exacerbate conflicts between competing interests. Where relatively advantaged groups and elites view changes in economic opportunities and wealth in terms of competitive disadvantage and relative deprivation, the result may be a backlash which is highly destabilizing in its consequences.[105] The success of a redistributive approach requires the right combination in each context of a number of variables—in particular, skillful leadership, effective political linkages, adequate public resources, and perceptions on all sides of mutual gains. In the absence of these, redistributive policies can provoke intense differences among the various state and ethnic elites and their constituents.[106]

Second, these perceptions of rival interests are not fixed and immutable but may shift as assessments of the intentions of adversaries alter over time. Kenya's Africans moved from essentialist thinking during colonial rule in the

1950s to pragmatic outlooks on relations with minority racial groups in the 1970s, as European and Asian visibility declined and group intermediaries became conscious of convergent needs and expectations.[107] In this process of shifting perceptions, the state may play an important facilitative role. As state elites enter into political exchanges with ethnoregional leaders and sponsor policies and programs that emphasize principles of proportionality or extra-proportionality, they may be encouraging predictable political interactions among rival group interests. It is as the flow of political exchanges gains regularity that political stability—and with it a change in perceptions about the intentions of adversaries—is most likely to materialize.[108]

And third, contrary to much superficial journalism on Africa, *the political elites of that continent have inclined more toward a pragmatic than an essentialist or reciprocative orientation.* Undeniably, there have been policies and programs inspired by essentialist and reciprocative outlooks, but the main thrust of political behavior has been in the direction of the pragmatic. Evidence of a concern for proportionality appears regardless of development strategy—transformation, reorganization, or accommodation—and in highly articulated as well as loosely structured hegemonial African political systems. The evidence is in the systemic outcomes, as seen in the four markets of political exchange noted above. In terms of our analysis, the upshot is to make a hegemonial exchange model an appropriate approach for the analysis of aspects of state-ethnic relationships in much of middle Africa.

## POLICY IMPLICATIONS

Clearly the control-consociational democracy dichotomy so often referred to by contemporary writers on state-ethnic relations fails to give an adequate insight into the complex interactions occurring within the countries of middle Africa. The control model, which focuses attention upon state efforts to repress, isolate, or dissipate ethnic and other interest demands by means of administrative or military coercion, presupposes a level of administrative effectiveness that most African states are far from possessing. And the consociational democracy model, which presupposes a more or less open organization of social divisions along party lines and a cooperative effort on the part of a "grand coalition" of elites at the top of the political system to manage ethnic and other demands, assumes a degree of elite collaboration, internal cohesion within groups, and public acquiescence in formal compromise that is hardly common in Africa at this time. Consequently a full understanding of the dynamics of current state-ethnic relations in these societies requires a new analytical model, one which allows full scope to informal procedures of reciprocity within these partially closed one- or no-party arrangements.

The alternative model adopted here—hegemonial exchange—seeks to reflect the contemporary situation of the African soft state and the inevitable political exchange relations between state and ethnoregional leaders arising from this reality. In an environment of pronounced economic scarcity, limited skilled manpower resources, and frail administrative institutions, the state, not surprisingly, adopts hegemony in form while in practice also entering into explicit or implicit political exchange relationships. Hegemonial exchange, then, emerges from the political necessity to engage in bargaining relations with subregional brokers and the central elite's general inclination to adopt a pragmatic rather than an essentialist outlook on intergroup relations. The result is a process of largely informal dyadic or coalitional exchanges within the hegemonial order. The hegemonial exchange systems manage conflict among disparate interests by means of joint elite participation in decision-making and conciliatory outcomes, largely determined by the use of the proportionality principle.

In addition to the examples noted above of a proportional (and even an extraproportional) operating guideline for use in determining resource allocation priorities, this neutral principle has also been applied within the African one- or no-party context in such issue-areas as coalition formation and elite recruitment. The employment of such a principle is designed to help reduce the intensity of group conflicts. It allocates scarce resources among rival interests on the basis of relative group numbers, thereby avoiding the adversarial politics of majoritarian competition. No interests are excluded and all are benefited, at least minimally, in the way that scarce and valued resources are distributed. Although the subject of proportional treatment of ethnoregional interests in the formation of political coalitions and the recruitment of elites has received more extensive analysis in another context,[109] a few examples seem pertinent here to indicate the widespread utilization of such a principle.

As is well known, Nigeria's 1979 Constitution included provisions on the "federal character" of the federal civil service and the appointments to federal political and administrative positions. The aim was to promote national unity by "ensuring that there [should] be no predominance of persons from a few States or from a few ethnic or sectional groups in that government or in any of its agencies" (Sect. 14[3]), and the federal government took steps to comply with the spirit of this provision by including representatives from all states in the federal cabinet. In line with this principle on greater representativeness, the federal government also acted to set quotas for admission to federal universities and to allocate postgraduate scholarships on a proportional, if not an extraproportional, basis. Its achievements in the latter area are plain to see. Whereas 33.2 percent of the applicants from the eleven states in the Federation designated as disadvantaged by the former Federal Military Government (and 46.2 percent in the nine disadvantaged states in the north) received postgraduate awards in the 1980–81 year, only 21.5 percent of those applying from the eight relatively advantaged states were given scholarships. This inclination toward corrective equity was even more apparent in the following year, as 60.9 percent of the applicants from the nine disadvantaged northern states received scholarship awards.[110]

What is less fully appreciated is the continuation of support by the Nigerian military, following its 31 December 1983 coup d'etat, for the guideline on "federal character" in central appointments. Upon seizing power, the administration of Major General Mohammed Buhari appointed an 18-member Federal Executive Council which included a member from every state except Bendel, and that state was compensated by the selection of a person from that subregion as head of the civil service.[111] Other African countries reflecting a geographical balance in high-level political appointments range across a continuum from Kenya's, the Ivory Coast's, and Cameroun's hegemonial exchange systems to Sékou Touré's tight one-party hegemony. Unofficial practices of proportionality also have been apparent, moreover, in civil service recruitment experiences in Ghana, Malawi, and various other Subsaharan countries. In these situations, the soft African state has made a virtue of political necessity. It has frequently responded to the reality of powerful ethnoregional demands for inclusiveness and for fairness in allocations by opting for the seemingly disinterested standard of proportionality.

What has the emergence of these diverse hegemonial exchange arrangements meant in terms of the twin policy objectives of conflict management and economic development? Certainly, in the short term at least, the strengths of loose and informal hegemonial exchange practices are more apparent than their weaknesses. By placing limitations upon intergroup conflict, hegemonial exchange seems more likely, under current conditions in middle Africa, to facilitate regularized patterns of reciprocity than would a formal system of consociational democracy. The latter's expectation of open party contestation, irrespective of hard- or soft-state circumstances, appears to run at cross purposes with the African dominant elite's general perception of the need, during a transitional period at least, for unitary state and party control. Many members of this elite, rightly or wrongly, assume that economic scarcity will give rise to intense competition over scarce public resources among ethnoregional and other interests. Their expediential mechanism under these circumstances, the single- or no-party state, places parameters around legitimate conflict; given their pragmatic bent, the members of this elite also recognize the political necessity of allowing for political exchanges within the hegemonic order, but only on the basis of a controlled reciprocity which does not weaken the government's formal capacity to shape and implement policy. The consequence is to reduce the intensity of conflict, channeling differences along cooperative rather than adversarial lines.

Even though the hegemonial exchange arrangement has displayed definite strengths in managing intergroup conflicts over a temporary period—a substantial achievement to be sure—this should not blind us to some of the model's apparent weaknesses. The pragmatism implicit in a hegemonial exchange approach may well help the soft states of middle Africa to live with ethnic diversity, even under conditions of economic scarcity, but conflict management is not tantamount to conflict resolution. The basic problem endures.

Moreover a hegemonial exchange arrangement is not without policy costs. Although this system does promote values of reciprocity and inclusiveness among state and ethnoregional leaders currently in power, it is by no means certain that such relationships among particular sets of elites will be flexible enough to allow for the cooptation of younger, more militant interest-group spokesmen into the ruling circle. Also the operation of informal norms of relationship under this model may prove difficult to sustain in the face of increasing populist demands brought on in part by a worsening economy. To the extent that an elite backscratching relationship at the top resists change and adheres rigidly to the principle of proportionality above competing values, it risks, to the extent it downplays recruitment on the basis of merit and achievement, becoming a cause of public frustration and leading to a possible decline in system legitimacy.

Some policy costs in the economic sphere are also recognizable. Not only is the dominant political elite constrained by aggregate economic scarcities—leaving them all too little to spread among many claimants—but also by the overriding need to allocate resources on a proportional, and preferably in terms of political objectives on an extraproportional, basis. Such a political use of the proportionality principle in the issue-area of resource allocation may involve a possible trade-off cost in terms of systemic efficiency. To the extent that the most productive ethnic and subregional interests see the outcome of their efficiency subsidizing the less productive, their incentive to remain productive—and to continue to acquiesce in reallocative policies—may decline sharply. In this event, mechanically enforced programs of proportional allocations, to say nothing of those policies with a redistributive thrust, can cause intensified conflict among ethnoregional and other interests, leading, paradoxically, to the very political instability that the hegemonial exchange arrangement is designed to prevent.

Clearly, then, hegemonial exchange is less than an ideal formula and may become a source for corruption, parochialism, conservatism, and immobility. Yet the alternatives may be less acceptable, especially where they lead to grave political instability and bitter resentments over possible acts of victimization and repression.[112] Hence one comments on the policy implications of an experiment with this type of system most cautiously. Hegemonial exchange is an expedient to be used during a transitional period when soft-state conditions and pragmatic perceptions of conflict prevail. However, the opportunity to manage conflict by such informal understandings and rules among elite spokesmen at the center in a one- or no-party system is likely to prove a fleeting one at best. It therefore seems prudent to make effective use of such a framework for collaboration to build more durable institutions and relationships. In brief, hegemonial exchange is a product of immediate political necessity; yet a longer term perspective requires a transition to institutions providing continuity and predictable channels for state-ethnic political exchanges.

## NOTES

I wish to express my appreciation to Professors Maure Goldschmidt, Arend Lijphart, Percy Hintzen, Edmond Keller, and Michael Foley for helpful comments on the first draft of the manuscript.

1. Charles E. Lindblom, *Politics and Markets* (New York: Basic Books, 1977), p. 139.

2. Alvin Rabushka and Kenneth A. Shepsle, "Political Entrepreneurship and Patterns of Democratic Instability in Plural Societies," *Race* 12, 4 (April 1941): 47.

3. See Richard Sklar, "The Nature of Class Domination in Africa," *Journal of Modern African Studies* 18, 4 (1979): 531–552.

4. See Donald Rothchild and Victor A. Olorunsola (eds.), *State Versus Ethnic Claims: African Policy Dilemmas* (Boulder, Colo.: Westview Press, 1983), p. 235.

5. On the soft state, see Gunnar Myrdal, *Asian Drama: An Inquiry into the Poverty of Nations,* vol. 2 (New York: Pantheon, 1968), pp. 895–900; and Goran Hyden, "Problems and Prospects of State Coherence," in Rothchild and Olorunsola, *State Versus Ethnic Claims,* pp. 73–74. A recent Ghanian document, commenting on the "inherent deficiencies" of the country's administrative apparatus, remarked that "it must have been obvious to all past governments that no efficient supervision of projects in the remote rural areas could be undertaken from the capital, Accra." Provisional National Defence Council (PNDC), *Outlines of the Decentralization Plan of the Provisional National Defence Council* (Accra: PNDC, 1982), p. 2.

6. John Saul, *The State and Revolution in Eastern Africa* (New York: Monthly Review Press, 1979), p. 361. On the critical role of group access to the state apparatus in systems of control in communally divided societies, see Percy C. Hintzen and Ralph R. Premdas, "Guyana: Coercion and Control in Political Change," *Journal of Interamerican Studies and World Affairs* 24, 3 (August 1982): 338.

7. Hyden, "Problems and Prospects," p. 74. Also see Henry Bienen, "The State and Ethnicity: Integrative Formulas in Africa," in Rothchild and Olorunsola, *State Versus Ethnic Claims,* p. 113; and Thomas M. Callaghy, "State and Ethnicity in Zaire: Prefects, State Formation and the Coverover Process" (Paper presented at the African Studies Association, Bloomington, Indiana, October 1981), pp. 5–6.

8. Aristide R. Zolberg, "The Structure of Political Conflict in the New States of Tropical Africa," *American Political Science Review* 62, 1 (March 1968): 73.

9. Naomi Chazan, "Ethnicity and Politics in Ghana," *Political Science Quarterly* 97, 3 (Fall 1982): 468, 484–85; and her book, *An Anatomy of Ghanian Politics* (Boulder, Colo.: Westview Press, 1983), p. 36. Also see Reinhard Bendix and Guenther Roth, *Scholarship and Partisanship: Essays on Max Weber* (Berkeley: University of California Press, 1971), p. 160.

10. On the need for a more systematic conceptualization of control models, see Ian Lustick, "Stability in Deeply Divided Societies: Consociationalism versus Control," *World Politics* 31, 3 (April 1979): 335–337.

11. Some of the major works on consociational systems include: Gerhard Lehmbruch, "A Non-Competitive Pattern of Conflict Management in Liberal Democracies: The Case of Switzerland, Austria, and Lebanon," in Kenneth D. McRae (ed.), *Consociational Democracy* (Toronto: McClelland and Stewart, 1974), pp. 90–97; Arend Lijphart, *The Politics of Accommodation,* 2nd ed. (Berkeley: University of California Press, 1975), *Democracy in Plural Societies* (New Haven: Yale University Press, 1977), (ed.), *Conflict and Coexistence in Belgium* (Berkeley: Institute of International Studies, 1981), *Power-Sharing in South Africa* (Berkeley: Institute of International Studies, 1985); Jürg Steiner, *Amicable Agreement Versus Majority Rule* (Chapel Hill: University of North Carolina Press, 1974), and "The Principles of Majority and Proportionality," *British Journal of Political Science* 1, 1 (January 1971), pp. 63–70; Val R. Lorwin, "Belgium: Religion, Class, and Language in National Politics," in Robert A. Dahl (ed.), *Political Oppositions in Western Democracies* (New Haven: Yale University Press, 1966), pp. 147–187; and Hans Daalder, "The Consociational Democracy Theme," *World Politics* 26, 4 (July 1974): 604–621.

12. G. D. L. Schreiner, L. Schlemmer, et al., *Buthelezi Commission Report,* Vol. 1 (Durban: Inkatha Institute, 1982): 126.

13. On the circumstances for negotiation, compare Roger J. Southall, "Consociationalism in South Africa," *Journal of Modern African Studies* 21, 1 (March 1983): 102–104; and Heribert Adam, "The Manipulation of Identity," in Rothchild and Olorunsola, *State Versus Ethnic Claims,* pp. 132–144.

14. Lijphart also includes Switzerland on the list; this is a somewhat difficult case to classify for consociational theory, however, because the referendum principle is a majoritarian device. See Brian Barry, "Political Accommodation and Consociational Democracy," *British Journal of Political Science* 5, 4 (October 1975): 485, 488; and Jürg Steiner and Jeffrey Obler, "Does the Consociational Theory Really Hold for Switzerland?," in Milton J. Esman (ed.), *Ethnic Conflict in the Western World* (Ithaca: Cornell University Press, 1977), pp. 324–342.

15. See F. van Zyl Slabbert and David Welsh, *South Africa's Options* (New York: St. Martin's Press, 1979), p. 76.

16. The four characteristics of consociational democracy are set out in Lijphart, *Democracy in Plural Societies,* p. 25.

17. See the discussions in Richard H. Dekmejian, "Consociational Democracy in Crisis: The Case of Lebanon," *Comparative Politics* 10, 2 (January 1978): 251–265; and David C. Gordon, *Lebanon: The Fragmented Nation* (London: Croom Helm, 1980), p. 105.

18. Dirk Berg-Schlosser, "Elements of Consociation Democracy in Kenya" (Paper presented at the International Political Science Association, Rio de Janeiro, 9–14 August 1982), p. 8.

19. Letter from Arend Lijphart to Donald Rothchild, 7 October 1983.

20. On the situational, variable, and overlapping nature of ethnicity in the African context, see Crawford Young, *The Politics of Cultural Pluralism* (Madison: University of Wisconsin Press, 1976), p. 65; and Dov Ronen, *The Quest for Self-Determination* (New Haven: Yale University Press, 1979), p. 53.

21. Brian Barry, "The Consociational Model and its Dangers," *European Journal of Political Research* 3, 4 (1975): 398.

22. Donald Rothchild, *Racial Bargaining in Independent Kenya* (London: Oxford University Press, 1973), chs. 1, 4, 13; and his "Changing Racial Stratifications and Bargaining Styles: The Kenya Experience," *Canadian Journal of African Studies* 7, 3 (1973): 419–431. Also Joel D. Barkan, "Legislators, Elections, and Political Linkage," in Joel D. Barkan with John J. Okumu (eds.), *Politics and Public Policy in Kenya and Tanzania* (New York: Praeger, 1979), p. 71.

23. T. Baumgartner and T. R. Burns, "The Structuring of International Economic Relations," *International Studies Quarterly* 19, 2 (June 1975): 128.

24. Warren F. Ilchman and Norman T. Uphoff, *The Political Economy of Change* (Berkeley: University of California Press, 1969), p. 94.

25. On the processes of facilitation and impedance, see Donald Rothchild and Robert L. Curry, Jr., *Scarcity, Choice, and Public Policy in Middle Africa* (Berkeley: University of California Press, 1978), pp. 61–77.

26. Ladipo Adamolekun, *Sékou Touré's Guinea* (London: Methuen, 1976), pp. 128–132. Claude Riviere comments, however, as follows: "The comparative balance in tribal representation that was reached among the cadres tends now to be upset by Malinké predominance and Peul underrepresentation in the policymaking decisions." *Guinea: The Mobilization of a People* (Ithaca: Cornell University Press, 1977), p. 217.

27. Gwendolen M. Carter and John H. Herz, *Government and Politics in the Twentieth Century* (New York: Praeger, 1961), p. 117. On the party as a machine, see Aristide R. Zolberg, *Creating Political Order* (Chicago: Rand McNally, 1966), p. 28; and Henry Bienen, "Political Parties and Political Machines in Africa," in Michael F. Lofchie (ed.), *The State of the Nations* (Berkeley: University of California Press, 1971), ch. 9.

28. On the general types of coordination processes, see Charles E. Lindblom, *The Intelligence of Democracy* (New York: Free Press, 1965), ch. 2. The emphasis in this definition upon mutually accepted norms and processes distinguishes it quite fundamentally from the "authoritarian consociational system" that another writer sees as characterizing state-homeland elite exchanges in South Africa. Not only are the homelands creations of South African power, but the inequities of exchange under the *hard*-state conditions of that country make for significantly different interactional experiences. See John Seiler, "Measuring Black Political Support in South Africa," *Politikon* (Pretoria) 1, 2 (December 1974): 23. Also see John Seiler, "Consociational Authoritarianism: Incentives and Hindrances Toward Power Sharing and Devolution in South Africa and Namibia" (Paper presented at the American Political Science Association, Washington, D. C., September 1977).

29. Richard M. Cyert and James G. March, *A Behavioral Theory of the Firm* (Englewood Cliffs, N. J.: Prentice-Hall, 1963), p. 277.

30. See the discussion in Rothchild, "Collective Demands for Improved Distributions," in Rothchild and Olorunsola, *State Versus Ethnic Claims*, pp. 189–192.

31. On the public's perception of legislators as "agents of the periphery at the center," see Joel D. Barkan, "Legislators, Elections, and Political Linkage," in Barkan with Okumu, *Politics and Public Policy in Kenya and Tanzania*, p. 67f.

32. This distinction between the state as partially autonomous actor and as an

organizing set of principles is discussed in my "Social Incoherence and the Mediatory Role of the State," in Bruce E. Arlinghaus (ed.), *African Security Issues* (Boulder, Colo.: Westview Press, 1984), ch. 6.

33. Nelson Kasfir, *The Shrinking Political Arena* (Berkeley: University of California Press, 1976), p. 163.

34. As Billy Dudley observes, the military "share the same cultural idiom with the people. . . ." *An Introduction to Nigerian Government and Politics* (Bloomington: Indiana University Press, 1982), p. 123. In this section, I have drawn heavily from my chapter: "State-Ethnic Relations in Middle Africa," in Gwendolen M. Carter and Patrick O'Meara (eds.), *African Independence: The First 25 Years* (Bloomington: Indiana University Press, 1985), ch. 4.

35. Robin Luckham, *The Nigerian Military* (Cambridge: Cambridge University Press, 1971), p. 296.

36. Ibid.

37. Interview, Professor Negussay Ayele, Berkeley, Calif., 1 June 1983.

38. Significantly, upon taking up his appointment as President for the High Executive Council for the Southern Region, Major General Gasmallah Rassas issued a statement through Radio Juba assuring Southerners that he hailed from Bahr el Ghazal province. "I am a Southerner," he told a *Sudanow* interviewer. "I was born in Bussere (11 miles south of Wau) and my brother and sister are still living there at our home. . . ." *Sudanow* 6, 11 (November 1981): 15. The importance of a regional identification is underscored by the experience in Darfur region, where the people rioted over Nimeiry's first choice as governor in 1981 on the grounds that he was not a native of Darfur and secured his replacement. See Colin Legum (ed.), *Africa Contemporary Record 1980–81*, 13 (New York: Africana Publishing Co., 1981): B102.

39. René Lemarchand, "Comparative Political Clientelism: Structure, Process and Optic," in S. N. Eisenstadt and René Lemarchand (eds.), *Political Clientelism, Patronage and Development* (Beverly Hills: Sage, 1981), p. 15.

40. Dunstan M. Wai, "The Sudan: Crisis in North-South Relations," *Africa Report* 27, 2 (March–April 1982): 26; also see his comments in "Geoethnicity and the Margin of Autonomy in the Sudan," in Rothchild and Olorunsola, *State Versus Ethnic Claims*, p. 326.

41. Donald Rothchild and Michael Rogin, "Uganda," in Gwendolen M. Carter (ed.), *National Unity and Regionalism in Eight African States* (Ithaca, N. Y.: Cornell University Press, 1966), pp. 378–79, 384, 394.

42. Colin Leys, *Politicians and Policies* (Nairobi: East African Publishing House, 1967), pp. 32, 44.

43. Fred G. Burke, *Local Government and Politics in Uganda* (Syracuse, N. Y.: Syracuse University Press, 1964), p. 229.

44. Kasfir, *The Shrinking Political Arena,* pp. 167–68.

45. A. Milton Obote, *Proposals for New Methods of Election of Representatives of the People to Parliament* (Kampala: Milton Obote Foundation, 1970), pp. 6–7.

46. Letter from J. M. Mutti to *Times of Zambia* (Ndola), 24 October 1970, p. 6. Mr. Mutti was a member of the controversial Chuula UNIP constitutional commission which called for equal provincial representation on the party's Central Committee.

47. Richard Hall, *The High Price of Principles* (New York: Africana Publishing Corporation, 1969), p. 195.

48. See the data in William Tordoff, "Introduction," in William Tordoff (ed.), *Administration in Zambia* (Manchester: Manchester University Press, 1980), pp. 14–15.

49. Jean-Pierre Langellier, "Zambia's Costly Mistakes," *Manchester Guardian Weekly* 128, 18 (1 May 1983): 14.

50. *Zambia Daily Mail* (Lusaka), 7 October 1970, p. 1.

51. *Sunday Times of Zambia* (Ndola), 9 July 1972, p. 1.

52. *Zambia Daily Mail,* 3 June 1971, p. 1.

53. Ernst B. Haas, "Technological Self-Reliance in Latin America: The OAS Contribution," *International Organization* 34, 4 (Autumn 1980): 552.

54. Although Sir Arthur Lewis's discussion of political coalitions refers to inter-party relations, his emphasis on the importance of inclusiveness and of allowing scope for ethnic "self-expression" is relevant to the hegemonic coalition as well. See his *Politics in West Africa* (London: George Allen & Unwin, 1965), p. 68.

55. Robert A. Mortimer, "Ivory Coast: Succession and Recession," *Africa Report* 28, 1 (January–February 1983): 5, 7.

56. Aristide R. Zolberg, "Politics in the Ivory Coast: 1," *West Africa,* 30 July 1960, p. 847.

57. Aristide R. Zolberg, *One-Party Government in the Ivory Coast* (Princeton, N. J.: Princeton University Press, 1964), p. 283.

58. Zolberg, "Politics in the Ivory Coast: 2," *West Africa,* 6 August 1960, p. 883.

59. Zolberg, *One-Party Government,* p. 234. On the deterioration of the political machine and the increase in Houphouët-Boigny's control of institutions of state in the 1970s, see Robert H. Jackson and Carl G. Rosberg, *Personal Rule in Black Africa* (Berkeley: University of California Press, 1982), p. 150.

60. Richard E. Stryker, "A Local Perspective on Developmental Strategy in the Ivory Coast," in Michael F. Lofchie (ed.), *The State of the Nations* (Berkeley: University of California Press, 1971), p. 134.

61. Colin Legum (ed.), *Africa Contemporary Record 1981–82* (New York: Africana Publishing Co., 1981), pp. B444–445.

62. See Robert H. Jackson and Carl G. Rosberg, *Personal Rule in Black Africa,* p. 102.

63. Goran Hyden and Colin Leys, "Elections and Politics in Single-Party Systems: The Case of Kenya and Tanzania," *British Journal of Political Science* 2, 4 (October 1972): 393; Cherry Gertzel, *The Politics of Independent Kenya 1963-8* (Nairobi: East African Publishing House, 1970), pp. 137-38; Henry Bienen, *Kenya: The Politics of Participation and Control,* (Princeton, N. J.: Princeton University Press, 1974), pp. 81-82; and John J. Okumu, "Party and Party-State Relations," in Barkan and Okumu, *Politics and Public Policy in Kenya and Tanzania,* p. 58.

64. Carl G. Rosberg, "National Identity in African States," *African Review* (Dar es Salaam) 1, 1 (March 1971): 86.

65. Robert H. Jackson, "Planning, Politics, and Administration," in Goran Hyden, Robert Jackson, and John Okumu (eds.), *Development Administration: The Kenyan Experience* (Nairobi: Oxford University Press, 1970), pp. 177-178. On public attitudes on allocations to the less favored areas, see Donald Rothchild, "Ethnic Inequalities in Kenya," *Journal of Modern African Studies* 7, 4 (December 1969): 696-701.

66. Vincent B. Khapoya, "Kenya Under Moi: Continuity or Change?" *Africa Today* 27, 1 (1st Quarter 1980): 22–23.

67. *Weekly Review* (Nairobi), 27 June 1980, p. 5.

68. Victoria Brittain, "Five Months That Took Kenya to the Brink," *Manchester Guardian Weekly* 127, 6 (8 April 1982): 7. Surprisingly, an unanticipated consequence of Charles Njonjo's ordeal at the hands of the Moi regime in 1983–84 has been a rise in his popularity among the Kikuyu elite in Central Province—and largely at the expense of his Kikuyu arch-rival, Vice-President Mwai Kibaki. Njonjo's newfound popularity has been attributable to a number of factors: public attention in parliament and at the judicial commission of inquiry, (real or imagined) ethnic grievances, and an inability of the current vice-president to speak openly against government policies perceived as disadvantageous to his constituents. "It is one of those strange ironies of politics on the African continent," commented one reporter, "that when all is said and done, tribal sentiment counts for a lot more than anything else." *Weekly Review,* 1 June 1984, p. 18.

69. *Weekly Review,* 7 October 1983, p. 4.

70. See Philippe C. Schmitter, "Still the Century of Corporatism?" *Review of Politics* 36, 1 (January 1974): 105. On the possible emergence of corporatism at some future time in middle Africa, see Aristide R. Zolberg, *One-Party Government in the Ivory Coast* (Princeton: Princeton University Press, 1964), p. 331.

71. Hyden, "Problems and Prospects," p. 73.

72. Ibid., p. 69.

73. Michael Holman, "Short of Everything—including Hope," *Financial Times,* 31 July 1981, p. 12.

74. Lindblom, *Politics and Markets,* p. 121.

75. For data showing multipartyism to be "particularly destabilizing when coupled with the presence of a dominant ethnic group," and the strong, one-party system as a stabilizing and integrative factor, see Robert W. Jackman, "The Predictability of Coups d'etat: A Model with African Data," *American Political Science Review* 72, 4 (December 1978): 1273–1274. Also see the discussion in Ralph R. Premdas, "Guyana: Violence and Democracy in a Communal State," *Plural Societies* 12, 3–4 (Winter 1981): 48.

76. See Samuel P. Hungtington, *Political Order in Changing Societies* (New Haven: Yale University Press, 1968), p. 421.

77. Cherry Gertzel, *The Politics of Independent Kenya 1963–8,* p. 145.

78. *Manchester Guardian Weekly* 128, 11 (13 March 1983): 8.

79. On choice possibilities, see the discussion in Rothchild and Olorunsola, *State Versus Ethnic Claims,* ch. 12.

80. Robert H. Jackson and Carl G. Rosberg, "Why Africa's Weak States Persist: The Empirical and the Juridical in Statehood," *World Politics* 35, 1 (October 1982): 21.

81. John Lonsdale, "State and Social Processes in Africa: A Historiographical Survey," *African Studies Review* 24, 2–3 (June–September 1981): 201.

82. Youssef Cohen, Brian R. Brown, and A. F. K. Organski, "The Paradoxical Nature of State Making: The Violent Creation of Order," *American Political Science Review* 75, 4 (December 1981): 904.

83. Ibid.

84. Robert A. Dahl and Charles E. Lindblom, *Politics, Economics, and Welfare* (New York: Harper and Row, Torchback ed., 1963), p. 472.

85. Goran Hyden, *Beyond Ujamaa in Tanzania* (Berkeley: University of California press, 1980), p. 30; and his "Problems and Prospect," pp. 73–74. Also see Barrington Moore, Jr., *Social Origins of Dictatorship and Democracy* (Boston: Beacon Press, 1967), p. 341.

86. Conor Cruise O'Brien, *States of Ireland* (New York: Pantheon Books, 1972), p. 303.

87. Klaus R. Scherer, Ronald P. Abeles, and Claude S. Fischer, *Human Aggression and Conflict* (Englewood Cliffs, N. J.: Prentice–Hall, 1975), p. 113.

88. Anatol Rapoport, *Fights, Games, and Debates* (Ann Arbor: University of Michigan Press, 1960), p. 255.

89. I have drawn heavily here from analyses of the role of perceptions in foreign policy formation. In particular, Alexander Dallin and Gail W. Lapidus, "Reagan and the Russians," in K. Oye, R. Lieber, and D. Rothchild (eds.), *Eagle Defiant* (Boston: Little, Brown, 1983), pp. 206–209; Miles Kahler, "The United States and Western Europe," Ibid., pp. 281–282; Robert Jervis, *Perception and Misperception in International Politics* (Princeton: Princeton University Press, 1976); Joseph H. de Rivera, *The Psychological Dimension of Foreign Policy* (Columbus, Ohio: Charles E. Merrill, 1968); David J. Finlay, Ole R. Holsti, and Richard R. Fagen, *Enemies in Politics* (Chicago: Rand McNally, 1967); and Herbert C. Kelman (ed.), *International Behavior* (New York: Holt, Rinehart and Winston, 1966). Also helpful in this regard were writings on third party consultation. On this, see Leonard Doob et al., *Resolving Conflict in Africa* (New Haven: Yale University Press, 1970); Marshall H. Segall, *Human Behavior and Public Policy* (New York: Pergamon Press, 1976), especially pp. 253–260; and Ronald J. Fisher, "Third Party Consultation as Conflict Resolution," *Journal of Conflict Resolution* 27, 2 (June 1983): 301–334.

90. Anthony D. Smith, *State and Nation in the Third World* (Sussex: Wheatsheaf Books, 1983), p. 93.

91. René Lemarchand, "Revolutionary Phenomena in Stratified Societies: Rwanda and Zanzibar," *Civilisations* 18, 1 (1968): 47. Ethclass, "the intersection of the ethnic group with the social class," is discussed in Milton M. Gordon, *Human Nature, Class, and Ethnicity* (New York: Oxford University Press, 1978), p. 134.

92. René Lemarchand, *Rwanda and Burundi* (London: Pall Mall Press, 1970), pp. 169, 179. Also see Leo Kuper, *The Pity of It All* (Minneapolis: University of Minnesota Press, 1977).

93. Thomas P. Melady, *Burundi: The Tragic Years* (Maryknoll, New York: Orbis Books, 1974), p. 72. Also see, René Lemarchand, *Selective Genocide in Burundi*, Report No. 20 (London: Minority Rights Group, n.d.), p. 8.

94. Michael Lofchie, "The Plural Society in Zanzibar," in Leo Kuper and M. G. Smith (eds.), *Pluralism in Africa* (Berkeley: University of California Press, 1969), p. 312; and Alexander A. Madiebo, *The Nigerian Revolution and the Biafran War* (Enugu, Nigeria: Fourth Dimension, 1980), p. 87.

95. Roger Fisher, *International Conflict for Beginners* (New York: Harper and Row, 1969), pp. 48–50.

96. For a discussion of the promotion of trust and reciprocity through exchange obligations in Kenya around the time of the transfer of power, see Rothchild, *Racial*

*Bargaining,* especially pp. 114, 145.

97. Jervis, *Perception and Misperception,* p. 43.

98. Peter M. Blau, *Exchange and Power in Social Life* (New York: John Wiley, 1967), p. 99.

99. Rothchild and Curry, *Scarcity, Choice, and Public Policy,* pp. 112–147.

100. Quoted in Donald Rothchild, "Military Regime Performance: An appraisal of the Ghana Experience, 1972–78," *Comparative Politics* 12, 4 (July 1980): 474.

101. On this, see C. L. G. Bell, "The Political Framework," in Hollis Chenery et al., *Redistribution with Growth* (New York: Oxford University Press, 1974), p. 58.

102. *Ibid.,* pp. 475–476.

103. Alan B. Amey and David K. Leonard, "Public Policy, Class and Inequality in Kenya and Tanzania," *Africa Today* 26, 4 (1979): 37–38.

104. See Donald Rothchild, "Africa: Hegemonial Exchange and Resource Allocation," in Alexander Groth and Larry Wade (eds.), *Comparative Resource Allocation* (Beverly Hills: Sage, 1984).

105. See Robert Melson and Howard Wolpe, "Modernization and the Politics of Communalism: A Theoretical Perspective," *American Political Science Review* 64, 4 (December 1970): 1117; and Howard Wolpe, *Urban Politics in Nigeria* (Berkeley: University of California Press, 1974), pp. 240–241.

106. Edmond Keller, "The State, Public Policy and the Mediation of Ethnic Conflict in Africa," in Rothchild and Olorunsola, *State Versus Ethnic Claims,* p. 263.

107. Rothchild, *Racial Bargaining,* p. 145.

108. Claude Ake, "Explaining Political Instability in New States," *Journal of Modern African Studies* 11, 2 (September 1973): 356.

109. See Rothchild, "State-Ethnic Relations in Middle Africa."

110. Calculated from *West Africa,* 10 May 1982, p. 1262.

111. The full list of high level appointments appears in Daniel G. Matthews, "Nigeria 1984: An Interim Report," No. 24, *CSIS Africa Notes* (February 29, 1984), p. 3.

112. On Lebanon's "National Pact" as a second-best arrangement for coping with the identity problem, see Michael C. Hudson, *The Precarious Republic* (New York: Random House, 1968), p. 45.

# 5 Ethnic Politics in Nigeria: A Conceptual Reformulation

John A. A. Ayoade

On December 31, 1983, the military took over the government of Nigeria and thus ended the Second Republic. The official explanation for the takeover did not include the resurgence and vitality of ethnicity, but every explanation, including corruption, was deeply rooted in the ethnic struggle for power. Although ethnicity was not conspicuously present as it was in the First Republic, it was more sophisticated and virile. Ethnicity had to be clandestine in the Second Republic because the constitution expressly forbade appeals to ethnic loyalties. But the actions of Nigerians were coded in ethnicity and were only meaningful when decoded as such. In fact corruption, which reached unprecedented proportions in the Second Republic, can in part be explained as one way of enhancing the relative competitiveness of the ethnic groups. Thus the constitution had succeeded only in changing the language and strategy of ethnic competition. In a way, this was to be expected because the constitution did not attempt to eradicate ethnicity; it only produced rules for participation in the ethnic game.[1] But in the attempt to regulate ethnic anarchy, the constitution ended up orchestrating it. The collapse of the civilian administration barely four years after the restoration positively proves the dangers of both laissez-faire and engineered ethnicity to the stability of a multiethnic society. Perhaps the constitution enshrined a system of equity between the ethnies in response to the changes of ethnic domination in the First Republic, but it soon became clear that it was difficult to build national unity via ethnic differentiation. The political parties were expected to have a national outlook by reflecting the ethnic composition of the country, just as executive appointments had to be inclusive or representative of the ethnic make-up of the country. The fact that the situation warranted a specific constitutional statement meant that people would ordinarily have been guided by ethnic political considerations. And the situation is still difficult, whether voluntary or compulsory processes are used to bring about change. But it has become clear that neither the strategy of deliberate constitutional engineering nor the paradoxical modality of achieving social homogenization through ethnic particularization has worked in Nigeria. The important question at this point is why these solutions failed to bring about the desired change. The argument in this study is that they failed because of wrong underlying assumptions that:

1. Modernization eliminates ethnicity.
2. Ethnicity is only a bourgeois pathology.
3. Ethnicity, paradoxically, is an urban phenomenon symptomatic of cosmopolitanism.

To a large extent, there is a linkage between the three wrong assumptions, because modernization tends to result in urbanization and the consequent emergence of classes. But more importantly the assumptions all derive from the near analytic anarchy that pervades the study of ethnicity. Paul Bohannan, as if to provide an alibi, has attributed the absence of conceptual and definitional clarity to the fact that ethnicity is the most mystical of all concepts.[2] The lack of intellectual consensus among ethnicologists has, therefore, produced conflicts that match the subject of their study. But more particularly it has produced solutions that suffer in both precision and adequacy. It is the purpose of this study to put forward a theory of ethnicity derived from the history of Nigeria in order to produce an explanatory schema for postcolonial, plural, developing countries.

## THE LIBERAL EXPECTATION

We have indicated that the view of ethnicity as a self-terminating "disease" is wrong. This view considered ethnicity to be a product of isolation, so that when contact and interaction is generated through industrialization and modernization there will follow a progressive attenuation of ethnic loyalties.[3] John Thompson, arguing in the same vein, posited a more controversial theory by saying that the differentiation of the division of labor and the penetration of the capitalist market will undermine ethnicity so that, within a modern society, ethnicity becomes a residual factor.[4] The reality in Africa, however, is that the inverse relationship between modernization and ethnicity is not true; rather modernization has catalyzed ethnicity. This situation tends to confirm that the premise of the liberal expectation was wrong. While it is true that isolation makes the *ethnies* visible and distinctive, contact, by definition, excites competition for human and material recognition which results in conflict. Thus, what Frederik Barth calls the ethnic ideology, i.e., disengagement and boundary formation, survives the flow of personnel across ethnic boundaries. Consequently, an ethnic group response, even in a cosmopolitan modernizing environment, by creating an inclusive socio-political arena, or Rupert Emerson's "terminal community." Thus, the result is an *imperio in imperium* in which Ferdinand Tönnie's organic totalities (*Gemeinschaft*) refuse to give way to the mechanical constructions (*Gesellschaft*). This is perhaps due to the natural resilience of people, such that, as in Africa, social and political change did not destroy the traditional social structure but prompted the adaptation of that structure to new circumstances.[5]

R. H. Jackson would not attribute this phenomenon to the natural tendency for adaptation. He argued that modernization in Africa resulted in social adaptation rather than social transformation because modernization did not include substantial industrialization.[6] But this is coincidental rather than causal because it does not explain ethnic rejuvenation in the industrialized societies.

Similarly, dependency theory does not explain why modernization does not occasion the homogenization of plural societies. Jackson argued that the dependent nature of most African economies arrested the development of social classes, particularly an African bourgeoisie.[7] While this may be true in global terms, incorporating the dependent economies into what Amilcar Cabral identifies as the nation class, it is not true that at the level of each African country classes were not gradually emerging. In fact, the lesson of dependence at the international level was to produce a similar order at the country level in the form of a patron-client relationship. The gap between patron and client may be blurred by an informal network of patronage and corruption exhibiting a superficial classlessness. This succeeds to the extent that the patron successfully plays the role of a "trans-class man" by holding a dual class identity. It does not, however, indicate the absence of classes. It only incorporates the ideology of patronage into class interaction in such a way as to entrench the upper classes through state financing. This symbiotic relationship continues until the political class matures and its survival no longer depends on the free and voluntary support of the masses of the people. At that time, when classes are fully evolved, the political class *demands* support without reciprocating in money or material.

The resistance of ethnicity to modernization can be better explained by the incomplete deracination of the African proletariat. The African proletariat retains a concurrent membership in the ethnic community and the modern society. The ethnic community still looks attractive to him because he always has a designated position there, so that he mitigates the insecurity of the urban setting by his ownership of rural land and kinship links with both urban and rural relatives.[8] Therefore, although he ceases to be a rural *volk,* he retains a rural affection. In the same way it is the double consciousness of the elite African that turns the African elite into a group of *interlocuteurs valables* still closely connected to the countryside and able to speak its language.[9]

## CONFLICT THEORY

While integration theory, which predicts the disappearance of ethnicity, fails in this case, conflict theory accounts for its persistence. The kernel of conflict theory is that the salience of ethnicity increases rather than decreases with interaction. Ernest Gellner saw ethnicity as a function of the unevenness of industrialization. Whenever such unevenness is coterminous with ethnic spatial boundaries, it results in the stratification of the geographically defined units.[10] But a country does not normally have an evenness of natural endowments, so that the geographical distribution of "ethnonational groups" into distinctive homelands is sufficient in itself to assure the existence of economic discrepancies among them.[11] Thus, ethnic groups residing *in situ* in areas with high resource differentials, but under the same government, have potentials for conflict. Such potentials can, however, become real when the government, which in developing countries is the principal allocator of economic resources, widens the differentials through uneven development. The statistically significant variations between the geographically distinguishable groups, therefore, create a perception of conspirational discrimination,[12] which M. Hechter characterizes as internal colonialism. For Hechter, this is a situation in which the superordinate or core group establishes and seeks to institutionalize a hierarchical cultural division of labor[13] such that cultural group membership determines life chances. This is different from the *Damnosa Hereditas* principle of ethnic ranking and martial races stereotype that the British adopted in their colonies. The feeling of the reliability of certain groups and not others grew from a hunch into a principle, but did not amount to internal colonialism because it was not tied to the development of the colonies.[14] Furthermore, Hechter's internal colonial model made the development of the core dependent on the underdevelopment of the periphery. It therefore generated what Thompson called "reactive ethnicity" from the periphery, which nurses a feeling of relative economic deprivation. Internal colonialism is a form of differential incorporation based on structured inequalities with real manifestations and high correlations with ethnic groups. It permits the general expropriation of economic resources by the dominant group, their control of access to education and technological resources, and their denigration of the culture of the subordinate section.[15]

Hechter's ethnicity thesis has been criticized by different authors. Pierre Van den Berghe makes the semantic observation that the domination of one ethnic group by the other can only result in imperialism and not colonialism, which he associates with the crossing of salt water by people of a different cultural, linguistic, technological, and racial origin.[16] But the more substantive criticism is that of Thompson, who argues that the Hechter thesis is too exclusively economistic. It is for this reason that Walker Connor contends that ethnonationalism depends not on relative economic deprivation, or even on economic change, but on the growing tendency of people to resent and resist alien rule.[17] For him economic argument only serves as the excuse for resisting domination.

Similarly, neo-Marxists like Edna Bonacich contend that that ethnic differentiation on its own is not adequate to initiate ethnic conflict. She attributed ethnicity to a split labor market in which two groups of workers are paid a different price for the same labor. This also results in reactive ethnicity, which Nairn completely disowns. According to Tom Nairn, it is inevitable that the core should develop at the expense of the periphery because even development is only a "metropolitan fantasy."[18] But more important is the ambivalence of the periphery to domination, because while the periphery objects to the dominance of the core it seeks to emulate its dynamism.[19] This explains why ethnicity persists after the peripheral area has itself become a core area and why ethnicity exists in core areas which have never experienced peripheral status.

Ethnicity is, therefore, not simply reactive or pathological. Max Gluckman characterizes it as a rational "organizing principle of social relations"[20] which amounts to a rational choice theory. Ethnicity operates as a form of situational selection, so that the individual's membership in a particular group in a particular situation is a function of the values, interests, and motives that influence his behavior in that situation.[21] The affirmation of ethnicity is, therefore, variable and dependent upon the immediate social situation. Thus primordialist identity is subjected to the optionalist identity, which is not permanently imprinted on the psyche but can be consciously emphasized and de-emphasized as occasions warrant.[22] Ethnicity is, therefore, a rational selection similar to the "familiar psychological mechanism by which discrepant ideas are segregated in different compartments of the mind."[23] It, therefore, results in what Leo Depres refers to as a pattern of segmentary opposition to attain what in Barthian terms is socially effective.[24] The rational choice theory of ethnicity of what John Paden terms situational ethnicity[25] is the process by which fitness maximization is achieved. And by emphasizing the individual as the unit of analysis it avoids the problem of reification, because social structures are the aggregate outcome of individual behavior.[26]

## ETHNIC ECOLOGICAL THEORY

All three theories—integration, conflict, and situational—assume the environment of ethnicity and emphasize variables like modernization, development, choice, and policy outputs that shape the environment in which ethnicity develops. The weakness of these approaches is the assumption that because of the givenness of the environment it can be assumed away. It will appear, however, that the problematic of ethnicity is a product of the policy outputs on the environment. Both factors are important and complementary.

The environment is important because it gives ethnicity in a particular place its defining characteristics, because the same policy outputs will yield different reactions in different environments. On the other hand, the policy outputs serve as the starter of the chain reactions or the accelerator of such reactions when they are already in motion.

The environment itself, therefore, needs to be defined. In broad terms, developed and developing polities will be an adequate differentiation, although they both are all too subsuming and require a further disaggregation. At the level of generalities, the dichotomy of developed and developing will approximate to industrialized and agricultural economies, which can each be subdivided into urban and rural (or agraria). This subdivision is particularly more significant in the developing countries because of the relative low level of the industrial penetration of agraria coupled with the significant presence of the agraria in the cities, thus creating distinct urban-agraria psychology. This situation of interpenetration creates a linkage but not an equal partnership between city and countryside. Each, therefore, has its own set of characteristics necessitating differences in how specific problems are confronted and, therefore, different systems of social dynamics.

Agraria is characterized by ascriptive criteria, which while not disincentives to competition, are regulators of competition. But these criteria are both inclusive and exclusive, because they operate within the lineage and keep out people outside the lineage. By their nature, therefore, they protect the lineage, and through that the ethnic entity against exogenous intrusion. Thus, the expansion of the traditional state can only be vertical rather than horizontal. The ethnic group in an agraria is therefore territorially discrete and emphasizes land as a patrimony; it cannot therefore ordinarily be transferred outside the confines of the lineage and the ethnic group. The result is the permanence of ethnic boundaries, which serve as built-in guarantees for ethnic survival. This situation creates an ethnic awareness that is based on the need and desire to protect cherished values. But such ethnic traits are only potentially significant until they are touched off by exogenous threat. It is at that point of confrontation that the individual becomes ethnically conscious and the salience of ethnic traits become "evident in the way it influences other cultural, social or territorial attributes and modes of individual identification."[27]

Rural ethnicity can, therefore, pass through four possible stages—potency, activity, dormancy or eradication, and reactivation. It has passed through potency to activation in Nigeria, and that has necessitated measures to move it at least to dormancy, if not complete eradication. But movement from one stage to the next presupposes the existence of change agents. The change agents that moved rural ethnicity from potency to activity were local and international territorial expansion. Local territorial expansion resulted from either population increase, resource decay, or the peculiarities of traditional grievance procedures. As population increased, resource requirements (grazing land, farm land, water, etc.) also increased, thus reducing the spatial distance between formerly distant ethnic groups. Through the resultant elimination of the buffer space, ethnic groups became contiguous and set in motion a process of resource negotiation.

Buffer space reduction also occurs in a situation of resource decay or resource exhaustion, leading to large-scale migration or transhumance living. Similarly, some grievance modalities have a tendency to narrow or even eliminate buffer space. For example, the traditional Ibo village democracies in Nigeria allowed dissenting groups the option of territorial relocation. The reduction of buffer space, therefore, has an implicit expansionist process, which because of the finite ethnic space was sure to be resisted or halted. At the critical point that land needs develop into land hunger, resource negotiations take the form of armed conflicts. Conflicts in such situations are further explained when viewed from the perspective of the differences between them—the greater the difference the greater the problem of ethnicity.

But is is not only local territorial expansion that leads to the social construction of reality in ethnic terms. International territorial expansion also results in the emphasizing of ethnic differences. Colonialism imposed new boundaries that superseded the existing ethnic boundaries and initiated a new form of ethnic movement that has an international dimension. It united all the colonized peoples in the struggle for independence so that the colonized and the colonizers crystallized into separate and antagonistic ethnic groups. In one sense, this complication reduced precolonial ethnic tension but this was by no means universal. In some places, the colonial system was welcome as a counterweight to more powerful neighbors. Such at-risk ethnic collectivities, therefore, valued colonialism. But in another sense colonialism increased ethnic tension by subsuming precolonial ethnic boundaries under the imposed international boundaries or sometimes by obliterating the precolonial boundaries. This process, therefore, introduced political changes that further threatened not just individual but also corporate ethnic survival. It resulted in state penetration of ethnic domains, and state formation, which in itself was a form of modernization, unsettled the countryside. Agraria was, therefore, no longer a separate entity with its own rules of social interaction but part and parcel of the larger polity through state penetration. This kind of change increases the density of ethnic stimulus in the rural areas and creates a consciousness of kind that approximates the urban ethnic phenomenon.

The urban setting is, however, different in several respects and provides many more instances of ethnic conflict than do the rural areas. In fact, state formation has occasioned such ethnic interpenetration that uni-ethnic cities have completely disappeared. This is particularly true in cities that serve as administrative or commercial centers. In effect, the national capital, the state capitals, and the provincial capitals have attracted a large number of people from outside the ethnic territory in which they are situated. It is no surprise, therefore, that the worst cases of urban ethnic clashes have occurred in Lagos, Jos, and Kano. The growth of the cities has resulted from the administrative and economic expansion of the modern sector, where the emphasis has been on the prescriptive criterion of functional rationality. Therefore, the cities are built on the assumption of a struggle for survival in which, by and large, merit and competence are at a premium. But this is not to say that all the people who live in the cities are *déracinés*. In fact it is because there are still people in the cities who are firmly rooted in the environment and who feel threatened by the influx of other ethnics that urban ethnicity becomes significant. But the modern state system in Africa weakens the primordial claims of the ethnics in whose territory such cities are established, because the success of the modern state apparatus depends on the protection of the life and property of the bureaucrats in both the private and the public sector. But this has not in any way prevented the expression of ethnic claims. In fact, the cities are characterized by two levels of ethnicity: the first is the level of ethnic conflict between the "sons of the soil" and the "native foreigners," and the second is ethnic conflict among the "native foreigners," a multiethnic group. The fact that the "native foreigners" can cooperate whenever they are threatened, but disagree whenever outside tension is reduced, shows up ethnicity as a rational strategem for working out life chances in a multiethnic society. Thus, the switching forward and backward, or the dissembling and assembling of ethnic identity, is calculated.

The urban ethnic turns to his ethnic base as a fallback position whenever the urban environment turns hostile. The urban ethnic group becomes the kinship referent for the migrant who otherwise would be adrift.[28] This is why Judith Nagata defines ethnic groups as "special kinds of reference groups, the invocation of which may vary according to particular factors of broader social situation. . . ."[29] Orlando Patterson also argues that ethnicity is neither an ascriptive, permanent characteristic nor a fixed anchorage, but a phenomenon that can only be seen in the dynamic context of the underlying socioeconomic interests of group members.[30] This phenomenon often does not amount to more than an existential solidarity, as distinct from ethnocentric solidarity, which is a conscious togetherness that may exist without existential solidarity. But there is only a thin line between the two, because existential solidarity easily converts to ethnocentric solidarity.[31] Similarly the dichotomy between the rural ethnic and the urban ethnic, while real, must not be overstressed. They are distinct and distinguishable but are characterized by economic and administrative linkages that we shall discuss presently.

## RURAL ETHNIC AND URBAN ETHNIC LINKAGES

Rural ethnicity has ceased to possess a sovereign status with the advancement of the modern state system in Africa. This is because the countryside, which paradoxically has been the backbone of the African economy as well as the abode of the majority of the Africans, has been relegated to a subordinate status following a colonial reordering of the hierarchy. A process of homogenization of the urban and the rural was set in motion under the terms favorable to the urban ethnics. Plural ethnicity became a subordinate social process, although it remained salient. In fact, the cash economy that accompanied modern state formation in Africa increased the value of land and thus reinforced interethnic boundaries. Boundary disputes increased, because razor-edge boundaries were introduced under the colonial system. Thus, the density of stimulus of ethnicity was higher in the boundary zones, and ethnicity has an inverse relationship with distance from interethnic boundaries.

Such boundary conflicts become the occasion for the further penetration of the modern state system into the countryside, resulting in the gradual narrowing of the gap between urban and rural ethnicity. The principal instrument of that process is the bureaucracy. But oftentimes while performing this function, the bureaucracy operates as a class which, because it still remains multiethnic, is better regarded as a "pluralistic class." It, however, continues as a class because it is united by a commonality of economic or political interest,[32] often sustained by a core-periphery mode of interaction. The urban centers, more often than not, exist in developing societies as parasites on the countryside. Collectively, there is an unequal sharing of rewards favoring the urban centers. But the intendant class in the urban centers does not shed its ethnic qualities. So for the "pluralistic class," interethnic cooperation is circumstantial. In a way, therefore, ethnicity does not wane as class waxes, because class is based on the commonality of interests that in developing societies are defined by culture. If culture, therefore, determines attitude to wealth, capital accumulation, or political obligation it can moderate class and class formation.

The persistence of ethnicity in the face of class is perhaps also due to the fact that members of the class sometimes need ethnicity to maximize their competitiveness in the urban setting. Thus, whenever class interest conflicts with individual interest, the individual emphasizes ethnic interest in order to have a comparative advantage. There is no problem whenever ethnic and class interests are collinear. But Thompson asserts that there is even a difference between class interests and ethnic economic interests in spite of their common material base. For him, ethnic economic interests "which are objective economic interests held in common by all members of an ethnic group regardless of their class position are a subset of ethnic interests, and not a subset of class interests."[33] Consequently, the vertical ethnic division of society and the horizontal class division of the same society create sluices and intersections that serve as the defining characteristics of that society. There is no dissonance between ethnicity and class at the sluices, but the intersection produces what Thompson terms a "structural ambiguity,"[34] because there is an overlap of two or more society-level structures. That overlap creates a problem of choice between alternative interests and alternative bases of political appeal and mobilization for the actors. Such a dilemma results in a situational selection between ethnicity and class, making the extent of the association between ethnicity and class variable in modernizing plural societies. There may therefore be interethnic cooperation, intraethnic conflict, cross-class interaction, and intraclass disagreement.

In recent Nigerian politics, however, there has been some emphasis on representative bureaucracy. The principle of the "federal character," which meant an unspecified representation of the component ethnics of the federation, was enshrined in the constitution. The argument was that a bureaucracy that was grossly "dissimilar in its composition from the general public might sacrifice its operational effectiveness or even lose its legitimacy."[35] The northern bureaucrats argued that social disproportions in the bureaucracy skew the mobility of opportunities and material rewards in the society and, consequently, reduce the ability of the bureaucracy to mobilize the masses of the people for development. The bureaucracy, therefore, cannot be the result of mere market forces or happenstance.[36] The bureaucrats need and use ethnicity to strengthen their professional claims. It is usually when this occurs that ethnicity is regarded as the concoction of manipulative elites. Unfortunately, the process may create an unintended awareness in the rural ethnics that may become a weapon in interclass conflict.

The bureaucrat also increases rural ethnicity by advocating the creation of new states and local governments. The creation of these new governmental structures helps to widen career opportunities for bureaucrats, but in the process new administrative boundaries are drawn, guided by the maintenance of traditional jurisdictional authority and linguistic affinity. The implication of this requirement is that hitherto common resources are located under one particular jurisdiction without proper interjurisdictional arrangements. Consequently, some people find their farms or pasture in one jurisdictional area and their homes in another. In order to facilitate their daily activities, they lay claims to resources on both sides of the boundary, thus occasioning border disputes. Such disputes are resolved by urban bureaucrats using rules that are more applicable to the solution of urban problems. This assumption of the congruence of rural-urban problems tends to complicate rural ethnicity. It puts rural ethnicity into an urban world, which is only a temporary solution and one that can be sustained only with the monopoly of urban-based force, and it confuses the intentionality levels of urban and rural ethnicity, thus producing a forced similarity of meanings. The process results in the progressive urbanization of the rural areas without a compensatory ruralization of the urban centers.

We have so far treated urban-rural interaction as a group phenomenon and generally as an epistructure. But at the level of the individual the dichotomy produces five main positions through ethnic hyphenations of exogamous marriages. These positions constitute a continuum with the "pure" ethnics at the two extremes. Thus there are:

1. The urban ethnic
2. The urban-urban ethnic
3. The urban-rural ethnic
4. The rural-rural ethnic
5. The rural ethnic

The ethnic hyphenations, i.e., the urban-urban ethnic, the urban-rural ethnic, and the rural-rural ethnic, occur whenever there is a difference between the individual and the group levels of intentionality, thus freeing the individual from group controls. However, ethnic hyphenations do not have the same salience as interracial hyphenations because they are intraphenotypical and, therefore, do not produce a distinct set of diacriticals. The progeny do not, therefore, constitute a distinct group, so that if ethnic hyphenations occur on a large scale, they blur ethnic distinctions and culminate in gradual assimilation. The progeny tends to be bilingual, but their acculturation reflects the fact that the acculturation of the parents has to be both additive and substitutive, depending on who the dominant partner is. All forms of ethnic hyphenation affect language, intentionality, and ethnic security maps in plural societies; each of these however, vary in size and salience.

The urban-urban ethnic hyphenation has been the most prominent in Nigeria, particularly because city life has been mixed rather than territory specific. People from different ethnic groups meet regularly at work, in market places, and in educational institutions. They, therefore, develop a rapport that is capable of generating effective ties. In addition, they speak a lingua franca, which breaks down the initial and possibly the most important barriers to interethnic interaction. And since ethnic hyphenations are symptomatic of individual freedom from group constraints, the urban ethnics are more likely to have that freedom because they have the greatest occupational and physical mobility. However, it must be noted that they also stand the greatest risk of status anxiety, thus occasioning value shifts in order to secure their positions.

There are examples of urban-urban interethnic marriages in the military and the civil service, as well as in the non-Westernized business community, where facility in the local language is a prerequisite of business success. But the Nigerian civil war (1967–1970) sounded notes of caution, because some Ibo wives of Yoruba or Hausa men were picked up for "security" reasons. It would be interesting to know whether such marriages have declined since then.

While contact and language facility helped urban-urban ethnic hyphenation, urban-rural ethnic hyphenation is hindered by the same factors. Generally, urban dwellers regard themselves as superior to rural people. Also, there is more often than not a language barrier between them so that contact and communication are minimal. Thus at the individual as opposed to the systemic level there is a very low process of urban-rural assimilation. However, at the intraethnic level there is the paradox that Nigerian males in cities sometimes show preference for an "unsophisticated" lady from their ethnic countryside. In such cases there is an emphasis on rural virtue.

Interethnic marriages of the rural-rural ethnic type are not common occurrences in Nigeria. This is perhaps because rural ethnics are tied more to their land and have very little physical mobility. There are also more protective of their property and culture, more for the purposes of ethnic "purity" than for the hatred of the other ethnic groups. The process of ethnic interaction in the rural areas is, therefore, principally determined by the boundaries as created by the modern state apparatus.

## CONCLUSION

The Nigerian government has been very much concerned with the problems posed by ethnic conflicts that have resulted in political instability. The late premier of the northern region, Sir Ahmadu Bello, argued that ethnic conflicts in Nigeria could have been avoided if the British colonial system had not amalgamated the north and south of Nigeria. But this assumed that the ethnic conflict in Nigeria was simply a north-south affair. In fact the east-west conflict has been more important in setting the political ethnic agenda of the country.

Almost confirming Sir Ahmadu Bello, Elizabeth Colson argued:

> At least in Africa, tribes and triablism as we know them today are recent creations reflecting the influences of the colonial era when large-scale political and economic organization set the mobilization of ethnic groups based upon linguistic and cultural similarities which formerly have been irrelevant in effecting alliances.[37]

While it is true that there is a relationship between colonialism and ethnicity, it is not mono-causal. In precolonial times rural ethnicity caused interethnic wars, which in some cases even made it easy for the colonial enterprise to succeed. Such conflicts determined interethnic relations in the colonial period and even after. But it is true that the administrative overrule of the colonial state made ethnicity a focus of identity and later a basis of organization in the anticolonial period.[38] The various ethnic groups, however, reverted to their precolonial positions after independence was achieved.

The solutions proffered by Nigeria to the ethnic problems in the form of multiethnic national political parties, representative bureaucracy, and multiethnic schools have tended to inflame more ethnic tensions. Ethnicity has come to be used as the instrument for opposing status inconsistency, and it thus became, as Crawford Young had asserted, an important factor in attaining collective upward mobility.[39] Even the rural areas that could have remained relatively immune from this kind of competition have been gradually incorporated into the urban ethnic conflict processes. The urban-rural dichotomy is gradually receding, to be replaced by only one kind of ethnicity, whose characteristics are urban. Consequently, ethnicity has not declined. Rather it has been reproducing itself, particularly through the incorporation of the rural periphery. And it will continue to be alive as long as it remains a viable strategy for the maximization of individual professional interests.

## NOTES

1. A. H. M. Kirk-Greene, "Ethnic Engineering and the 'Federal Character' of Nigeria: A Boon of Contentment or Bone of Contention?" *Ethnic and Racial Studies* 6 (1985). Compare Ugbana Okpu, "Nigerian Political Parties and the Federal Character," *Journal of Ethnic Studies* 12 (1984); R. Ayo Dunmoye, "Ethnic Ideology, Bourgeois Democracy and Nigerian Politics," *Journal of Ethnic Studies* 12 (1984); and John A. A. Ayoade, "Ethnic Management in the 1979 Nigerian Constitution," *Publius, The Journal of Federalism* (forthcoming).

2. Paul J. Bohannan, "Our Two Story Culture," *Saturday Review* 55 (1972): 39–41.

3. Richard Sinnott and E. E. Davis, "Political Mobilization, Political Institutionalization and the Maintenance of Ethnic Conflict," *Ethnic and Racial Studies* 4 (1981): 400.

4. John L. P. Thompson, "The Plural Society Approach to Political Mobilization," *Ethnic and Racial Studies* 6 (1983): 87.

5. R. H. Jackson, "Political Stratification in Africa," *Canadian Journal of African Studies* 17 (1983): 201.

6. Ibid., p. 202.

7. Ibid.

8. Ibid., p. 203.

9. Henry Bienen, "State and Revolution: The Work of Amilcar Cabral," *Journal of Modern African Studies* 15 (1977): 564.

10. Ernest Gellner, "Nationalism," in *Thought and Change,* ed. Ernest Gellner (London: Weidenfeld and Nicolson, 1964), pp. 171–72.

11. Walker Connor, "Eco or Ethno-Nationalism," *Ethnic and Racial Studies* 7 (1984): 343.

12. Ibid., p. 344.

13. M. Hechter, *Internal Colonialism: The Celtic Fringe in British National Development, 1536–1966* (London: Routledge and Kegan Paul, 1975), p. 39.

14. A. H. M. Kirk-Greene, "*Dammosa Herdeitas:* Ethnic Ranking and the Martial Races Imperative in Africa," *Ethnic and Racial Studies* 3 (1980): 393.

15. Thompson, "The Plural Society," p. 141. Compare M. G. Smith, "Some Developments in the Analytic Framework of Pluralism," in *Pluralism in Africa,* ed. Leo Kuper and M. G. Smith (Berkeley: University of California Press, 1969), p. 430.

16. Pierre L. Van den Berghe, "Class, Race and Ethnicity in Africa," *Ethnic and Racial Studies* 6 (April 1983): 222.

17. Connor, "Eco- or Ethno-nationalism," p. 349.

18. T. Nairn, *The Breakup of Britain* (London: New Left Books, 1977), p. 347.

19. Ibid.

20. Max Gluckman, "The Analysis of a Social Situation in Modern Zululand," *Rhodes-Livingston Paper, No. 28* (Manchester, England: Manchester University Press, 1958), p. 26.

21. Ibid., p. 21.

22. Philip Gleason, "Identifying Identity: A Semantic History," *Journal of American History* 69 (1983): 901–31; and "Americans All: World War II and the Shaping of American Identity," *Review of Politics* 43 (1981): 483–518.

23. Arnold L. Epstein, *Ethos and Identity: Three Studies in Ethnicity* (London: Tavistock Publications, 1978), p. 26.

24. Jonathan Y. Okamura, "Situational Ethnicity," *Ethnic and Racial Studies* 4 (1981): 458.

25. John N. Paden, "Situational Ethnicity in Urgan Africa with Special Reference to the Uausa" (Paper presented at the African Studies Association Meeting, New York, 1967); and "Urban Pluralism, Integration and Adaptation of Communal Identity in Kano, Nigeria," in *From Tribe to Nation in Africa: Studies in Incorporation Process*, ed. K. Cohen and J. Middleton (Scranton, N. J.: Chandler Publishing, 1970), p. 268.

26. Van den Berghe, "Class, Race and Ethnicity," p. 230.

27. James McKay and Frank Lewins, "Ethnicity and the Ethnic Group: A Conceptual Analysis and a Reformulation," *Ethnic and Racial Studies* 1 (1978): 415.

28. Stephen Holphe, "The Significance of Barth and Geertz Model of Ethnicity in the Analysis of Nationalism in Liberia," *Canadian Journal of African Studies* 4 (1973): 243.

29. Judith A. Nagata, "What is a Malay? Situational Selection of Ethnic Identity in a Plural Society," *American Ethnologist* 1 (1974): 333.

30. Orlando Patterson, "Context and Choice in Ethnic Allegiance: A Theoretical Framework and Case Study," in *Ethnicity*, ed. M. Glazer and D. P. Moynihan (Cambridge: Harvard University Press, 1975), p. 305; and *Ethnic Chauvinism: The Reactionary Impulse* (New York: Stein and Day, 1977), pp. 43–44.

31. Van den Berghe, "Class, Race and Ethnicity," p. 229.

32. Cynthia Enloe, "Ethnicity, Bureaucracy and State Building in Africa and Latin America," *Ethnic and Racial Studies* 1 (1978): 340.

33. Thompson, "The Plural Society," p. 129.

34. Ibid., p. 131.

35. Enloe, "Ethnicity, Bureaucracy and State Building," p. 340.

36. Ibid., p. 343.

37. Elizabeth Colson, "Contemporary Tribes and the Development of Nationalism," in *Essays on the Problem of Tribe: Proceedings of the 1967 Annual Spring Meeting of the American Ethnological Society*, ed. June Helm (Seattle: University of Washington Press, 1968), pp. 201–02.

38. Jackson, "Political Stratification."

39. Crawford Young, *The Politics of Cultural Pluralism* (Madison, Wis.: University of Wisconsin Press, 1976), Chapter 4.

# 6 State Creation and Ethnicity in a Federal (Plural) System: Nigeria's Search for Parity

Omo Omoruyi

One of the recurring themes in Nigerian political development is the search for a stable government and representation of the polyglot society. Two facts seem to be well established about this search in the history of Nigeria.

One is that Nigeria started as a geographical entity that was brought together and held together by various colonial agents: traders, religious missions, and later official colonial agents. Whatever was put together before 1914 was grouped into different units—Lagos protectorate with headquarters in Lagos, the protectorate of Southern Nigeria with headquarters at Calabar, and the protectorate of Northern Nigeria with headquarters at various times at Lokoja, Jebba, and Zungeru. The Lagos and Southern protectorates were amalgamated to constitute the Southern protectorate with headquarters in Lagos in 1906. Between 1906 and 1914, there were two distinct units or parts of Nigeria—the North and South. By 1914 these two parts were formally brought together. Throughout these divisions and amalgamations, the inhabitants (i.e., the people constituting the areas) were never consulted about what later formed the entity called Nigeria. In this sense Nigeria was a colonial creation. The overriding importance in the minds of the colonial officials was to find the minimum administrative cost for running the occupied territory.[1]

The other development was the creation of provinces in both Northern and Southern Nigeria. The criteria for creating any number of provinces were subject to changes from one British administrator to another. Consequently these official actions formed the basis of future political agitation because neither the protectorates nor the provinces formed homogeneous ethnic entities. This fact was to form the basis of nationalist agitation after World War II. The nationalists opposed the artificial nature of the regions and the provinces and urged the dismantling of the regions and the creation of provinces based on ethnic communities. They believed that provinces should be created along ethnic lines. The two most outspoken of the nationalists, Dr. Nnamdi Azikiwe and Chief Obafemi Awolowo, advocated the right of ethnic communities to states or regions of their own as the only basis for a federal system of government in Nigeria.[2]

At the base of politics of state in Nigeria is the conflict between two notions of representation—ethnic groups or states. This conflict poses the problem for successive governments of how to balance *ethnicity* and *statism*. While ethnic units form the units of representation in a plural society, states are the units in a federation.[3] The number of ethnic groups in Nigeria was and still remains unknown. For the protagonists of states, the critical question is how to balance these two concepts of society—plural society and federation—and this question will continue to constitute a source of stress for the system. In the history of Nigeria since nationals became involved in its politics and government, advocates for more states have been involved in the search for parity among ethnic groups in the name of states.

## SEARCH FOR PARITY

One issue that dominated the political history of Nigeria up to 31 December 1983 was the creation of more states as a solution to the ethnic problem. Even at the terminal stage of military withdrawal from the political arena in 1978, it was erroneously felt then by some members of the Constituent Assembly[4] that the Constituent Assembly ought to and would be able to find a lasting solution to that problem. It failed and it couldn't. The issue of state creation broke and shattered a voting group (Ngwo group) in the Constituent Assembly; it put together a new voting group which successfully transformed itself into a political club (National Movement) and later into a political party, the National Party of Nigeria (NPN).[5] Yet the Constituent Assembly was able to wind up short of finding a solution. The controversy continued throughout the Second Republic until the military intervention put an end to it on the 31st of December 1983.

Historically there have been different arguments made for more states in the Federation of Nigeria, depending on who is making them. The linguistic argument is that those who speak the same language should be grouped together. There cannot be an end to linguistic states because Nigeria is reputed to have over 200 such groups. The linguistic argument seems to be uppermost in the minds of those who were agitating for Anioma state in Bendel state because of their separateness, being Ibos, from the other inhabitants of Bendel state. But the linguistic argument does not explain the position of those who want Oshun state in the present Oyo state, because the inhabitants of the present Oyo state are all Yoruba-speaking people; nor does it explain the agitation for Wawa or New Anambra or Abakaliki states out of the present Anambra state where they are all Ibos; nor does it explain the agitation for Kaduna or Katsina state in the present Kaduna state where the people of both Kaduna and Katsina are more or less of the Hausa—Fulani cultural—linguistic group. But language can partially explain some agitation in a somewhat negative fashion, just as the case for Port Harcourt state in Rivers state was based on the getting together of non-Ijaw-speaking elements on the mainland of the Rivers state to constitute a state. I will not be able to examine all the cases that dominated the newspapers after the Constituent Assembly, nor can I find explanation for the series of delegations to the National Assembly after the 1979 elections that lodged petitions before either the Senate President or the Speaker of the House or both.[6] What will be examined here is the issue of harmonization of certain parities, including parity between ethnic groups in the polyethnic federal political system.

Parity is not an argument for equality between entities or states. Neither is it an argument for a movement toward equality between existing entities. Parity in this context means the search for a maintenance of the precolonial or colonial equilibrium between groups or states. It is the argument of this study that primordial groups consciously seek some primordially defined status quo or parity. The introduction of political parties later tended to complicate the search for harmony and drive the primordial impulse underground.

I shall put forward six types of parities that existed in Nigeria's political history, and are still consciously being sought, for the purpose of bringing about some order as we study the polyethnic political system and agitation for states.

1. North-South Parity
2. East-West Parity
3. Yoruba-Ibo Parity
4. Hausa/Fulani-Yoruba-Ibo Parity
5. Majority-Minority Parity
6. Party-Party Parity

This search for parity did not occur in state creation alone in Nigeria's history. It has to do with anything that involves sharing, touching on power and power sharing, such as *census, elections, revenue allocation, appointments and other forms of representation.*

Nigeria's Northern and Southern protectorates were amalgamated in 1914. Beginning from that year, the parity between the two parts of Nigeria was guided by successive colonial rulers and in the various constitutional experiments. This applied to the distribution of seats on the basis of 50-50 to the two parts of Nigeria in the Central Legislature between 1951 and 1959. The wrong assumption then was that the two parts of Nigeria were soon to be split and built around two ethnic groups: the West (Yoruba) and the East (Ibo) respectively. This parity was not disturbed even with the allocation of equal numbers of ministers to three regions according to the 1951 Constitution, because the ministers were not actually endowed with power. It was not a big surprise that when General Yakubu Gowon, the head of state of Nigeria (1966–1975), created the 12 states in 1967, he had to allocate six states to the North and six states to the South. The states in the North were North East, North West, Kano, North Central, Benue/Plateau, and Kwara, and the states in the South were East Central, South East, Rivers, Western, Midwest, and Lagos. This was not an accident at all. This was in keeping with the principle of parity between the North and the South. (Figure 6.1 shows the states under General Yakubu Gowon.)

The 12-state system also enunciated two other principles of parity: the East-West Parity and the Yoruba-Ibo Parity.

Under the first principle, General Gowon created three states on each side of the Niger. The western side of the Niger had Lagos, Western, and Midwestern states and the eastern side had East Central, South Eastern, and Rivers states. The other principle was the Ibo-Yoruba parity which left the East Central state as the state of Ibos and the Western state as the Yoruba state. Lagos was not considered a Yoruba state for the purpose of balancing the Ibo-Yoruba parity.

The Murtala Muhammed/Olusegun Obasanjo regime (1975–1979) upset these three parities by creating 19 states (see Figure 6.2). First, by allowing 10 states in the original North and nine states in the original South, the Muhammed/Obasanjo regime, after over 60 years (1914–1975), distorted the North-South Parity which the colonial government initiated in 1914 and successive governments had maintained since then. Secondly, by allowing five states in the former Western region and four states in the former Eastern region, the East-West parity maintained by successive government for over 40 years (1914–1967) was destroyed. Thirdly, by creating three states out of the former Western state of Gowon (Ogun, Oyo, and Ondo) and two out of the East Central state of Gowon (Anambra and Imo), the Muhammed/ Obasanjo regime destroyed the Yoruba-Ibo parity. And if Lagos were to be added to the Yoruba states, the Yoruba-Ibo parity would have been further distorted. This was the beginning of the distortion. The reason for this distortion was that since the Ibos were not adequately represented in the Muhammed/Obasanjo military government, they could not expect justice from the hands of their historical adversaries, the Yorubas. The impact of the Ibos, an ethnic group, on the political process or decision-making process was very maximal during the ensuing years of Muhammed/Obasanjo. There was another implication. It was generally believed that General Murtala Muhammed (a Kano man) might have created 10 states in the North to give some advantage to the North to the disadvantage of the South. On the other hand, it was also believed that General Olusegun Obasanjo (an Ogun man) influenced a ratio of three or four to two in favor of the Yorubas in the South to the

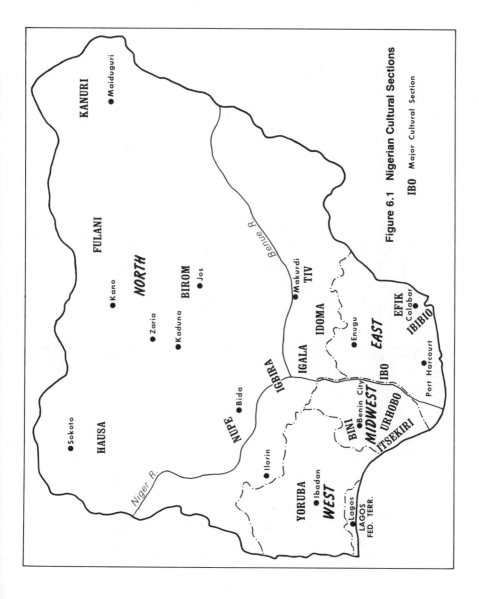

**Figure 6.1   Nigerian Cultural Sections**

IBO   Major Cultural Section

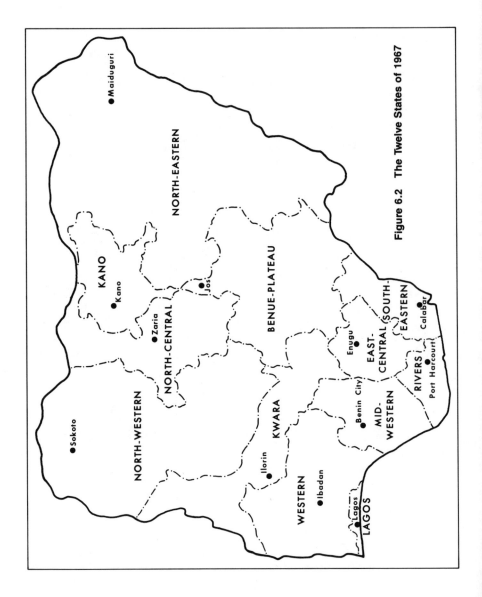

Figure 6.2   The Twelve States of 1967

disadvantage of the Ibos. The Muhammed/Obasanjo government did not realize how potentially destabilizing the whole exercise of state creation of 1976 was at the terminal stage of military disengagement.

By allowing 10 states in the old North, the country was faced with an octopus that then threatened the rest of the country and distorted meaningful discussion among entities in the country on the basis of equality of known entities for the purpose of forming political parties in 1978. The disparity between the North and the South led to a general belief that since the North was united and could operate from a position of a ten-state North, it was suicidal for the rest of Nigeria, the disunited nine states, to want to stay in opposition to that octopus. The south, thinking as nine separate states, developed the opposition mentality *ab initio,* even though the 1979 Constitution was supposed to kill the notion of government and opposition on the British model.

The same position was taken by some Southerners who argued against playing second fiddle to the party that originated in the North. On the basis of unfair geographical distribution of states in the federation, they too wanted to return to a status quo ante. It was the general feeling among politicians in the south that linkages should be initiated with the Northern political leaders because of the belief that the preexisting ten Northern states would be acting together as one in opposition to the disunited Southern states. The Southern political leaders took the Northern politicians as the ordained rulers, because their "headstart" in number of states and population made them most likely to provide the needed leadership in 1979. They did not see the rationale for organizing political parties that did not take this disparity for granted.

The 19-state system constituted the greatest threat to a meaningful dialogue among Nigerians on the basis of equality of states, where states were supposed to be taken as the units of representation. The erosion of states as units of representation in the federal system was the greatest problem that was ever posed to the Southern minorities of Bendel, Cross River, and Rivers state. The older political leaders of the First Republic in these three Southern states blackmailed the young ones who were then representing the area in the Constituent Assembly to the extent that they were sending emissaries to Northern members of the Constituent Assembly disassociating themselves from the position taken by the Southern members of the Constituent Assembly. This was the reason why many political leaders from the Southern minorities, and even the majorities, flocked to the North at the time the ban on partisan political activities was lifted to search for and cultivate the mythical ruler. After the two communal champions (Zik and Awo) had collected the votes of the Ibos and Yorubas respectively, the Southern minorities helped to enthrone the Northern candidate.

On the other hand, a 10-state North gave the leaders of the North a false sense of security and strength, a belief that they had been ordained by virtue of a "headstart" in number of states and population to provide the leadership for the country. They made it known to the Southern politicians that the claims of the Northern leaders were based on their ability to rally the ten Northern states into a millenium of *Arewa,* "one north." This was the reason that when two or three Hausa-Fulani leaders got together in the Constituent Assembly they then boasted that they spoke for 10 states, or for the North. The Southern minorities had serious difficulty in understanding that assertion in the face of the Northern minorities' (Benue, Plateau, Gongola, and Kaduna) determination to convince the rest of Nigeria that state creation had given them the needed autonomy, a home from which they could work with the rest of Nigeria.[7]

## PARITY AMONG MAJORITY ETHNIC GROUPS

Parities among ethnic groups were rarely openly used by protagonists of state creation as an argument for agitation for states. One has to read between the lines. Certainly the Ibo quest for justice in Nigeria's polyethnic society manifests itself in the agitation for an equal number of states for the Yorubas in the West of Nigeria and the Ibos in the East of Nigeria. The Ibos have always been critical of the continued dominance of the economy and the bureaucracy by the Yoruba and they want it changed; on the other hand the Yorubas and younger Southern minorities in the Constituent Assembly saw the continued dominance of the political system by the Hausa-Fulani, especially when the definition "federal character" in the 1979 Constitution takes states as the units of representation, as highly unacceptable. It was the Ibo-Yoruba disparity that the Ibo leaders wanted very badly to change. Dr. K. O. Mbadiwe and Dr. Chuba Okadigbo, aides of the former president, Alhaji Shehu Shagari (1979–1983), had been the greatest exponents of parity between the Ibos and the Yorubas. Dr. Nnamdi Azikiwe, the national leader of the banned Nigerian Peoples Party (NPP), later had to join those agitating for Ibo-Yoruba parity as a response to the Constituent demand. The Ibo leaders believed that to be the greatest factor making for a sound federal political system, as if the two ethnic groups together constitute the Nigerian federation.

The Ibo leaders ignored the disparity between the Hausa-Fulani and the Ibos. They would rather tag on to the Hausa-Fulani than to the Yorubas. While the Hausa-Fulani would want to control the political realm, they were not opposed to sharing power with others. The Ibos had this experience of sharing power with the Hausa-Fulani in the Northern Peoples Congress (NPC) and National Council of Nigerian Citizens (NCNC) coalition of government between 1959 and 1966 and would want a return to that period. For the Ibos, the use of the states as units of representation according to the notion of federal character was skewed in favor of the Yorubas and they wanted it changed.

The various sections of the 1979 Constitution put emphasis on states as units of representation, thus providing a definition of federal character in the appointment of ministers, ambassadors, and judges and in revenue allocation, etc. The Ibos saw the principle of states forming the units of representation as working against their interest. In the Constituent Assembly the two assembly "voting groups" (the Ngwo and Kaduna groups) came under severe stress and strain when the issue of recruitment into the armed forces and the system of election of the president came up for consideration.[8] Take the case of Section 166 of the draft constitution dealing with the composition of the armed forces.

The amendment to Section 166 of the draft constitution, which was spearheaded by the Ibo members of the Constituent Assembly in ominous cooperation with some Northern elements, took the Assembly by surprise. The amendment sought to add a new subsection (2) as follows:

> The composition of officers corps and other ranks shall reflect the Federal Character *based on population of each state.*[9] (Emphasis added.)

This amendment, which was proposed by Dr. Okadigbo, an Ibo from Anambra state, from the floor of the Constituent Assembly, found support among the Kaduna group to the utter embarrassment of the Ngwo group who saw this newfangled alliance as a prelude to the development of a new voting group involving the majority of the Ibos and the Kaduna group. This matter was not seriously tackled by the leaders of the Ngwo group. It did enter the minds of the Ibo theoreticians that that amendment might be a clue to finding a solution to their problem of powerlessness. They openly condemned General Obasanjo's government, which they believed consciously worked to reduce the Ibos to a position of a minority group in Nigeria. During the debate on this amendment in the Constituent Assembly the Ibos were disappointed to hear the Yoruba lawyers arguing that the amendment was not only unconstitutional but was also impracticable. The Ibos were very impressed by the Kaduna group who persisted in promoting the amendment, not that they believed that the amendment was practicable, either. It should be noted that throughout the Constituent Assembly, it was generally observed that the votes of Ibo members could not be relied upon by any clique or group as long as they perceived their environment as promoting injustice prompted by disparity in the number of states among ethnic groups.

The idea used in Dr. Okadigbo's amendment was not the notion of federal character found in the draft constitution. In the final version approved by the Constituent Assembly, it was stated as "the distinctive desire of the peoples of Nigeria to promote national unity, foster national loyalty and give every citizen of Nigeria a sense of belonging to the nation."[10] The amendment was, therefore, superfluous.

Adding a new subsection (2) to Section 166 in order to redefine federal character was meant to reflect the Ibo distaste of the predominant position of the Yoruba in the officer corps or in other ranks in the armed forces. It was also meant to protest their relative powerlessness in the armed forces and to call the nation's attention to the need for justice in a vital federal institution like the armed forces. This new development did not win the admiration of the "Fourth Dimension"[11] members from the Middle Belt who saw the new move by the Ibos as a direct indictment of the preponderant position occupied by the Middle Belt in the armed forces. The Hausa-Fulani joined the Ibos in the Constituent Assembly to get the provision to form part of Section 166, but the Supreme Military Council (SMC) removed it at last. Again the Ibos had to blame General Obasanjo, who was the head of the SMC, for removing that provision.

In the context of search for parity, the movers of the amendment were sure that any distribution of offices according to states would always have the Ibos worse off vis-à-vis the Yorubas, who were operating from four states (including Lagos). But if it were to be done on the basis of state population, the Ibos believed that the disparity would be bridged or narrowed considerably because of the near equality of the population of the majority ethnic groups.

This quest for parity also came up during the consideration of the procedure for electing a president in the Constituent Assembly. The minority caucus argued that a certain weight should be given to the states and the rest spread according to population. The Ibos and members of the Ngwo group in the Constituent Assembly voting group, which included the Yorubas, the Ibos, and the "Fourth Dimension," had to split on this issue. A lot of negotiating had to be done to bring some sanity to the issue. The Ibos were not interested in attaching too much weight to the states. Yet the notion of territorial spread was based on certain minimum support (25 percent) in at least two-thirds of the states of the federation. It should be noted that this was an article of faith which the minority caucus believed in and around which they cohered from the beginning of the discussion of the 1979 Constitution.

## PARITY BETWEEN MAJORITY AND MINORITY ETHNIC GROUPS

In all the discussion about state creation and the agitation for the redrawing of boundaries, there was a complete absence of discussion of the question of parity between the majority and the minority groups in this country. The majority ethnic groups took it as a way of redrawing the power game among them. In the new politics, which gave rise to the notion of the "Fourth Dimension" in the wake of the new dispensation leading to the 1979 Constitution, the minority ethnic groups in the North and South started to see their future as linked. In keeping with the kernel of faith of the "Fourth Dimension," members of the "Fourth Dimension" were poised to fight against the disequilibrium in the relationship between the majority and minority ethnic groups in the country. Therefore, to the "Fourth Dimension" theoretician any agitation for more states that does not recognize the need for parity between the majority and minority groups will run into difficulties with the "Fourth Dimension" states, because no state can be created without the participation of other preexisting states according to the 1979 Constitution. The critical question here is whether this new parity could or should be superimposed on preexisting parities or on newfangled parities. This matter was to be explored by theoreticians in all the parties and groups.

In the present 19-state system (Figure 6.3), the minority ethnic groups claim the states of Bendel, Cross River, and Rivers (in the South), and Benue, Plateau, Gongola, and Borno (in the North). The largely Hausa-Fulani states are Kano, Kaduna, Sokoto, Niger, and Bauchi. The Ibo states are Anambra and Imo, and the Yoruba states are Oyo, Ondo, Ogun, and Lagos.

In the agitation for states the theoreticians of the "Fourth Dimension" believed that it would gain a lot from the splitting of some of the minority states. It therefore supported (1) the splitting of Cross River into two states: Mainland and Qua Iboe states; (2) the splitting of Rivers state into two states: Port Harcourt and Ijaw or Delta, encompassing part of Bendel state; (3) the splitting of Gongola state into two states; and (4) the splitting of Bendel state into three states: Anioma, Delta, and Edo states. The minority caucus spearheaded the agitation for these states throughout the country as a way of enhancing the power of the "Fourth Dimension" in the polyethnic society.

The relative advantage that would likely accrue to one group or the other governed the intensity with which one issue or the other was pursued. The minority caucus believed throughout this period that since the majority groups were already powerful under the existing 19-state system, to give them more states would be endowing the majority groups with more power to the disadvantage of the minorities in the country.

## PARTY-PARTY PARITY

Political parties are geared to calculate their gains in the general overall calculation of party-party parity. This is an aspect of the agitation for states that is not highlighted by analysis.

Certainly the support that the National Council of Nigerian Citizens (NCNC) gave to the agitation for the Midwest state in the 1950s to early 1960s and the campaign that leaders of the Action Group (AG) led against the Midwest state during the same period had to do with the relative advantage that the NCNC was likely to gain by the creation of the Midwest state and the relative disadvantage that the AG would be getting by the creation of the Midwest state. The NCNC wanted to increase its advantage while the AG wanted to cut its losses. The support that the Northern Peoples Congress (NPC) gave to the NCNC in this regard was meant to weaken the AG, a party

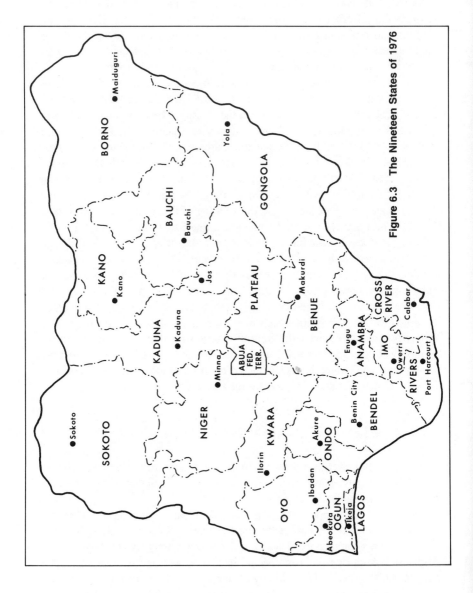

Figure 6.3   The Nineteen States of 1976

that was already splitting into two factions.[12]

The backing that the AG gave to the Calabar-Ogoja-River (COR) states in the East and the Middle Belt in the North arose from the need for the AG to reap the electoral advantage (votes) by supporting their creation. It did get these votes in the 1959 and 1964 federal elections.[13] This was the reason why the All-Party Conference which President Shagari summoned in February 1982 would not have been able to find any lasting solution to the issue of state creation. Parties would not have been able to solve their problems that way. As the Committee report shows, all the parties tended to support all the cases that had been presented to the National Assembly.[14] The relative advantage that a party was likely to gain may not be easily communicated to another. Unless we are operating on the basis that one political party would facilitate the goal attainment of another party we are likely to find that it would be a fruitless exercise for political parties to converge around a table presided over by the president, a leader of a political party, to haggle on state creation. Those who attended the first meeting confirmed that it was an exercise in futility.

It is now an open secret that the lack of congruence between party demands and ethnic demands became evident at the All-Party Conference. The National Party of Nigeria (NPN) was reported to have read a prepared statement of policy on states and indicated that the NPN as a party would support the creation of three states: Oshun state, New Cross River state and Katsina state. Of course when the Ibo elements in that party raised question about the projected Anambra state or Abia state, they were not recognized, since the Conference had to do with parties and was not a collection of ethnic leaders. Chief A. M. A. Akinloye represented the NPN and spoke for the NPN. He was facilitating his interest in Yorubaland by advocating the Oshun state.

## PROBLEM WITH COMMISSION OF INQUIRY

The setting up of the Irikefe Panel was the first time a specific question about state creation was assigned to a panel of inquiry, but the panel unwittingly did not address itself to the complex parity argument. Instead, it focused on criteria for state creation as if there could be criteria that could be said to be sancrosant for all times. There could be none.[15]

The population argument may be worthwhile for consideration as a reason for state creation, but there is no optimum population for a state in a federation. Some analysts talk of a certain desirable number of states as if there is an optimum number of states in a federation that could be related to a certain population. Table 6.1 shows the fallacy of these two points. In my view the parity argument will dominate the quest for states in the future, unless the military decrees a certain number from time to time. Creation of states through the political process would, for the reason of parity, elude

**Table 6.1    Statistics on Federal States**

|  | Nigeria (1963) | U.S.A. (1976) | India (1961) | Switzer-land | Canada (1961) |
|---|---|---|---|---|---|
| Total Area (Sq. Km) | 915,064 | 9,363,166 | 2,919,812 | 41,258 | 9,976,146 |
| Total Population (000) | 56,000 | 218,184 | 482,480 | 5,429 | 18,238 |
| No. of States | 19 | 50 | 15 | 22 | 10 |
| Average size of states (Sq. Km) | 43,056 | 183,591 | 1,875 | 1,875 | 831,340 |
| Average Population of states (000) | 2,926 | 4,278 | 20,611 | 247 | 1,615 |
| Maximum Population of states (000) | 5,800 (Kano) | 15,717 | 73,752 | 952 | 15,409 |
| Minimum Population of states (000) | 1,200 (Niger) | 226 | 11,831* | 32* | 15* |
| Minimum size of states (Sq. km) | 3,345 | - | 38,857* | 238* | 5,656* |
| Maximum Area of states (Sq. km) | 16,400 (Borno) | 1,513,770 (Alaska) | 443,432 | 17,198 | 6,236 |
| Federal District | 1 | 1 | - | - | - |

protagonists. Unless the various parities are understood and consensus is built around one or the other, there may never be additional states in the Federation.

We should understand parity as the ingredient that makes for a balanced federation. A balanced federation is one in which the different parities outlined above are harmonized. The committee set up in both Houses of the National Assembly of the defunct civilian government (1979–1983) ought to have had this at the back of their mind when they were moving from one part of the country to another examining cases. They did not. This ought to be realized before the invocation of relevant sections of the 1979 Constitution. More importantly, the moment the creation of states was moved to the political platform the various political parties had to assume advocacy of one position or the other.

The condition for creation of states is very well entrenched in the suspended 1979 Constitution. From my experience with the Technical Committee on Revenue Allocation in 1977, then a military function, I believed that the 19-state system would be a permanent feature. Even when the issue of amending or modifying the condition for creation of states arose in the Constituent Assembly, the debate cut across known partisan tendencies in the

Assembly, and in the end the condition was made stiffer than the military would have thought of. Like the issue of local government and revenue allocation, state creation will be an issue that the country's leaders must continue to debate whenever the desire to resolve outstanding issues arises in the country.

## CONCLUSION

There are certain lessons that we can learn from the creation of states, starting with the creation of the Midwest (now Bendel) state in 1963 and continuing with the 12-state system (1967) and the 19-state system (1976).

First, the creation of the Midwest state in 1963 was meant to balance ethnic forces in the old Western region, which was then perceived by the minority groups—Edos, Urhobo, and Ibo—as belonging to the majority ethnic group, the Yoruba. These minority groups together believed that a new state would be a panacea for the perceived discriminatory practices of the government of the Western region dominated by the Yoruba ethnic group. Intraregional ethnic balance or conflict are also linked with outside political parties, who engaged in the balance of political power game. The Nigerian political parties generally acted as political entrepreneurs.[16] For instance the NCNC/NPC alliance did not favor state creation in the North and in the East of Nigeria which they controlled respectively. But they would support the creation of the Midwest state in the West of Nigeria because of the perceived damage the act would do to the AG, a Yoruba-dominated political party, regionally and nationally.[17]

Second, the perceived rigidity in the Constitution may become flexible once the political climate is ripe and favorable to the creation of states.[18] The Midwest case showed that. After all, the three regions participated in the creation of that state and the rigidity of the 1979 Constitution, which the protagonists of states today fear, may become flexible and surmountable once the political climate is ripe for it. A favorable political climate could mean the kind of political climate that occurred in the country in 1962 under a military government where decrees can be used to create states as in 1967 or in 1976. Political process cannot create more states.

Third, the objective factors like viability (economic, manpower, or administrative efficiency), size, and population were never applied to the states that were created in 1963, 1967, and 1976 for obvious reasons. The Willink Commission of 1957 was to take objective factors into account should it consider the creation of states as the last resort to alleviate the grievances of the minorities.[19] This was a colonial trick meant to turn down the wishes of the minorities. After all the creation and running of the 12 or 19 states in 1967 and 1976 respectively showed that the issue of viability could no longer be a problem because of the integrated financial or economic structure of the federation. This means that as long as the federation was viable, the parts, states, *ipso facto* will just have to be viable.

Fourth, the question of optimality is theoretical from the available statistics in federal political systems. There is no optimum number of states for a federation; there is no optimum population for a state in a federation, and there is no optimum size for a state in a federation. In Table 6.1, the statistics on five federal political systems (Nigeria, U. S. A., India, Switzerland, and Canada) illustrate the fact that states in federation arise from different circumstances, and Nigeria could not be an exception.

Fifth, the number of criteria enumerated in 1967 and 1976 would never be examined in future state creation exercises because they were tied to the various conceptions of optimality. For example, in 1967 in General Yakubu Gowon's speech announcing the creation of 12 states the following criteria were enumerated as the reasons for the creation of the 12 states:

1. No one state should be in a position to dominate or control the central government.
2. Each state should form one compact geographical area.
3. Administrative convenience, the facts of history, and the wishes of the people concerned must be taken into account.
4. Each state should be in a position to discharge effectively the functions allocated to regional government.
5. It is also essential that the new states should be created simultaneously.

Criteria 1 to 3 are veiled ethnic criteria, while 4 and 5 were meant to accord the ethnic group equality of treatment.

The Federal Military Government did not arrive at the foregoing criteria empirically, but if we relate them to the states that grew out of the criteria we would find that the exercise succeeded in giving locus of power to some groups. It also succeeded in whetting the appetite of others. It turned out that no exercise would ever completely satisfy state agitators. Whereas for some, especially the Ibos, the exercise was seen as punitive because it excised the minorities (Cross River and Rivers) from them. These minorities had to contribute to the federal effort in fighting the war of succession (1967-1970). The never-ending agitation was reopened after the civil war. The military successor to Gowon in 1975 had to include the issue of state creation on its political program. The Murtala Muhammed regime that replaced Gowon's government in 1975 had to set up a Panel on State Creation. This act showed that the criteria and method used in the 1967 exercise were not satisfactory. In addition to the criteria used in 1967, the Irikefe Panel on State Creation used the following criteria:

1. The need to bring the government nearer to the people.
2. Even development.
3. The need to preserve our federal structure of government.

4. The need to maintain peace and harmony within the federation.

5. The need to minimize minority problems in Nigeria.[20]

Again they are veiled ethnic criteria.

In the final analysis state creation will continue to be a political decision and the criteria will be at best *ex post facto,* as in the 1967 exercise, or suggestive of the kind of rationalization that can be put forward for one kind of state or the other. After all, the 1976 exercise deviated in many respects from the Irikefe recommendation. Yet the criteria of Irikefe served as the rationalization for the 1976 exercise. The parity question is, and will continue to be, at the base of the five criteria that the Irikefe Panel added to the 1967 criteria.

## NOTES

1. For the history of Nigeria see the Ibadan History series published by Longman.

2. Dr. Nnamdi Azikiwe and Chief Obafemi Awolowo were the foremost nationalist leaders in the mid-1950s and their concept of a federal system was one superimposed on ethnic units. See Nnamdi Azikiwe, *Zik, A Selection from the Speeches of Nnamdi Azikiwe* (Cambridge: Cambridge University Press, 1961), and Obafemi Awolowo, *Path to Nigerian Freedom* (London: Faber, 1947).

3. I highlighted this problem in 1976. See Omo Omoruyi, "Representation in Federal (Plural) Systems: A Comparative View," in A. B. Akinyemi et al., *Studies in Federalism* (Lagos, Nigeria, 1979).

4. The Constituent Assembly which was composed partly of elected and partly of nominated members debated a draft constitution (1977/78) prepared by the Constitution Drafting Committee (1975/76) set up by the Military Government in 1975.

5. For the development of political groups, cliques, and alliances in the Constituent Assembly see my work, *Constituent Assembly and the Origin of the Nigerian Peoples Party* (forthcoming), especially chapter 2.

6. The number of new states supported by the political parties ranged from 21 to 27 as of 31 December 1983.

7. The Northern minorities in Benue, Plateau, Gongola, and part of Kaduna and Bauchi constituted themselves into a solidarity group called Council for Unity and Solidarity (CUS), whose purpose was to convince the Southern minority of Bendel, Rivers, and Cross River that they should team up in the Constituent Assembly and seek friends together. This was the origin of Club 19. See Omo Omoruyi, *Constituent Assembly and the Origin.*

8. Ibid., chapter 2, for the origin of these two main voting groups in the Constituent Assembly.

9. Draft Constitution, Section 166(2). The Supreme Military Council removed this amendment later.

10. 1979 Constitution of the Federal Republic of Nigeria, Section 14(3).

11. "Fourth Dimension" was a term coined by the minority caucus in the constituent Assembly as distinct from the three majority ethnic groups—Hausa, Ibo, and

Yoruba—termed First, Second, and Third Dimensions.

12. See Omo Omoruyi, "The Criteria for the Creation of the Midwest Region in 1963," in Omolade Adejuyigbe et al., *Creation of States in Nigeria* (Lagos, Nigeria, 1982), pp. 34–37.

13. See K. W. J. Post and Michael Vickers, *Structure and Conflict in Nigeria, 1960–1965* (London: Heineman, 1973).

14. "The Report of the 17-Man-Committee," in K. O. Mbadiwe, *Marching Towards National Integration* (Eagle Press Publication, 1982), pp. 35–40.

15. Mr. Justice Ayo Irikefe of the Supreme Court presided over a panel for the examination of cases for more states in 1975. See *Report of the Panel on the Creation of More States* (December 1975).

16. For the concept of political entrepreneur, see Richard E. Wagner, "Pressure Groups and Political Entrepreneur," in *Papers in Non-Market Decision-Making,* ed. Gordon Tullock (Charlottesville, Va.: Thomas Jefferson Center for Political Economy, 1966); and Alvin Rabushka and Kenneth A. Shepale, "Political Entrepreneurship and Patterns of Democratic Instability in Plural Societies," *Race* 12 (April 1971).

17. Omo Omoruyi, "The Criteria for the Creation."

18. Ibid., pp. 161–68.

19. See *Report of the Commission Appointed to Inquire into the Fears of Minorities and the Means of Allaying Them* (London: Her Majesty's Stationary Office, 1958).

20. Justice Irikefe, *Report of the Panel,* pp. 39–46.

# 7 Ethnicity in Economic Crisis: Development Strategies and Patterns of Ethnicity in Africa

## Naomi Chazan

The relationship between ethnicity, economic resources, and the state is fundamental to most analyses of political trends in the contemporary world. A variety of approaches to their interconnection, based on widely differing assumptions and leading to significantly divergent conclusions, have emerged over the years.[1] Initially ethnicity was viewed as a residual object which, since it was antithetical to state-building and national integration, should be eliminated by the careful deployment of resources and the nurturing of economic growth. As ethnic manifestations persisted even during periods of rapid economic expansion, ethnicity came to be viewed as a by-product of development and political consolidation. "Ethnic groups persist largely because of their capacity to extract goods and services from the modern sector and thereby satisfy the demands of their members."[2] In this connection, some observers have insisted that ethnic salience is a result of natural competition, whereas others uphold an epiphenomenal outlook which maintains that ethnicity has been manipulated by elites in order to amass resources for their own use. In both instances, ethnicity is nevertheless seen as a viable means of obtaining highly valued goods.

Instrumental notions of ethnicity have not been discarded as economic scarcity has defied visions of progress and as the realities of the soft state have replaced concepts of the overdeveloped one. "The effect of the soft state, with its relatively weak institutions and fiscal capacity, is certainly to produce a situation in which ethnoregional leaders may seize the initiative and issue unreasonable demands which cannot be absorbed by the state."[3] In these circumstances ethnic groups may unite not only to avert neglect but also—wary of the predatory designs of their highly centralized and weak state

137

networks—perhaps to protect themselves against unwarranted state incursions.[4]

Common to all these (frequently contradictory) interpretations of the political economy of ethnicity is the affirmation of the centrality of the state. The iron grid of the state purportedly informs social encounters and serves as the foremost arena for conflict over resources.[5] This state-centric viewpoint stems from two core assumptions: that the state has something to offer and that people therefore want to participate in its activities. Neither of these proportions can be taken for granted in today's Africa.

Most African countries are in the midst of a monumental and seemingly relentless economic crisis. As the population has expanded, food production has dropped by over 11 percent in the past decade alone. Agriculture has been neglected and transportation is virtually at a standstill. Foreign debts continue to rise at an unprecedented pace while most citizens scurry to cope with hyperinflation. Fully half of the continent has been declared a disaster area by the Food and Agriculture Organization. These twenty-four countries are incapable of meeting the most basic of needs. Too many of their citizens are on the brink of outright starvation. It is not at all clear that African states have anything to distribute or that people think that association with their state is worthwhile.

The purpose of this study is to explore what happens to ethnicity when the economy is at a standstill and when the centrality of the state is no longer a given. Specifically, it first examines in detail patterns of ethnicity at different phases of economic deterioration; it then isolates some of the reasons for these particular expressions of ethnicity and their relationship to development strategies; and finally, it outlines some implications for analysis and practice.

If ethnicity is, indeed, both intermittent and fluid, then the study of its variations can go a long way towards uncovering the meaning behind major socioeconomic and political processes.[6] This study attempts to show that in situations of drastic economic fluctuation, the forms of ethnicity multiply and the social distance between them increases. As ethnicity ceases to be an effective tool for economic interaction within the state framework, the ethnic community, variously defined, becomes a substitute for the state and assumes many of its characteristics. At this juncture ethnicity no longer serves an integrating function and new categories of power relations, solidarity, and binding values are established.[7] The type and direction of ethnic adjustments is determined, to no mean degree, not only by the content of development policies but also by the manner of their implementation.

Since ethnicity changes in relationship to economic and political trends, marked vacillations in ethnic presentations are an indication of flux elsewhere. The relativity of ethnic politics takes on different meanings as social fluidity becomes more apparent. The tracing of these dynamic shifts therefore has a crucial bearing on the understanding of the boundaries of state coherence and on the ramifications of state decomposition for human well-being.[8] These issues can no longer safely be ignored in a continent where the formal state system frequently lacks relevance and misery abounds.

## ECONOMIC CRISES AND PATTERNS OF ETHNICITY

African states have experienced three different kinds of economic crises in recent years: of dwindling resources, of maldistribution, and of poverty verging on economic collapse. Each of these forms of economic deterioration derives from different sources, affects specific groups in a variety of ways, evokes its own set of coping mechanisms, and precipitates certain unique patterns of ethnicity.

### Crises of Dwindling Resources

Virtually every state in Africa has experienced a reduction in the resources at its disposal since independence. If twenty years ago credit was easy, imports flowed, and new tastes for expensive consumer products were developed, today the quantity of goods has decreased and the cost of those available has risen. Most African leaders have watched as state coffers have been depleted, production has slowed down, foreign indebtedness has grown, and external dependency has increased.

The problem of dwindling resources may be attributed, to a large extent, to a consistent pattern of policy mismanagement. Most African states encouraged cash-cropping for export to augment government revenue and to satisfy urban demands for Western goods. Consumption patterns, facilitated by the active intervention of multinational firms, were altered in many African urban areas. But as the price of imports leaped and export revenues dropped in the aftermath of the oil crises, many governments persisted in subsidizing expensive imports.[9] Inflation has set in, many items are priced beyond the reach of the average citizen, and the lack of essential commodities is everywhere apparent.

Those most directly affected by these scarcities are urban dwellers. Unskilled labor has been unable to keep up with rising costs. Consequently, urban poverty has proliferated. Skilled workers, salaried employees, and even the professional middle classes have been hurt by the rapid expansion of the inflationary spiral. To be sure, rural residents have cut production as high prices for imports have reduced export incentives. But those most seriously caught in the crisis of dwindling resources have been those directly dependent on the state and hence closely bound to its reservoirs.

Adjustments to this manifestation of economic crisis have involved various mechanisms of managing and suffering.[10] People, however reluctantly, have become accustomed to the periodic absences of electricity and water, of medical supplies and soap, of petrol and batteries. They have altered their diets and adjusted their consumption habits to accord with existing supplies. This perforce has also led to changes in the use of time. Many hours have been devoted to the search for basic commodities, following tips received from friends. Worker output has diminished and absenteeism has increased, putting an even greater strain on the already precarious economies of these countries. At the same time, however, many urban dwellers have begun to cultivate vegetable gardens for home consumption. Housewives and children, formerly outside the labor circle, have found some ways to make money to contribute to family income. Home crafts have been converted into cottage industries. And moonlighting, always a prevalent phenomenon, has increased considerably. Barter techniques and the communal use of vital goods such as water and candles have been refined. More people are suffering in the large cities and fewer are managing than in the past.[11]

The social consequences of these reactions have been manifold. Cynicism and alienation have become widespread. But disaffection has been demonstrated in a variety of ways. In some instances, fatalism has set in. Urban residents have closed up, narrowed the circle of their social interaction, and come to rely more heavily on kin and close friends.[12] In other cases social tensions have risen palpably. Some of these social tensions do retain ethnic features, especially where patronage networks are still effective. But increasingly, dissatisfaction with resource supplies has led to the exacerbation of class tensions, which have taken on both populist and radical forms. A rash of strikes and demonstrations, now commonly called "IMF riots," has spread throughout the continent.[13] These activities have provided a funnel for the venting of popular frustrations and a significant outlet for the cry for reform. Despite the salience of such outbursts, however, they have been confined to major cities and have been directed specifically at policymakers.

The suffer-manage syndrome reflects the reaction of those who are unable to extricate themselves from the malfunctioning state arena. It has therefore been accompanied by social strife and at times even bifurcation. New forms of interaction, resting periodically on communal considerations but mostly organized in a class rubric, have emerged. Class and ethnicity not only coexist but, increasingly, intersect in this setting.[14]

Social responses to the problem of diminishing resources have charged the atmosphere in many African states, making the exercise of state authority all the more difficult and the proliferation of disorder, if possible, more salient. But even when conflict has taken on rejectionist overtones, solidarity with the state has scarcely been affected. Foci of identification and association have been retained at the same time as the instrumental benefits to be derived from continued reliance on state dispensations have been severely reduced. The loss of resources depletes state power, but it does not necessarily reduce the significance of ethnic (and class) competition.

## Crises of Maldistribution

Many economic problems in Africa today relate less to scarcities than to issues of availability. Basic necessities are visible both in the town and the countryside, but they are not accessible to large portions of the population. The monopolization of productive assets by the powerful few renders many constantly needy.[15] The vision of ample bread in some neighborhoods and no bread at all in others is a familiar sight in many African towns. Flour and sugar, eggs and yams may not be available in the marketplace, but they do appear at the dinner tables of government officials. Some people walk miles to work because spare parts cannot be purchased at any price, while new Mercedes whisk by at high speeds. Virtually every flight out of African capitals is booked to capacity, but budgets for feeder roads have been frozen. Glaring inequalities in accumulation and distribution networks make the issue of access to resources sometimes more prominent than that of actual supplies.

Lopsided distribution patterns date back to dualistic colonial economic policies. The uneven development of the countryside, propelled by a penchant for production for export at the expense of food cropping, was supported not only by land tenure policies that bolstered relatively large independent producers, but also by the development of transportation and marketing networks with a heavy urban and coastal bias. After independence, the propensity to manage access to food on the basis of criteria of power rather than economic rationality or need continued apace. The inherited structure of most economies was not altered by successor elites, who often improved upon the inequities initiated by their predecessors. Western temptation created an environment that sanctioned official accumulation through malfeasance to the detriment of the creation of suitable domestic supply routes. Agriculture in general and food production in particular was neglected.[16]

The structural roots of economic management were not always apparent when basic commodities were abundant. But as scarcities began to surface, access to supplies became noticeably circumscribed. Tendencies towards centralization were accentuated as governments tried to control the movement of goods, to increase their monopoly over essential commodities, and to oversee all distribution. In short, economic inequities have their roots in biased power structures and consequently evoke power concerns.

Economic maldistribution especially affects those most removed from the centers of political life. In the urban areas, it is the workers and lower echelons of salaried employees. In the countryside, peasant producers and seasonal laborers are less likely to have access than are independent farmers engaged in market production. Everywhere, women and children are relatively dependent and disadvantaged.

Responses to ineffective or discriminatory distribution practices have focused on the expansion of the parallel economy. The growth of the informal sector is a result of the increased domestic demand for final and intermediate goods.[17] Those who have few means of gaining access to supplies have attempted to maximize their options by devising their own economic, social, and institutional linkage networks. In every African country where the parallel economy is on the ascendance, the initiative may be traced back to those engaged in trade rather than production. These individuals and groups are positioned at the conjuncture of both domestic and international production and exchange, and are therefore in an enviable position to manipulate the market to their own ends.

This group has spearheaded a series of activities aimed at reorienting accumulation and distribution patterns. The first of these is smuggling. Although a familiar pursuit since independence, smuggling has become rampant in recent years. It is particularly apparent in countries like Ghana, Zaire, Uganda, Tanzania, and Guinea, where commercial restrictions and scarcities in most essential commodities have given farmers and traders very powerful incentives to sell their products in neighboring countries in which consumer goods and desirable currencies can be obtained.[18]

Closely linked to smuggling is hoarding and black marketeering. The former occurs when it is unprofitable to market goods because of stringent price controls. The latter flourishes when diminishing supplies of hoarded goods enable their sales at prices much higher than the ones set by the state. The regulation of supplies to the parallel market is facilitated by the creation of unofficial transport monopolies.

The parallel system cannot be sustained without a heavy dose of official collusion. Government personnel repeatedly capitalize on their positions in order to funnel state resources to meet personal needs. Corruption, fraud, and embezzlement are fast becoming the salaried technocrat's response to inadequate food supplies. By diverting official aid resources and operating budgets to the parallel system, bureaucrats have been able to augment their own incomes and meet the needs of their families and dependents. Many of those responsible for the skewed lines of food supply are reacting to the situation by further intensifying the problem.[19]

Impoverished urban inhabitants have not, however, been able to utilize these channels effectively. They have either returned to the rural areas, remained in the cities to be subjected to growing poverty, or resorted to theft to avert starvation. The rising crime rate is but a meager indication of the desperation attendant upon the inequality of economic mechanisms in many African states.

The diverse responses to the challenges of maldistribution have become an acceptable way of life in contemporary Africa. In some countries full-fledged parallel distribution systems—*magendo* in Uganda or *kalabule* in Ghana—have emerged.[20] The cumulative effect of these methods of beating the system has been an overriding cynicism towards official channels and generalized noncompliance with the law. These popular strategies are anti-government in orientation and substance.

Patterns of ethnicity which emerge in these economic conditions differ qualitatively from those apparent in crises of dwindling resources. Engagement in the parallel system promotes loyalty to the individual and the specific group above support for the system as such. The pattern of social conflict in these circumstances is distinctly communal. Social cleavages are highlighted and the structural inequality between city and countryside is accentuated.

In this context, social groups tend to cohere around ethnic collectivities and regional agglomerations. Ethnic ascription and ethnicity become indispensable avenues to the attainment of vital goods. Just as in the past ethnicity served as a means of benefiting from what the state had to offer (education, employment, development funds), so in conditions of unequal distribution ethnicity serves as a protective device which either guards past gains and/or offers a tool for divesting the system of its resources.[21] Ethnic diversity grows, therefore, and ethnic divisions become firmer.[22] So, too, do regional links. Differential demands of geographic entities are intensified. Richer regions, those that suffer most when austerity sets in, tend to increasé their demands on the state and simultaneously seek alternative routes to their satisfaction. Poorer regions attenuate their pressures, content to make do with the handouts they might receive from the central government.[23] In this process the differences between various sections of the country are highlighted: the divergence between north and south in West Africa and the Sudan and between core areas and peripheries in East and Central Africa have become more pronounced.

These manifestations of ethnicity do not, however, occur in a vacuum. They are closely linked to class politics emanating from the state core and the patronage web that these formations generate. As patron-client relations of a fluid sort have been replaced by more structured mechanisms of political control, in many cases ethnic consciousness is being employed to further the narrow class interests of ruling elites.[24] This pattern of unequal ethnic manipulation has been demonstrated repeatedly in Ghana and in Kenya, in Zaire and in Nigeria, in Guinea and in Uganda.[25] Thus, the consolidation of different forms of ethnicity ". . . is played out within the boundaries of a class system shaped and dominated by the state through its various distributive and redistributive policies."[26]

Patronage itself, however, may now be undergoing change. Unsuccessful ethnic patrons are being displaced. Local and regional figures have emerged in various places. Since they link producers and distributors in innovative networks beyond the reach of the official apparatus, new forms of patronage and clientage may eventually emerge.[27]

The social outcomes of economic inequality rotate around power and power concerns. Growing political awareness, suspicion of government and the establishment, and a general wariness are evident in the growth of lawlessness and the precipitous drop in participation rates.[28] These sentiments have erupted into strikes and demonstrations aimed directly at altering the composition of state officeholders. And as the parallel economy expands, coup attempts and military takeovers recur.

The struggle for access to power and its concomitant control of allocations has accentuated the differential interests of various social agglomerations. Previously fluid patterns of association and identification have ossified under the growing pressure of instrumental concerns. Specific groups—be they ethnic, regional, occupational, or personal—have undergone a process of politicization that has enhanced their salience and increased their cohesion.

The social outcomes of economic maldistribution have serious consequences for governmental viability. The symbolic significance of the state crumbles as occupants of official positions misuse their trust and themselves become the object of distaste and suspicion. Disorder thus provides a framework within which new patterns of interaction take shape. Solidarity with the state is provisional. To be sure, some well-organized groups may wish to supplant existing coalitions in order to use the fruits of office for their own purposes. In a growing number of cases, entire communities continue to operate within the state framework but distance themselves from overexposure to governmental vagaries. If formal resources and institutions still exist, their original purposes are often distorted. The intrusive nature of state activities cannot be overlooked, but contact becomes both intermittent and highly conditional. The maldistribution of economic goods therefore undermines the structure of state power. Differential ethnicity becomes a tool that substitutes for state inadequacies without replacing the state framework. Beneath the surface other contiguous, interweaving, and frequently overlapping communally defined networks flourish.

## Crises of Poverty

In some African states, problems of resource utilization and distribution have given way to an all-encompassing crisis of poverty. Absolute shortages exist in many portions of the continent. Scarcities proliferate. In most areas supplies simply cannot meet existing needs. In places where agricultural output has dropped, there is not enough to feed those who in the past could eke a living out of the land. Undernourishment, malnutrition, rural impoverishment and starvation are spreading throughout the continent.[29] Human energy is drained, motivation is reduced, and prospects for amelioration are dimming. The margins of the fragile economies of many African states are subsuming their cores in a debilitating cycle of passivity and helplessness. The absolute lack of food lies at the source of underdevelopment and constitutes its most debilitating outcome.[30]

Scarcity and poverty are the final stages in the dreary process of policy misdirection and resource misuse. All the factors contributing to the diminution of resources and their skewed distribution converge to yield monumental problems of production. These difficulties have been compounded by demographic increases, misplaced development priorities, ignorance, the inability to make use of technological advance, and poor training and extension services. When accompanied by natural disasters, civil strife, and inadequate central guidance, these pitfalls have resulted in declining production rates and virtually complete impoverishment.[31] The state in such situations becomes incidental to the desperate struggle for survival.

Poverty, though it affects everyone, has its roots in the persistent neglect of the countryside. It nevertheless impinges, albeit unequally, on all sectors of society and on all social groups. Hunger fuels widespread social disarray and therefore provokes heterogeneous, often contradictory, reactions. Spatial, gender, and generational differences become more pronounced. Class divisions increase. Ethnic, communal, and religious cleavages are highlighted. All these social manifestations constitute efforts to find alternatives to existing patterns of production and exchange. Forms of social reorientation constitute, in and of themselves, frameworks for coping with real scarcity. These changes are by their very nature radical. The community, however defined, assumes the multifarious roles of the state. Social life is reorganized, priorities are rearranged, and the context of human interaction is drastically altered.

Two main forms of confronting the challenge of poverty through the radical redrawing of communal frontiers have been devised in recent years. The first is withdrawal or self-enclosure. Where people are hungry, entire communities are consciously, if only temporarily, disengaging from the state. Local self-reliance is facilitated by the preservation of strong community ties, by the persistence of local group solidarity, by a perceived threat to survival, perhaps by the emergence of an articulate leadership.[32] But above all patterns of withdrawal are influenced by the availability of some means of production, and usually by a combination of land and labor.

Instances of constructive disengagement from the formal polity permeate Africa today. Rural self-help schemes, entirely autonomous of government control, have flourished in remote areas of Zaire and Senegal. They are evident in Ghana and Mozambique, in Guinea and Chad.[33] In Uganda farmers have returned to subsistence agriculture with renewed energy. In Niger peasants devised rat-traps to protect their crops and have consequently increased yields.[34] In Ethiopia different communities have begun to grow their own food and repeatedly shun government overtures. "Today millions of people in the Third World have turned their back on official development strategies and are trying to improve their living conditions through their own efforts."[35]

The process of conscious self-enclosure from the formal and the nonformal markets is predicated on a growing need to produce in order to survive. Local self-reliance is based on agriculture, although the injection of new skills and techniques by returnees from the urban areas makes these processes more than just an atavistic return to subsistence modes of production.

Withdrawal therefore generates fairly autonomous enclaves that vary in location, economic base, symbolic orientation, and historical grounding. Some withdrawal processes revolve around the local or regional geographic community.[36] Some are formed within religious entities. Still others are grounded in culturally defined ethnic or linguistic frameworks. And in some instances kinship is reasserted or previously cohesive agglomerations break down into new collectivities. Self-enclosure breeds diversity and nurtures many different variations of ethnic articulation.

Self-encapsulation, whatever specific form it takes in any given setting, involves much more than a strategy of mere economic survival. Traditional modes of stratification have been revised and adjusted. Novel instances of status incongruence have emerged. New struggles for power have surfaced as traditional leaders have vied with each other and with pretenders for increasingly variegated power and authority roles. Rural interethnic relations have shifted, and the force and texture of ethnicity in the local context has changed.[37]

As ethnic units have become frameworks for interaction, and as local interests have displaced national ones, preoccupations with identities *per se* have frequently been replaced by utilitarian concerns. Indeed, local disputes, factional alignments and contests over resource allocations receive particular attention at the ethnically defined community level.[38]

Not all self-reliance efforts, however ingeniously pursued, have been successful. In areas overrun by wars or pestilence, shifts to local production do not always constitute a viable option for the rural hungry. In these instances migration has been employed as an alternative to withdrawal. To be sure, temporary migration has been prevalent in Africa for many years. Motivated by declining economic opportunities, restrictions on personal freedoms, political harassment, or the promise of greener pastures elsewhere, many African states have been depleted of some of their best citizens over the years. Escape mechanisms of this sort have been adopted by the highly educated and the unemployed, by rural wage earners and by urban skilled labor.[39] In recent years, however, large population movements have occurred when local possibilities have been exhausted and no real prospects for minimal sustenance could be expected from remaining in place. The refugee problem in Africa has now reached alarming proportions, with estimates ranging between 5 and 10 percent of the entire population of the continent.[40] The wandering hungry have gravitated to potential food distribution centers in neighboring countries. The refugee problem is most severe in the Horn of

Africa. But growing pockets of refugees can be found throughout the continent.

Migrations (conducted mostly on a rural-rural basis) are another form of boundary redefinition. Patterns of ethnicity among migrants vary substantially. In some cases, groups assimilate easily into new local communities. In other instances they reconfirm their original identities.[41] In still other examples, broader identities have broken down, or new identities have been formed.[42] Even within the same group, new settlement in different locations has evoked different expressions of ascription and affiliation.[43] These modes of self-expression blur international boundaries and create transnational communities whose outlines are still indistinct.

Not all migration has been successful. When initiatives to change the boundaries of one's existence fail, helplessness sets in. Such revelations of utter despair, where survival is open to question and famine reigns, are becoming all too familiar.[44] Having tried every possibility to no avail, some people can do no more than to put themselves at the mercy of others. Hopelessness breeds social anomie.

Responses to poverty involve basic alterations in the settings of social interactions. These very diverse reactions have heterogeneous political ramifications. Other foci of political conflict have developed; class conflict has penetrated into the countryside, new forms of populism have emerged. Political involution has taken place where local self-reliance mechanisms have thrived. And paradoxically, pressures on existing states have increased.

The responses to the crisis of poverty call into question the foundations of state power. The issue is no longer how power is used or who controls the government, but the validity of state power itself. The integrity of the existing political networks is assailed and social tensions are no longer integrative as diffuse, multidirectional and mass-oriented modes of conflict proliferate. By tugging on the existing system from many different directions, these responses necessarily alter solidarity and instrumentality, values and norms. Impoverishment raises new questions about the frameworks and contents of governance in many parts of the continent.

## Patterns of Economic Challenge and Ethnic Response

Different economic challenges in Africa have yielded quite distinct social consequences. Problems of dwindling resources have highlighted class and situational concerns at the expense of inherited affiliations. Maldistribution has accentuated differential ethnicity as a tool for contending with structural and class inequalities. The crisis of poverty, in turn, has transformed ethnicity from an instrument into a framework for human survival. As economic difficulties have become more severe and more pervasive, ethnic permutations have multiplied and the distance between groups has increased. In this process, the boundaries of state capability, state solidarity, and state relevance have shifted. The greater the isolation of individuals and groups, the greater, too, the prevalence of state incoherence.[45] The position of states in Africa has fluctuated in accordance with the economic problems they have had to confront and the reactions these crises have evoked.

Each African state, and especially those seriously affected by economic regression, has exhibited differing combinations of social manifestations in response to its present situation. Details of the condition of Ghana do not coincide with those of Zaire, which in turn diverge from Sudan and Tanzania, Nigeria and Uganda, Chad, Ethiopia, Zimbabwe, or Niger. In each of these countries the nature of economic difficulties varies and so, too, do economic coping strategies and their ethnic outcomes.

Six distinct patterns of ethnicity have emerged in specific countries in recent years. The first involves the continued salience of large ethnic agglomerations.[46] The second highlights the decomposition of large ethnic groupings and the consolidation of social interaction in smaller, frequently kin- or geographically based, units. The third underlines regional separation. The fourth brings forth the significance of the local collectivity. The fifth centers around the religious community.[47] And the sixth still accentuates the predominance of class over ethnic concerns. In some areas, a combination of these patterns has developed in different parts of the country.

Thus, specific constellations of historical, ecological, external, cultural, social, and political factors have come together to create unique, complex, and distinctive types of ethnic presentations and patterns of state-society interaction in various settings. It is this highly fluid picture of ethnic diversity in the face of economic adversity that requires further explanation.

## DEVELOPMENT STRATEGIES AND ETHNIC REDEFINITION

The connection between economic resources and the state has molded social relationships in functioning political entities. Patterns of ethnicity in conditions of economic crisis may themselves be viewed as outcomes of the failure of development strategies and the particular types of state disintegration they set in motion. Just as the construction of ethnic collectivities in existing state networks is a function of the sequential pattern of economic growth and political consolidation, the diversity of ethnicity in situations of flux may be the result of the systematic reversal of these processes. Social fluidity, it is suggested, is the overt manifestation of an inverted cycle of economic failure and political breakdown.

The progression of ethnic delineation within post-colonial African states is fairly well known and need be recapitulated only briefly. Precolonial social entities possessed specific features defined by ecological, historical, economic, cultural, and symbolic factors. When the Europeans first arrived on the shores of Africa, they were greeted by vibrant political formations that possessed their own complex social dynamics. Foreign incursions remolded existing frameworks and created new patterns of social interaction.[48] Colonial contacts were accompanied by the introduction of alternative sources of wealth and social differentiation. Competition over resources introduced new lines of stratification. Ethnic reorganization was a crucial by-product of these readjustments.[49] It was granted added coherence by the extremely alien, hegemonic, and instrumental nature of the colonial state. By the time African countries began to emerge from the colonial period, the relationship between power, dominant classes, and the state had coalesced.[50] The political bases of class formation, consolidation, identification, and action have been documented superbly elsewhere.[51] During the first years of independence, ethnic manipulation became a crucial mechanism for elite entrenchment. In these conditions, the interests of tribalism as social pluralism and tribalism as elite ideologies converged.[52]

The centrality of government as purveyor of development and distributor of social goods meant that state intervention contributed heavily to the sharpening of the social realities of ethnicity and class.[53] The rhythm of ethnic politics was largely a function of state actions and of the fluctuations in the composition of state officeholders. The activation of ethnicity could be traced back to the makeup, structure, policies, and performance record of specific ruling coalitions at various points in time. These initiatives were rarely egalitarian or disinterested. Ethnicity was employed as a resource to expand bureaucratic control around the state. Governments, concerned with their own survival, often promoted a siege mentality by isolating ethnic scapegoats. In time, they evinced little concern for national integration in terms unrelated to state and dominant class concerns.[54] Ethnicity, used as a way of asserting state power, proved, however, to be a double-edged sword. The process of purposeful depoliticization in many African states has also made politically defined ethnic groups into a bulwark against rampant bureaucratization.[55] As state capacities have diminished and ruling classes splintered, specific ethnic constellations have become more prominent.

The standard sequence of ethnic definition in Africa has therefore followed a clear pattern, which started from primordial roots and then progressed through economic competition and political control to manipulation and conflict within an integrative setting. Ethnic interactions have been perceived as the end products of conventional political processes. "Hierarchy has to be admitted as an important factor in keeping states going. So does conflict."[56] Ethnicity is reflective of these requisites.

The diversity of the expression and uses of ethnicity in recent years and the social fragmentation and isolation that has ensued are, in stark contrast, the final stages in the reversal of these (however unequal) integrative movements. The process of social reordering commenced with the almost pervasive failure of development efforts.

In the first decade of independence, most African states undertook to promote growth and expand social services in accordance with development perceptions largely imported from abroad. Although these varied in specifics—from state capitalist and state socialist to Marxist-Leninist forms— the overriding objective of plans was to increase production and thereby enrich the quality of life.[57] By the end of the decade pessimism had replaced hope and economic disparities had grown. The reasons for this failure lie not only in environmental, demographic, and ecological factors, but also in poor policy planning, inadequate implementation, institutional weakness, and personal frailties.[58] Whatever the precise combination of variables brought to bear on this topic, by the beginning of the 1970s economic targets had to be scaled down and priorities redesigned.

In the second stage emphasis therefore shifted from development to persistence. Attempts were made to fortify domestic autonomy, to exploit local resources, and to reverse the abject neglect of agriculture and the rural areas that characterized the ambitious plans of early independence. Notions of self-reliance, variously defined, became the passwords if not the determinants of economic action. But as African states entered the 1980s concerns over stagnation had given way to an almost complete preoccupation with questions of survival. Policy-rooted explanations could no longer account for these realities. They were clearly related to deep structural factors both domestically and internationally.[59]

Africans are today confronted with the enormous burden of dealing with misery with little resources and almost insurmountable structural restraints. As they grope for solutions to these well-nigh intractable problems, exploitation, withdrawal, dependency, and anomie become widespread. Social redefinition can be attributed, first and foremost, to the almost complete breakdown of development.

The type and direction of ethnic adjustments do, however, vary. These patterns are related to the specific political ramifications of economic failures. The frailty of the political economy has almost inevitably weakened many African states and reduced their salience, sometimes to the point of disintegration. Variations in state coherence are reflected in the structure of interethnic ties.[60] Here the content of policies, especially economic ones, has played an important role.[61] Different regimes have rested their persistence on divergent formulas for linking people, resources, and values to the state. In some cases the coercive and exploitative apparatus has been magnified and participation circumscribed. In these instances class antagonisms have become pronounced. In some other countries ethnic mobilization has been encouraged to induce legitimacy and facilitate order. In these instances large ethnic agglomerations have congealed. In some cases, official favoritism has been practiced to strengthen support bases and enrich ruling coalitions. In these instances kin and subethnic concerns have surfaced. In some other countries an ethnic economy of affection has been elevated to the highest policy levels.[62] In these instances regional rifts have become pronounced. Where kleptocracies have ruled localization patterns of ethnicity have coalesced.[63] And the formal resort to new symbolic models has evoked religious responses.[64]

Specific substantive approaches have therefore provided, in all probability unwittingly, channels for the delineation of the nature and direction of state decomposition. The problems of the reduction of political control have been raised either to state authority, to state legitimacy, to state power, or to some combination of these factors.[65] The loss of some instrumental, symbolic, and/or solidarity functions has meant that other entities have taken over these tasks. The substance of state enfeeblement has therefore contributed directly to redefining the parameters, structures, and roles of increasingly autonomous and isolated ethnic collectivities.

"Scarcity thus underlines and exacerbates the main problems of governability in middle Africa—namely social incoherence, overdeveloped state structures, insufficient state legitimacy, and inadequate state coercive power."[66] As African states gradually forfeit more and more of the essentials of "stateness," the terms of reference of social interaction are shifting. A real, albeit not official, redrawing of political, economic, and social boundaries is taking place. New types of connections between economic, social, and political factors are being refined, and these in turn nurture other forms of relativity and a differing dynamic between these polities and the social orders they encompass. This situation is the result of the undoing of the particular sequence of the interconnection between the economy, the state, and ethnicity which helped to delineate communal relationships in the past. The failure of development strategies made association with the state less worthwhile. The content of these policies differentially influenced various facets of state coherence. The loss of specific elements of statehood has generated a multiplicity of separate ethnic expressions. The relationship between political economy, ethnicity, and the framework of political interactions is still indispensable to understanding political and social processes. But new sequences are being devised, their diachronic progressions are shifting, and the dialectic relationships they foster are yet to unfold. Ethnic expressions provide an important clue to their properties and implications.

## IMPLICATIONS FOR ANALYSIS AND PRACTICE

The political economy of ethnicity in Africa generates a multifaceted regressive cycle. "In something of a dialectical process, scarcity undermines institutional effectiveness, which in turn worsens the constraints of scarcity."[67] The interconnection between misplaced development efforts, weakened state structures, and manifestations of social dissolution has yielded four major political patterns in contemporary Africa: dissent, alienation, disintegration, and total external dependence. The direction of changes implied by these processes varies: certain states are being fortified while others are being undermined; some states are collapsing rapidly as others extend their grasp. Though the imperative of change is inescapable in all these situations, the possibilities that are presented follow many different courses.[68]

The relationship among economic change, ethnicity, and the state is neither fixed nor uni-directional. By questioning the assumptions underlying current patterns of interaction, it has been possible to get another view of social and political processes and their ethnic reverberations. The analysis of ethnicity as a descriptive variable has highlighted the significance of responses and not only actions, of margins as well as the core, of sub-units and the state, of diverse social formations together with society as a whole. The fluidity of ethnic presentations can only be understood by reference to models drawn from the literature on nationalism and ethnicity, on development and the state. The mutability of social organisms in contemporary Africa also endows this body of knowledge with new meaning and may demand significant adjustments and clarification.

Isolated ethnic diversity is a sign of fundamental social, economic, and political uncertainty. The human ramifications of political collapse and social anomie can no longer be safely ignored. And the implications for practice must be confronted head-on. "What ultimately matters is whether African states can effectively exercise their right to self-determination and in the process mitigate the incoherence of their ethnic environments."[69]

Several different methods may be suggested for averting the many negative by-products of economic scarcity, political breakdown, and social fragmentation. The first focuses on policy changes. There is hardly a voice in Africa today that does not advocate increased concentration on rural and agrarian matters. Advances in these areas require greater attention to foreign relations and pricing mechanisms, to modes of resource utilization and program design. A modicum of order is a precondition, however, for the effective formulation of policy and its implementation. For this reason, some observers have suggested a second, social, approach to dealing with the current crisis. By attenuating ethnic and regional demands and reducing their intensity, it has been suggested that it might be possible to generate a constructive bargaining process between social groups and the state.[70] This method implies social accommodation and the opening up of avenues for participation.

A third way of coming to terms with current crises rests on the presumption that social quiescence may not be attainable without structural change. Emphasis in this view is placed on representation and public supervision as much as on participation. There are those who claim that structural reordering cannot be attained unless major symbolic shifts take place. In this fourth perspective ideology and political culture assume center stage. If the consummatory underpinnings of social behavior are altered and identities redefined, it might be possible to redirect modes of rational interaction as well.[71]

A group of political realists, relying on state-centric concepts, contend that symbolic mechanisms are meaningless in situations where the framework of political action is obscure. They suggest, in a fifth approach, a reconcentration on means of augmenting state capabilities. In this context, some analysts have suggested that state institutions should be bolstered from the outside. Others have focused on decentralization and the directed devolution of decision-making.[72] In their minds, regardless of whether the state should be strengthened or whether it should become less in order to become more, reconstruction is impossible without state rehabilitation.[73] Pessimists have offered a sixth method: one which calls for a total redefinition of the domestic, regional, and global structure of power.[74]

Whatever the merits of employing any of these methods of grappling with economic decline and political uncertainty—either individually or in concert—it may be necessary to reconsider not only substantive needs but also modes of interaction. A new school has set out to reconsider the relationship between economy and the state, between society and political values, between ethnicity and policy. In this intriguing approach, it is posited that solutions to underdevelopment and disorder may lie as much in rearranging the links between these basic components of human behavior as in revising their contents.[75]

Regardless of the precise approach selected and refined (and in all probability a combination of these methods is called for), both the understanding of current trends and the prescription for their rectification cannot be adequately tackled without a thoroughgoing review of the concepts of nationalism and ethnicity, development and the state. Those truly concerned with ameliorating the exigencies of the contemporary African experience must first face the preliminary challenge of changing the perception and operationalization of these fundamental processes and reassessing their interrelationship.

## NOTES

The assistance of several people was invaluable in the preparation of this paper. Katya Azoulay assisted with the research, Etti Yacobovitz provided some vital details, and Victor Azarya gave important comments at various stages. The Harry S. Truman Research Institute of the Hebrew University of Jerusalem furnished the environment and facilities for fruitful research.

1. An excellent overview is provided in Nelson Kasfir, "Explaining Ethnic Political Participation," World Politics 31 (1979): 365–88.

2. Robert Bates, "Modernization, Ethnic Competition and the Rationality of Politics in Contemporary Africa," in State Versus Ethnic Claims: African Policy Dilemmas, ed. Donald Rothchild and Victor Olorunsola (Boulder, Colo.: Westview Press, 1983), p. 161.

3. Donald Rothchild and Victor Olorunsola, "Managing Competing State and Ethnic Claims," in their *State Versus Ethnic Claims*, p. 10.

4. For one view see Goran Hyden, "Problems and Prospects of State Coherence," in *State Versus Ethnic Claims*, ed. Rothchild and Olorunsola, pp. 67–84.

5. Crawford Young, "Patterns of Social Conflict: State, Class and Ethnicity," *Daedalus* 3 (1982): 72. Also see his *The Politics of Cultural Pluralism* (Madison, Wis.: University of Wisconsin Press, 1976).

6. On the fluidity of ethnicity and the possibilities ingrained in utilizing it as a descriptive concept see Naomi Chazan, "Ethnicity and Politics in Ghana," *Political Science Quarterly* 97 (1982): 461–85.

7. For quite a different view, compare Henry Bienen, "The State and Ethnicity: Integrative Formulas in Africa," in *State Versus Ethnic Claims*, ed. Rothchild and Olorunsola, pp. 100–24.

8. Bernard Schaffer, "Organization Is Not Equity: Theories of Political Integration," *Development and Change* 8 (1977): 19–43. Also see Pierre L. van den Berghe, "Class, Race and Ethnicity in Africa," *Ethnic and Racial Studies* 6 (1983): 221–36.

9. The typologies employed in the analysis of economic crises in Africa were developed in Naomi Chazan and Timothy Shaw, "The Political Economy of Food in Africa: Contradiction, Crisis or Collapse" (Paper presented at the Twenty-Sixth Annual Meeting of the African Studies Association, Boston, 7–10 December 1983). On pricing policies, consult Paul Streeten, "Food Prices as a Reflection of Political Power," *Ceres* 16 (1983): 16–22.

10. Examples are drawn from Ghana, Guinea, Ethiopia, Zaire, Tanzania, Liberia, and Uganda. For a preliminary analysis see Naomi Chazan, *An Anatomy of Ghanian Politics: Managing Political Recession, 1969–1982* (Boulder, Colo.: Westview Press, 1983), pp. 192–93.

11. Richard Sandbrook, *The Politics of Basic Needs: Urban Aspects of Assaulting Poverty in Africa* (London: Heinemann, 1982).

12. Jean-Marie Gibbal, Emile le Bris, Alain Marie, Annik Osmont, and Gerard Salem, "Situations Urbaines et Politiques Sociales en Afrique," *Cahiers d'études africaines* 21 (1981–1983): 7–10, and the entire issue.

13. Chazan and Shaw, "The Political Economy of Food in Africa."

14. Michael G. Schatzberg, "Ethnicity and Class at the Local Level: Bars and Bureaucrats in Lisala, Zaire," *Comparative Politics* 13 (1981): 461. For a similar analysis on the Ivory Coast see Michael Cohen, *Urban Policy and Political Conflict in Africa: A Study of the Ivory Coast* (Chicago: University of Chicago Press, 1974).

15. Frances Moore-Lappé and Joseph Collins, "While Hunger is Real, Scarcity Is Not," *Internationale Entwicklung* 4 (1980): 24–27 and passim.

16. René Dumont and Marie-France Mottin, *Stranglehold on Africa* (London: Andre Deutsch, 1983). The neglect of agriculture is a constant theme in the economic literature on Africa. For a specific case study see Timothy M. Shaw and Malcolm J. Grieve, "Africa and the Environment: The Political Economy of Resources," *The African Review* 9 (1982): 104–24.

17. Sara S. Berry, "Custom, Class and the Informal Sector: Or Why Marginality is not Likely to Pay," African Studies Center Working Paper No. 1 (Boston: Boston University, 1978), p. 5.

18. For some examples see Deborah Pellow, "*Kalabule* Out, *Warabeba* In: Coping in Revolutionary Ghana" (Paper presented at the Twenty-Fifth Annual Meeting of

the African Studies Association, Washington, D. C., November 1982); and Donald Rothchild and John W. Harbeson, "Rehabilitation in Uganda," *Current History* 80 (1981): 115–19.

19. Official malfeasance of this sort has been documented for virtually every African country. For one example see Thomas Turner, "Mobotu's Zaire: Permanently on the Verge of Collapse," *Current History* 80 (1981): 124–28.

20. Rothchild and Harbeson, "Rehabilitation in Uganda," and Richard Jeffries, "The Political Economy of Underdevelopment in Ghana," *African Affairs* 81 (1982): 307–17.

21. Rothchild and Olorunsola, "Managing Competing State and Ethnic Claims." Also see Anders Hjort, "Ethnic Transformation, Dependency and Change: The Iligira Samburu of Northern Kenya," *Journal of Asian and African Studies* 16 (1981): 50.

22. This finding repeats itself consistently. See Minion K. C. Morrison, *Ethnicity and Political Integration: The Case of Ashanti, Ghana* (Syracuse: Maxwell School of Citizenship and Public Affairs, Syracuse University, 1982); Peter Osei-Kwame and Paul P. W. Achola, "A New Conceptual Model for the Study of Political Integration in Africa," *The Journal of Developing Areas* 15 (1981): 585–604.

23. Donald Rothchild, "Collective Demands for Improved Distributions," in *State Versus Ethnic Claims,* ed. Rothchild and Olorunsola, pp. 172–98, gives an excellent overview of differential demand and expectation patterns in various parts of the continent.

24. M. Catharine Newbury, "Colonialism, Ethnicity, and Rural Political Protest," *Comparative Politics* 15 (1983): 253–80.

25. Kathleen A. Staudt, "Sex, Ethnic and Class Consciousness in Western Kenya," *Comparative Politics* 14 (1982): 147–67; Larry Diamond, "Class, Ethnicity and the Democratic State: Nigeria, 1950–1966," *Comparative Studies in Society and History* 25 (1983): 457–89; Wyatt McGaffey, "The Policy of National Integration in Zaire," *Journal of Modern African Studies* 20 (1982): 87–105; and David Brown, "Sieges and Scapegoats: The Politics of Pluralism in Ghana," *Journal of Modern African Studies* 21 (1983): 431–60.

26. Schatzberg, "Ethnicity and Class at the Local level," p. 479.

27. Young, "Patterns of Social Conflict," p. 93. Also see Bruno Jobert, "Clientelisme, Patronage et Participation Populaire," *Revue Tiers Monde* 95 (1983): 537–56.

28. The problem of nonparticipation in elections has become fairly acute in recent years. Participation rates in Nigeria, Kenya, and Ghana were exceptionally low in the past decade. For a discussion of the latter see Chazan, "Ethnicity and Politics."

29. Carl K. Eicher, "Facing Up to Africa's Food Crisis," *Foreign Affairs* 60 (1982): 153–74.

30. This cycle is well documented in Assefa Bequele, "Stagnation and Inequality in Ghana," in *Agrarian Policies and Rural Poverty in Africa,* ed. Dharam Ghai and Samir Radwan (Geneva: ILO, 1983), esp. pp. 24–45.

31. For one example see Michael Bratton, *The Local Politics of Rural Development: Peasant and Party State in Zambia* (Hanover: N. H.: University Press of New England, 1980).

32. Roy Prieswerk, "Self-Reliance in Unexpected Places," *Geneva-Africa* 20 (1982): 64.

33. See Victor Azarya and Naomi Chazan, "Disengagement from the State in Africa: Reflections on the Experience of Ghana and Guinea" (Paper presented at the Twenty-Seventh Annual Meeting of the African Studies Association, Los Angeles, October 1984).

34. John-Pierre Gontard, "When the Cat's Away the Rats Will Play: The Kornaka Trap in Niger," in *Self-Reliance: A Strategy for Development*, ed. Johann Galtung, Peter O'Brien, and Roy Prieswerk (London: Bogle l'Ouverture, 1980), pp. 330–36.

35. Prieswerk, "Self-Reliance in Unexpected Places," pp. 58–59.

36. Martin Staniland, *The Lions of Dagbon: Political Change in Northern Ghana* (London: Cambridge University Press, 1975); Paul Andre Ladouceur, *Chiefs and Politicians: The Politics of Regionalism in Northern Ghana* (London: Longman, 1979).

37. Hjort, "Ethnic Transformation, Dependency, and Change." Also see Hector Blackhurst, "Ethnicity in Southern Ethiopia: The General and the Particular," *Africa* 50 (1980): 55–56.

38. Chazan, "Ethnicity and Politics in Ghana," pp. 472–73. Also see Walter L. Barrows, "Comparative Grassroots Politics in Africa," *World Politics* 26 (1974): 283–97; and Maxwell Owusu, "Policy Studies, Development and Political Anthropology," *Journal of Modern African Studies* 13 (1975): 367–82.

39. These patterns are traced by Aderanti Adepoju, "Migrations and Socio-Economic Change in Africa," *International Social Science Journal* 31 (1979): 207–25.

40. Michel Ndoh, "Les réfugiés africains: Status juridiques et réflexions politiques," *Geneva-Africa* 20 (1982): 9–38.

41. For one interesting example of both these possibilities see Ulrich Braukamper, "Ethnic Identity and Social Change Among Oromo Refugees in the Horn of Africa," *Northeast African Studies* 9 (1982–1983): 1–15.

42. Gerald W. Kleis, "Confrontation and Incorporation: Igbo Ethnicity in Cameroon," *African Studies Review* 23 (1980): 89–110.

43. This pattern has been documented most extensively for the Fulbe. See Charles Frantz, "Fulbe Continuity and Change Under Five Flags Atop West Africa: Territoriality, Ethnicity, Stratification, and National Integration," *Journal of Asian and African Studies* 16 (1981): 89–115; "Image and Reality in African Interethnic Relations," *Studies in Third World Societies* 2 (1980); and Victor Azarya, *Aristocrats Facing Change: The Fulbe in Guinea, Nigeria and Cameron* (Chicago: University of Chicago Press, 1978).

44. Geoffrey Lean, "Three Disasters Hit Africa," *Africa Now,* October 1983, pp. 128–29.

45. Ndiva Kofele-Kale, "Patterns of Political Orientations Towards the Nation: A Comparison of Rural-Urban Residents in Anglophone Cameroon," *African Social Research* 26 (1978): 469–88.

46. Richard Hodder-Williams, "Conflict in Zimbabwe: The Matabeleland Problem," *Conflict Studies* 151 (1983), would disagree. But this observation is based not on an analysis of the ethnic roots of the Zimbabwe crisis, but on the pattern of conflict that results from the current situation.

47. Paul M. Lubeck, "Islamic Networks and Urban Capitalism: An Instance of Articulation from Northern Nigeria," *Cahiers d'Etudes Africaines* 21 (1981-1983): 67-78.

48. These points have been made by many scholars. For a good summary see Robert Bates, "Ethnic Competition and Modernization in Contemporary Africa," *Comparative Political Studies* 6 (1974): 457-85.

49. For a good overview see Bernard E. Segal, "Ethnic Stratification and Political Cleavage," *Issue* 8 (1978): 10-13. Specific examples may be found in Edmond J. Keller, "Education, Ethnicity and Political Socialization in Kenya," *Comparative Political Studies* 12 (1980): 442-69; and Lois Weis, "Ethnicity in Ghanaian Schools: A Re-Assessment," *Journal of Asian and African Studies* 15 (1980): 229-41.

50. Young, "Patterns of Social Conflict." Also see Newbury, "Colonialism, Ethnicity, and Rural Political Protest."

51. Richard L. Sklar, "The Nature of Class Domination in Africa," *Journal of Modern African Studies* 17 (1979): 531-52.

52. David Brown, "Who Are the Tribalists? Social Pluralism and Political Ideology in Ghana," *African Affairs* 322 (1982): 37-70.

53. On the centrality of the state see John S. Saul, *The State and Revolution in Eastern Africa* (New York: Monthly Review Press, 1979), esp. pp. 169-70. This point is also made by Guillermo O'Donnell, "Comparative Historical Formations of the State Apparatus and Socio-Economic Change in the Third World," *International Social Sciences Journal* 32 (1980): 717-29.

54. Brown, "Sieges and Scapegoats," p. 459 and passim.

55. Cynthia H. Enloe, "Ethnicity, Bureaucracy and State-Building in Africa and Latin America," *Ethnic and Racial Studies* 1 (1978): 336-51.

56. Schaffer, "Organization is Not Equity," p. 30.

57. For a comprehensive analysis of ideology and development, see Crawford Young, *Ideology and Development in Africa* (New Haven: Yale University Press, 1982).

58. Michael F. Lofchie and Stephen K. Commins, "Food Deficits and Agricultural Policies in Tropical Africa," *Journal of Modern African Studies* 20 (1982): 1-25, gives a good overview of the various approaches to explanation.

59. Amartya Sen, "The Food Problem: Theory and Policy," *Third World Quarterly* 4 (1982): 447-59; and Robert L. Paarlberg, "Shifting and Sharing Adjustment Burdens: The Role of the Industrial Food Importing Nations," *International Organization* 32 (1978): 655-78. Also see Rolf Hanisch and Rainer Tetzlaff, "Agricultural Policy, Foreign Aid and the Rural Poor in the Third World," *Law and State* 23 (1982): 120-43.

60. René Lemarchand, "The State and Society in Africa: Ethnic Stratification and Restratification in Historical and Comparative Perspective," in *State Versus Ethnic Claims,* ed. Rothchild and Olorunsola, p. 64.

61. J. F. Bayart, "La revanche des sociétés africaines," *Politique Africaine* 11 (1983): 95-127.

62. Hyden, "Patterns and Prospects of State Coherence," pp. 71-73.

63. Terminology taken from Jeffries, "The Political Economy of Underdevelopment in Ghana." Also see Chazan, *An Anatomy of Ghanaian Politics.*

64. See the situation in Sudan today for one example.

65. John Lonsdale, "The State and Social Processes in Africa," *African Studies Review* 24 (1981): 139–226. For another view see Robert Jackson and Carl Rosberg, "Why Africa's Weak States Persist: The Empirical and the Juridical in Statehood," *World Politics* 35 (1982): 1–24.

66. Donald Rothchild and Michael Foley, "The Implications of Scarcity for Governance in Africa," *International Political Science Review* 4 (1983): 311–26.

67. Ibid., p. 319.

68. Timothy M. Shaw, "Debates About Africa's Future: The Brandt, World Bank, and Lagos Plan Blueprints," *Third World Quarterly* 5 (1983): 330–44. Also see Timothy M. Shaw, ed., *Alternative Futures for Africa* (Boulder, Colo.: Westview Press, 1981).

69. Lemarchand, "The State and Society in Africa."

70. Rothchild and Olorunsola, "Managing Competing State and Ethnic Claims," pp. 10–11.

71. For one example, see Theodore Natsoulas, "Pluralism and Instability in Ethiopia and Somalia," *Plural Societies* 12 (1981): 13–24.

72. I. William Zartman, "Issues of African Diplomacy in the 1980s," *Orbis* 25 (1982): 1030; Thomas O. Hoglin, "Scarcity and Centralization: The Concept of European Integration," *International Political Science Review* 4 (1983): 345–60; and Naomi Casswell, "Death Wish in West African Economies?" *Africa Now,* October 1983, pp. 70–71.

73. Rothchild and Foley, "The Implications of Scarcity for Governance," pp. 126–127. Also see Crawford Young, "Comparative Claims to Political Sovereignty: Biafra, Katanga and Eritrea," in *State Versus Ethnic Claims,* ed. Rothchild and Olorunsola.

74. This is rampant in the dependency literature. For one example see Mohamed Said, "Integration as a Mode of Ethnic Conflict Resolution in Africa," *International Interaction* 8 (1981): 349–72.

75. For two examples: Larry Diamond, "Cleavage, Conflict and Anxiety in the Second Nigerian Republic," *Journal of Modern African Studies* 20 (1982): 629–68; and Goran Hyden, *No Shortcuts to Progress: African Development Management in Perspective* (Berkeley: University of California Press, 1983), who both make a plea for the separation of economic processes from the state.

# 8 Political Identities and Communal Identities: Shifting Mobilization Among the Lebanese Shî'a Through Ten Years of War, 1975-1985

Elizabeth Picard

How long will there be a Lebanon? Savage and endless fighting all over the country induces one to despair. Today, no price would seem too high to secure peace, even if national territory had to be divided and independence lost. Moreover, one wonders: has Lebanon ever existed as a unified entity? Lessons of history and analysis of current political management clearly show that at no time has the country been consistent with the Western nation-state model. Thus, the real bases on which the Lebanese state has managed to preserve its uneven existence during more than sixty years are still to be discussed. Not only would such a study be of historical interest in order to explain the processes of wars, but it might also be useful at the time Lebanon is rebuilt.

When trying to analyze the political processes at work in Lebanon, especially during war, social scientists are confronted with two antagonistic ranges of theoretical hypothesis as far as mobilization is concerned: 1) Social and economic identities (class identities) are the real ground for political identities. Thus, their development is the unique condition and the decisive proof of state modernization. 2) Ethnic and religious identities (communal identities) are taken for the only relevant deep-rooted political identities as far as Middle Eastern populations are concerned. This is the reason why attempts at ignoring them or at rubbing them out of the picture lead traditional Arab societies to trouble and conflict.

Keeping the two proportions in mind, this study will investigate political identities and political mobilization among a major group of Lebanese: the Shî'a, and more precisely the Shî'a from southern districts, throughout ten years of regional and civil war.

## SOCIAL AND ECONOMIC CHANGES: TOWARD MODERNIZATION AND CRISIS

Specialists of the Near-Eastern Arab states and Lebanese political administrators agree on the amplitude of the economic changes that have taken place in Lebanon since the end of the 1960s: rapid growth of the gross national product, increase in foreign trade, increase in monetary reserves, etc. Yet while the successive oil booms of 1973 and 1979 were giving an exceptional lift to Lebanese commerce and banking, these indicators were becoming increasingly fragile. Half of the gross domestic product consisted of money sent into the country from abroad, and these transfers accounted for fully 80 percent of deposits in local banks. This meant that the new prosperity brought with it a marked degree of vulnerability which was further aggravated as the already wide gap between incomes became wider still.[1]

The rapid growth in industry, now second in importance in the Arab East, is a characteristic of the change which took place in Lebanon during this period. In 1975, a quarter of the active population (675,000 people) worked in the industrial sector which provided 20 percent of GNP. The majority of workers had progressed from an independent status to that of salaried employees.[2] Most important of all was the rise of a working class, which that year became some 135,000 strong, and simultaneously the beginnings of a labor movement exemplified by the strikes of 1972 and 1973.[3]

The economic growth was accompanied by profound demographic and social changes of which the most significant features were: 1) the numerical superiority of the Moslems who, at the end of the seventies, accounted for 55 to 60 percent of the Lebanese population in the country (a study published in *The Wall Street Journal* puts the figure as high as 70 percent);[4] 2) the size of the Syrian and Palestinian populations, which numbered respectively 500,000 and 400,000 people in 1975, out of a total of 3,000,000 inhabitants; and 3) a massive rural exodus, followed by the precarious settlement in the suburbs of Beirut of tens of thousands of families, coming from all the surrounding regions and especially from the south (Jabal 'Amil). A brief reference must be made to a third aspect of the change that took place in Lebanon. This was a cultural change. Development in communications and progress in education facilitated among the 15- to 30-year-old age group the spread of ideas and modes of behavior borrowed, above all, from the West. It was possible to discern a distancing from traditional religious and family values, together with the diffusion of class cultures. These were most marked in the upper classes ("bourgeoisie") and among industrial workers. And these various class cultures tended at the time to transcend communal cleavages.

Against this background of radical change, war broke out in April 1975. The detonator was the development of the Palestinian Resistance in Beirut and South Lebanon from 1968 onwards. Lebanon had become the battlefield of the Israeli-Arab conflict. However, the regional and international aspects of the conflict, important though they are, cannot obscure the fact that it was, from the outset, a civil war about social issues—a war between the periphery and the core, a war between rich and poor.[5]

Indeed, the economic and social upheavals which Lebanon had been subjected to in the years preceding the war found an echo at the political level. Is it possible to talk about a "political modernization" at this point? Without being excessively optimistic,[6] or making the mistake of identifying political modernization solely through a series of indicators borrowed from the Western model,[7] such as the parliamentary system, respect for civil liberties, and mobility of the elites, it is possible to conclude that the progress made in schooling, in the diffusion of a dominant culture, in the growth of a state bureaucracy, or in the beginnings of redistribution (all characteristics of Lebanon at the time) can be taken to be indicative of modernization. Above all, the desire for a secularization of public life became so widespread amongst the urban middle classes that certain participants in the Lebanese system of government, including leaders, became convinced that Lebanese contradictions could only be resolved through the suppression of confessionalism. This is illustrated by any army instruction booklet (written prior to 1967) and by various school textbooks on civic education common in the sixties. The following example is taken from one of the latter:

> It is the duty of the Lebanese to join forces in abolishing confessionalism once and for all. In so doing, they will show that they have acquired a national awareness and political maturity. Communal representation is a transitory stage which cannot be prolonged without damaging both the interests of the state and those of the Lebanese people.[8]

It would be difficult to find a clearer condemnation of the consociational system of representation of religious communities adopted by the Lebanese state after its creation in 1920,[9] a system that was reinforced on independence by the "National Pact" and one that was founded and supported by a cartel of elites who were always ready to give away public possessions in exchange for political stability.[10] These elites watched in consternation the progress of political modernization in the country and, in particular, the diffusion of secular ideology among the petty bourgeoisie in the towns who were eluding their control. Every year, members of political parties proposing universal ideals and laying the foundations of a profound transformation of the whole system increased in number. In 1970, a few weeks before the new 'ahd (regime) of S. Frangiah, Kamâl Junblâtt, then Minister for the Interior, legalized the

Communist party, the Social Nationalist party, and several other left-wing parties. On 18 August 1975, they drew up a program of reforms calling for the abolition of sectarianism, the reform of the administration and of the election law, the reorganization of the army, and the election of a Constituent Assembly.

The "leading poles" *(aqtâb)* of the elite had received their first warning shot in the shape of clashes between the army and the Palestinian Resistance in 1969, and a further, more serious one, in May and June of 1973. When it became clear to them in 1974 and 1975 that peace negotiations conducted under the American wing were doomed to fail, they precipitated Lebanon into war in an effort to halt the process of change that was taking place. This is why many political scientists—of which I was one[11]—at the time analyzed the outbreak of the war as the translation into a military conflict of social conflicts which had not been able to develop at the political level.

Today, it would be important to evaluate the precise role played by the various partisans of social and political change in Lebanon, both before the war and during the first few years, to measure their influence on trade unions and student organizations, and to measure their ability to mobilize support both at the core and at the periphery of the country. Account should also be taken of the support they received from abroad; the presence in Lebanon of the PLO should also be borne in mind. However, at the beginning of 1975, considering the country as a whole with its various communities and regions, Lebanon seemed destined to undergo profound transformations. Mass demonstrations were clamoring for such a change.[12]

## SOUTH LEBANON SHÎ'A AND THE POLITICAL CONTEST

Since the adoption of the Lebanese constitution in 1932 and the signing of the "National Pact" between the head of the state and the prime minister in 1943, political organizations and governmental power were shared by seventeen religious communities *(tâ'ifa,* plur. *tawâ'if).* Among them, five were historically and/or demographically predominant: the Maronites, a Catholic sect; the Sunnîs, or regular Muslims; the Druze, on the contrary heterodox Muslims; the Armenians, the majority of whom are non-Catholics; and the Shî'a. The latter, who counted 104,000 members in 1922 (17.2 percent of the population of Lebanon) and 154,000 in 1932 (19.6 percent), had become, according to each of the two official censuses, three times as numerous, between 451,000 and 970,000 according to contradictory sources.[13] About 80 percent of them originated from the southern *muhâfaza* (district). A part still lived there but many had migrated to Beirut and its suburbs: Nab'a, Burj al-Barajnih, 'Ain Remmanih. The remaining 20 percent lived in the northern part of the Biqâ' valley, Hirmil and Ba'albak districts. Of all the different segments of the Lebanese society, the Shî'a of South Lebanon were the most solidly motivated to adhere to the ideologies of change and to demand a radical modification of the political system.

*First, there were historical reasons:* The Shî'a of South Lebanon had been kept at a distance from the formation of the Lebanese state under the French mandate and, above all, after independence in 1943, on the basis of a compromise between Sunnîs and Maronites. Traditionally, they had leanings toward Palestine but the frontier divisions of 1920 and the creation of Israel in 1948 cut them off from their true capital, Haifa.[14] Ever since the Palestine war (1948–1949) and even more so after 1968, their land had become the battlefield for the Israeli-Arab conflict, while the rest of Lebanon remained—for a time at least—out of the war zone. Thus, although the Shî'a belonged to the state of Lebanon, they resented the fact.

*There were also economic reasons* behind the Shî'a desire for a change: Shî'î South is a mainly agricultural region and the majority of the working population are sharecroppers, semisalaried employees of the Régie des Tabacs, or workers in the citrus fruit orchards. The closing down of the frontier with Palestine, together with increasing insecurity and underequipment in the region, placed tens of thousands of families in a precarious situation. Average individual earnings in South Lebanon are five times less than those in Beirut,[15] although landlords and powerful patrons (*zu'amâ'*) prosper there, just as they do in other parts of the country. Hence emigration has taken place since the sixties to the main towns and even to Africa.

*Religious reasons:* While maintaining a rather strict control on solidarity and communal discipline by means of its clerical network, Shî'î Islam engenders a relationship with state power which is different from that of other religious communities in the Arab East, including Muslim communities. For the Shî'a, a legal power collapsed with the assassination of *Imâm* Husayn in the year 61 Hegira. Ever since that date, Shî'a have transmitted down the centuries a collective refusal to accept any political power which does not have its origins in the religious hierarchy of the community. Consequently, they are predisposed to join parties contesting established authority.[16]

*Social reasons:* In common with the rest of Lebanon, the South Lebanese Shî'a live under the domination of local notables (*a'yân*), such as the 'Usayrâns in Sidon, the Zayns in Nabatiya, or the Khalîls in Tyre. The greatest influence is still exerted by members of the leading feudal (*muqata'jî*) family, the As'ads who have their own parliamentary block of eight southern deputies from Marjayun, Bint Jubail, and Nabatiya—the Independent Parliamentary Bloc (*al-Takattul al-Niyâbî al-Mustaqil*). Confronted with the sudden penetration into the region of a capitalistic economy, which made its appearance by means of agricultural ownership through the money sent by expatriates and also through the growth of a working class both in the region and in the suburbs of Beirut, these dominant lineages tightened their hold on their cliental networks in order to retain their influence, and they succeeded in checking the process of social mobility.

*Cultural reasons:* The Shî'î community of the South suffered from a serious lack of schools[17]—so much so that the illiteracy rate in 1975 was as high as 31 percent for men and 70 percent for women (as against 13 and 20 percent respectively in the Christian communities). From the middle of the sixties onwards, Shî'a have made tremendous efforts to narrow the cultural gap, and this is exemplified by the frequent attribution of the portfolio of Education Minister to a Shî'i.

All of these motivations are, of course, closely linked with political inequalities. The Shî'a are the most populous community in Lebanon. They are, however, represented in Parliament by only 19 members out of a total of 99, with only 11 for South Lebanon, which numbers a quarter of the entire population of the country. They were not given top positions in the civil service until 1974 and still cannot boast of a Shî'i President of the Republic or a Shî'i President of the Council. The first office is reserved for a Maronite and the second for a Sunnî. By and large, the community has been overshadowed by the Lebanese Sunna whose traditional leaders kept to themselves any benefits arising from common Muslim struggles, as they did, for example, in the aftermath of the 1958 civil war.[18]

"The Shî'a are the proletariat of the earth; the class the most subdued in appearance and the most revolutionary at heart. The revolt of the Shî'î masses could become a revolt in the name of all the communities." This analysis is by a political observer who could hardly be suspected of being a radical.[19] It is similar to one made by Lebanese left-wing parties at the beginning of the seventies. At the time, the Arabist parties who had established themselves in Sidon and in South Lebanon—Nasserists amongst the Sunnîs and Ba'th above all amongst the Shî'a—were undergoing the backlash following the severe Arab defeat in 1967. Young Shî'a, particularly those without civil status (students, the unemployed) who had often lost touch with the family tradition of solidarity, began to turn at this point to radical and Marxist groups which were rapidly gaining ground. Nineteen sixty-nine saw the simultaneous founding of *Lûbnan al-Ishtirakî* (Socialist Lebanon) and the *Munazzamat il-Ishtirakiyyin l-Lubnâniyyin* (Lebanese Socialist Organization), which amalgamated the following year under the title of *Munazzamat il-'Amal al-Shuyû'î fî Lubnân* (Organization for Communist Action in Lebanon). It was the head of the OCA, Muhsin Ibrâhîm himself, who conceived at this time the "community-class" concept with reference to the Shî'a, a concept which was to remain in vogue for half a decade. Indeed, it is clear from research carried out by Kamal Hamdân's *Markaz al-Abhâth al-Iqtisâdiyya* or by the Family Planning Organization (*The Family in Lebanon,* sample survey, June 1971), that the average earnings of the Shî'a were inferior to those of all the other communities in the country, and that a greater proportion of Shî'a were to be found amongst the proletarian and semi-proletarian classes. In the Lebanese Communist party (LCP), whose administration had been largely Christian since its second Congress in August 1968, Shî'a became as numerous from the beginning of the seventies as Christians. But Shî'a were also to be found in the small groups making up the Lebanese progressive constellation: for example, in the pro-Syrian Ba'th whose secretary general Asim Qansô was a Shî'î, in the Social Nationalist Party, and even in Junblâtt's Progressivist Socialist party.

The political awakening and the organization of the Shî'i masses developed on a social and economic basis, in particular through the activity of the Lebanese General Labor Confederation during the serious tobacco plantation strikes of 1973 in the Nabatiya area,[20] and among Sidon fishermen. But it developed simultaneously within a communal framework, with specific relevance to the Shî'îs. Under the pressure of new elites in the sect, a law was passed on 19 December 1967 which organized the community separately from the Sunnîs. It instituted the Islamic Shî'î Higher Council (IHSC), destined to direct the internal affairs of the community and its relations with the Lebanese state in accordance with the *Ja'farî (Shî'î)* rite. In May 1969, 820 Council members, politicians, intellectuals, and business managers, together with the *'Ulamâ* college, elected as president of the ISHC Mûsâ Sadr, a Tyre *imâm*, a native of Qom in Iran. They reelected him for his lifetime in 1975.[21]

The Higher Council created more Shî'î social and medical organizations, sports clubs, etc. In conjunction with the Greek-Catholic authorities, it participated in an organization with humanitarian and charitable aims, the "Social Movement." But it became more committed when it demanded state protection for South Lebanon against Israeli attacks which were becoming more frequent. While the progressive parties increased their following, Mûsâ Sadr also became more influential. In 1974 he founded the *Harakat al-Mahrûmîm* (Movement of the Disinherited). And in June 1975 he created *Amal (Afwâj il-Muqâwamat il-Lubnâniyya)* (the Battalions of the Lebanese Resistance)—"hope"—which has since become a symbol for Lebanese Shî'a to rally round.

It is significant that the *Amal*, like many of the progressive Lebanese parties, benefited at the time from the active support of the Palestinian Resistance in Lebanon, which took the form of financial and logistical aid. Hence, the militiamen who perished in July 1975, when a Ba'albak barracks was blown up, were commanded by Fatah officers. Just as Lebanese Communists fought side by side with the PLO in the *Ansâr* militia, Shî'î commandoes supported Palestinian *fidâ'in* in Khyâm (a village that was devastated by the Israeli army in 1972) and in Kfar Shûbâ, in January 1975. Thus, at the beginning of the Two-Year War (1975–1976), the Lebanese progressive parties, united in a National Movement (NM) round the August 1975 program, and *Amal* organization happened to be rivals on the Lebanese scene and especially among the Shî'a.

While in South Lebanon doing research on an annual Shî'î ceremony called *Ashûrâ*, I had the opportunity to compare the attitude and strategy adopted by each of the two groups—the Leftists and *Amal*—toward this traditional religious rite, and to analyze their political meaning. For the Shî'a, *Ashûrâ* (the Decade) commemorates the murder of Husayn, second son of 'Alî (the Prophet's cousin) in 680, an assassination which marked a final break between them and the Sunnî orthodox caliphate. The ritual lasts ten days and consists of three main elements: 1) public relation of the murder; 2) processions of mourners and flagellants; and 3) performance of the tragedy before hundreds of spectators. In South Lebanon, dominant Shî'î elites used to intervene in the preparation of the ceremony. They had succeeded in ritualizing *Ashûrâ* and making it an instrument for political domination.[22] Not only did it mirror a collective guilt for an ancient treachery, but it was also performed in response to the disastrous social and economic conditions in the district. While local Shî'î elites were protected from criticism by their historical legitimacy, the ceremony was turned against the people celebrating it and changed into a submission rite,[23] at variance with the community culture and tradition of contestation and insurrection. During the procession through Nabatiya in 1970, young men belonging to the LCP and to OCA publicly urged the people of the town to stop chastising themselves and to turn their anger "against the enemies of both class and nation." They were immediately arrested and the local *imâm* gave a solemn reminder of the necessity for the rite.[24] But four years later people could hear a similar political admonition, issued this time by religious authorities, at the head of whom was Mûsâ Sadr. The *imâm* declared in his *khutba* (religious speech): "Our community is ready to stage a revolution."[25] The very next day, he helped to found a "People's Committee Against Inflation" and marched in Sidon, heading a giant procession of strikers and students.

## FAILURE OF THE SECULARIST LEFT WING; SUCCESS FOR COMMUNAL MOBILIZATION

The contrast between the secularist Left's failure to mobilize the masses celebrating *Ashûrâ* in 1970, and Mûsâ Sadr's success only four years later, announces and illustrates the arrival of these two movements on the Lebanon scene and, in particular, in the Shî'î South. They were concurrent, as I have already pointed out, because their struggle shared two essential characteristics: the sociological content on the one hand, and the cooperation with the Palestinian Resistance on the other.

Despite the *imâm's* insistence that he is "neither of the right nor of the left" but follows the "path of the Just" (*al-sirât al-mustaqîm*), *Amal* and the Left are concerned with similar problems and their demands, as far as development is concerned, are similar. This becomes immediately obvious if one compares the list of Shî'a demands, published in the form of a manifesto in *al-Hayât* on 12 February 1974, with contemporary LCP publications, particularly their study of the agrarian question.[26] Moreover, the attitude of both toward the state is equally legalist: they reproach it with being too "soft," demanding the extension of its authority and an increase in its interventions in order to end the power of the traditional elite and to solve the growing social crisis. Both show the same solidarity toward armed Palestinians in South Lebanon. Like *Amal,* the NM approved the Cairo agreement of November 1969, which gave the *fidâ'în* a territorial autonomy for the struggle. Increasingly frequent Israeli "deterrent" or "retaliation" attacks on the villages and civil populations of the Jabal 'Amil and the coast south of Sidon inspired a solidarity which was publicly proclaimed by the LCP at its third Congress in 1972, by all the progressive parties which created in 1974 a Solidarity Front with the Palestinian Resistance, and by the people in the Shî'î community and their leaders.[27]

Finally, there is a third similarity in the position adopted by the NM in its early days, and that of *imâm* Sadr's group: both criticized and even condemned the political sectarianism on which rests the equilibrium of the Lebanese state. Here again, the similarity is evident if one compares the text of Shî'a demands as published in *al-Hayât* or even *Amal*'s charter, Article 7, which looks beyond the limits of the Shî'î community and refuses confessionalism, with the NM's program for reform which was published the same year.[28]

While they were both fully engaged in the process of change in Lebanon, the left of the NM and *Amal* were to develop along opposing lines during the war years of 1975 to 1985. The NM's decline and loss of credibility contrasted with the rise of political Shî'ism—a rise which was a main characteristic of Lebanon's evolution during these ten years, and of which 1978 was the decisive year. In the first months of the war, left-wing parties lost the majority of their militants in the zone under the domination of the Lebanese Front (LF), around that zone, the North controlled by Frangiah, and in Matn occupied by the Syrian *Quwwât al-Redde'.* More than a hundred of them died in combat in the winter and spring of 1976. Most of the others had to abandon their communist or progressive affiliations in favor of their Christian identity. When territorial divisions were settled in 1978 between the LF, Syria, the PLO and the NM, the LCP—whose leaders were still mostly Christian—had become a largely Muslim party. However, between 1978 and 1981, during three years of stagnation and a wait-and-see policy in West Beirut and in the South, the NM alienated the Muslim population, and especially the Shî'îs, to the point where armed confrontation with *Amal* became inevitable. The latter claimed to supervise social, political, and, above all, military matters in the southern regions. The battle for control of the crowded suburbs of Burj al-Barajnih at the beginning of July 1981, which then transferred to Nabatiya, and from the 9th onwards to the nearby village of Deir, gave the advantage to the Shî'î organization, which denounced the progressive parties and their Palestinian ally, calling them "oppressors" and even "parasitic foreigners." The following Year, *Amal* showed itself a major force for mobilization against Israeli invasion, particularly south of Beirut (Khaldeh). Although the movement had owed much to the personal charisma and strong personality of Mûsâ Sadr, his disappearing in August 1978 had not, as might have been expected, weakened it. Instead, it conferred on him the image of the "absent imâm" *(imâm ghâ'ib)*, which galvanized the militants during the next few years while their new leader was a follower of Mûsâ Sadr, the member for North Biqâ', Husayn al-Husaynî.

## POLITICAL CULTURE AND COMMUNAL CULTURE

As fratricidal dissension in the NM progressive parties undermined them from within and the optimism and hope of the early war years turned sour, the intellectuals began to reflect on the causes of the failure. According to one theory, it was the language used by the Left—of the Lebanese Left in particular and the Arab Left in general—which was responsible. Those who had sought to change the *Ashûrâ* ceremonies in 1970 had failed to get their message across to the people for the simple reason that they had expressed imported concepts in unfamiliar terminology. In direct contrast, Mûsâ Sadr and the new Shî'î leaders had, it was argued, appealed to the community's very own culture using familiar religious terminology. It was obvious that this criticism was not only directed at the way the message was expressed, but also at its content: merely changing the form would not have made it any more real to the people. For the progressive intellectuals had failed to understand the changing culture in the Arab East since the defeat of 1967, as Elias Khoury pointed out in his reflections on the failure of the NM.[29]

Criticism voiced as the war in Lebanon worsened accused the leaders of the progressive parties of having ignored or underestimated communal cultural values, especially religious and family ones, and of having reduced them to "a superstructure designed to mask class contradictions."[30] But this criticism fails to explain why these same progressive parties had been so successful during the first half of the seventies, when their success was precisely based on a transcommunal ideology. Above all, it is at variance with many other criticisms which seem to be largely well founded, namely, that the various components of the NM and the secularist, Marxist parties allowed themselves to drift into the very sectarian splits and conflicts that they had themselves condemned. This was apparent in their agreeing, as early as October 1975, to negotiate a new intercommunal balance within the Committee for Dialogue based on religious criteria. A few months later, they gave up their demand for the suppression of sectarianism. Soon the war, originally opposing Left against Right, became a war of "Christian conservatives" against "Islamic progressives" and finally a war between Christians and Muslims.

As the Lebanese population was returning to primordial identities and allegiances (which alone withstood the torments of war and even emerged revivified), many intellectuals were tempted to fall back in an ideological about-turn when analyzing the situation. They were prompted in this by the political mobilization of the Lebanese masses, particularly of the Shî'a, along community lines. Thus a new literature flourished, devoted to the harmonious coexistence of the different communities and the economic development under the emirate of Bashirll Shihâb (1788-1840). It also celebrated another period thought to have been blessed by peaceful intercommunal cooperation: that of President Fu'ad Shihâb (1958-1964). In the legal institutional field, the key word used by the partisans of communalism in Lebanon became "consociatio," because they believed that only a consensus between elites of the various communities would be able to safeguard Lebanese unity.[31] They seemed to underestimate the political blockages engendered by this same "consensus," in 1952, 1958, 1970, and 1973, even to ignore the warning of the author of the "consociational model" himself, A. Lijphart, to the effect that a consociational arrangement has the effect of polarizing the society and that it can become a source for corruption, parochialism, conservatism, and immobility.[32]

In search of a theoretical frame in which to analyze this withdrawal on primary solidarities, many scientists turned to the work of the great philosopher Ibn Khaldûn, who studied Arab society at the beginning of the fifteenth century. After him, they discovered, or rediscovered, the power of 'asabiyya, the agnatic solidarity, which binds families together.[33] Simultaneously, some historians and orientalists assumed that the Ottoman system of autonomous administration for religious communities—the millet system—had been the best adapted to the social and cultural structures of the Near East. Their conclusions happened to link up with some theories developed from the beginning of the war among the conservative Christians in the Lebanese Front, precedents of "political Maronitism" and partisans of separate communal administration on a territorial basis. In a way, they also comforted an inclination of some Israeli leaders for splitting the Arab states of the Near East in order to "balkanize" the whole area.[34]

But a full understanding of the shift from class to communal identities requires consideration of two points which are of prime importance in the analysis of the Left's failure and of the success in communal mobilization, not only in the Shî'î South but in all Lebanon and, perhaps, even in the entire Arab region. The first concerns foreign intervention and the evolution of political forces in the Near and Middle East. I have mentioned the failure of the 1974 Geneva Conference as a signal of the outbreak of war in Lebanon. For it is obvious that the size (10,400 sq km), the enclosed geographical situation, and the ethnic balance of Lebanon, all give rise to a close connection between domestic and foreign and even lead to a blurring of the distinction between the two fields. Another example of foreign influence—decisive for the Lebanese Shî'a—is to be found in the events of 1978. Their *imâm* "disappeared" in Libya where he had gone to negotiate the use of a gift from Colonel Khaddhafi to *Amal*. The Iranian revolution against the Shah gained force, as was reported by Iranian *hizbollahîn* in South Lebanon. Israel invaded Jabal 'Amil, the 'Arqûb, and the coast up to Litânî; the Security Council decided to establish the United Nations Interim Force in Lebanon and, simultaneously, intensive Syrian bombing brought a reduction of the zone controlled by the LF. More generally it has to be admitted that every single Middle Eastern state and the two Great Powers sought to undermine or deflect efforts made to change the domination system in Lebanon, since those efforts were a threat to all established regimes. Money played a major role in this patronage of Lebanese political forces as it did in their mobilization along confessional lines, since the 25 million or so dollars paid every month to the militia by foreign powers was a means of controlling the military force of each party and, consequently, their political weight.[35]

But this deviation of a mobilization originally based on a secularist social and political project, and then turned into a sectarian mobilization, was taken up within Lebanese politics by the dominant elites themselves. Change threatened these elites, especially the Maronite leaders, whose community had lost its numerical superiority and was hard hit by the economic modernization crisis.[36] The themes of "Christianity," "Libanity," and "cultural pluralism" were given prominence in order to regain control, first of the Maronite community and then of the entire Lebanese population.[37] The result of this ideological and sectarian mobilization on the battlefield was the spread, as early as 1975, of conflict and even murder and collective massacre on the basis of communal identities. This was symbolized and even made almost "official" by "Black Saturday," December 6th, when tens of innocent civilians were murdered in Beirut.

In spite of, and perhaps even because of, their rigid theoretical stance, the various components of the NM, and even the Marxist parties, obeyed these "rules of the game" imposed on them from outside by their enemy, and accepted to appear as "Muslims," with the OCA and LCP to be labeled as the Shî'a parties. They were thus led to negate their own theses and to annihilate the very foundations on which their mobilization was based. In this respect, the self-criticism of Muhsin Ibrâhîm, like that of Georges Hâwî, are only a belated recognition of phenomena that had already been denounced in West Beirut and in the South as early as 1977.[38] These had become worse between 1979 and 1981, with the wait-and-see policy toward the Sarkis regime, and did not, unfortunately, disappear after the Israeli invasion in the summer of 1982. They consisted of abuse, extortion, and various kinds of sectarian excesses; an inability to assert their independence; and, above all, the persistence, even the spread, of traditional attitudes. Because of the flagrant contradiction between the Left's original intentions and the way it actually acted during the war, "many Amal recruits may in fact have been leftists simply adapting to their difficult environment."[39]

## THE NEW SHÎ'Î AND THEIR STRATEGY

However, the errors and contradictions of the Left, even aggravated by foreign intervention, are not sufficient to explain *Amal*'s success among the
Shî'a and all over Lebanon. Two factors seem to be crucial in the analysis of
the contrast between the uneven success of *Amal* and the uneven failure of the
Left. The first refers to the new social classes on which *imâm* Sadr's movement rested: at the beginning, in 1974–1975, Sadr called the "disinherited"
in his community, and through them every disinherited in the country, whatever his religion. Since that period, Shî'î masses have made up the bulk of
*Amal* forces. As Nabih Berrî told *Le Monde,* "I have a million fighters."[40]
But while still invoking social priorities, the new generation who inherited
the communal movement after *imâm* Sadr's disappearance in 1978 represents
middle classes. They are supported by bourgeois and petit-bourgeois elements, having recently prospered through emigration and education.[41] Nabih
Berrî, a barrister born in Sierra Leone, is particularly representative of these
Shî'î newcomers who speak out in the Higher Council, in Parliament, and in
the southern towns against the traditional oligarchy. This new elite rejects
traditional alignment not only according to family or patronage but also according to ideological beliefs either panarabist or Marxist. It chooses instead
to rely on religious identities in order to achieve an alignment along communal lines.[42]

It can be noticed that this new kind of communal mobilization, definitely
different from traditional mobilization, leads to "class collaboration" within
the Shî'î community on the ground of a vague populist program, *Mithâq
harakat Amal* (*Amal*'s Pact). In fact, this program hardly disguises the ambitions of the new Shî'î of sharing in the economic and political power. For
they simultaneously try to substitute their own authority for the traditional
leadership inside their community, and to supersede the Sunnî leaders on the
national field.

Here again, Nabih Berrî exemplifies the Shî'î evolution. He went to the
inter-Lebanese conferences of Geneva (November 1983) and Lausanne (April
1984), bringing the claims of poor Shî'î masses from the South, and from
Beirut suburbs, who had just successfully confronted the army. He arrived
there with maximalist requests for the abolishment of communal representation and the adoption of the simple majority system. But when he was
granted a portfolio in Rashîd Karâmih's government, he accepted the much
more modest principle of a restoration of the intercommunal balance. Sharing in a new elite consensus might meet his expectations and content the elite
around him, but it is certainly not the answer to mass demands upon the
state. That is why communal consent around these new leaders is finally

precarious and leaves *Amal* leadership vulnerable to either political or religious contest.

This adoption of a new communal strategy is not specific to *Amal*. It should be paralleled with the Maronite "warlords' " hold on the Christian communities and with the ambitions of prosperous mountain dwellers, as Jumayyils of Bickfaya, to become part of the establishment. *Amal* and the younger heads in the Lebanese Forces share a common will to restore a strong state as well as their opposition to Palestinian armed presence in Lebanon. This "affinity" between Maronite conservatives and the Shî'î movement is a blatant manifestation of political segmentarity in Lebanon, because through their cooperation with the Maronites, the Shî'a try to challenge the Sunnî community, who have retained the Muslim leadership in the country.

However, it appears necessary to mention the radical changes which took place on the Lebanese stage during ten years of war, even if the direction and the meaning of these changes do not appear clearly yet. For instance, the destruction of nearly three quarters of the country's industries as early as 1976 obliged many wage earners to turn to the local and regional militias and to become semiproletarian fighters. The new organization of the production and trade around various urban poles resulting from Beirut's division should also be kept in mind, because it laid the basis for a new communal social structure, even more segmented than before. And last but not least, warfare has contributed to reshaping political identities when security became more and more a priority.

Does all this mean that class identities upon which Shî'î masses were being mobilized before the war were a myth? The contrast between class mobilization and communal mobilization has been debated at length.[43] The study of processes at work in South Lebanon confirms this contrast to be a false dilemma when reality is read as a whole in its complexity. Class identities are still precarious because of recent formation; they combine with ethnic and religious identities, which are more essential because they are linked to group survival. In a crisis like the war in Lebanon the logics of essential identities thus tend to supplant the logics of precarious identities.

## A NEW TERRITORIAL COMMUNALISM

In order to fully understand the revival of communal identities in the process of political mobilization in Lebanon, the geographical dimension of each group's strategy has to be taken into account.

As far as the Shî'a are concerned, they have always regarded Lebanon with its 1920 frontiers as a "definite" fatherland, with no Syrian or Palestinian alternative. Even *Amal*'s link to the Syrian army since the beginning of the war, and the military equipment it was supplied with, did not succeed in clientelizing the movement, as the leftist parties had been under successive "national fronts." If we consider Shî'a apart from eastern parts of the country, from Hirmil and the Biqâ', who have been living under direct Damascus control since June 1976, most members of the community are of peasant origin, rooted in their land since the second century of Islam and used to living in a Lebanese political frame. This characteristic explains why, from its creation on, *Amal* steadily claimed the reinforcement of state structures and of its authority all over national territory by development of the army. It should also be noticed that, until 1983, when Shî'î mobs and fighters challenged the regular army in Beirut southern suburbs, the whole community had maintained its obedience to the state and its respect of legality. This attitude clearly opposes the Shî'a to the Sunnîs, whose ideal political reference would rather be a unified Arab state or at least a Near-Eastern "greater Syrian" state, enlarging upon Syria, Jordan, Lebanon, and Palestine (i.e., Israel).

In a different manner, the geographical dimension of the Shî'î project for Lebanon also opposes the Maronites' and this gives the new communal mobilization a special meaning. For, unlike the Maronites in the Lebanese Front, who chose to withdraw back to a "smaller Christian Lebanon" and stood for a new communal federalism on a territorial basis, the Shî'a reject any division between geographical minorities. In this respect, their strategy clearly differs from that of Bashîr Jumayyil who favored in 1980–1982 the reconquest of the entire national territory starting from his Christian stronghold.[44] Against any territorial division, a communal religious authority was issued in July 1984, a *fatwa* (formal legal opinion) forbidding Muslims to sell their land. In the same period the Shî'a began to take a decisive part in the struggle against Israeli occupation. And following their path, they fought Palestinian militias in Beirut suburbs in May–June 1985. Thus, *Amal*'s mobilization appeared positively correlated with a national Lebanese mobilization and its ability to check the country's partition.

*

It is certainly too soon to draw conclusions about the meaning of this new communal mobilization in Lebanon, to compare it with similar communal mobilization all over the Arab East, or to discuss the chances to restore the country's political balance. The part played by *Amal* on the Lebanese stage is still going on, and it meets with successes and setbacks. The movement's successes in 1983 and 1984 over most of its Muslim partners, especially the Sunnîs and the Palestinians, prompted its leaders to demand to be allowed a new political majority, not on a social and electoral but on a communal military basis. Their claim is thus contradictory to an efficient political communalism, which requires a steady balance of power and a minimal elite *consensus*. Shî'a ambitions, when articulated as communal ambitions, lead Lebanon into a dead end and finally to the care for Syrian arbitration, i.e., the ruin of an independent political system.

*Amal*'s setbacks contribute even more to undermining Shî'î collective strategy towards the Lebanese power. For the community search for an economic and political new balance comes up against the Maronite, and Christian as a whole, needs for guarantees and security. It is also impeded by the Sunnîs' will to cling to their first-rank status in such a way that any readjustment of the political system becomes impossible to carry out. As a result, extremist groups develop at the fringe of *Amal,* like the Hizbollahîn, *Amal islâmî,* or the Jihâ. Their common characteristics are a refusal of concessions to non-Muslim communities and a demand for an Islamic constitution applied to every inhabitant of Lebanon, including the Christians, who would then be returned to their Ottoman status of "protected" citizens (*dhimmis*).

These current developments suggest a controversial discourse on the return of communal identities in the political mobilization processes in Lebanon, a discourse which might apply to the phenomenon through the Middle East as a whole. While it can be identified as the mark of an authentic rooting in local cultures, in order to renew the political system this return must also be acknowledged as the consequence of the failure of a more secularist mobilization for the development of a modern relation between state and citizens.

## NOTES

1. A. Dagher, "La grande détresse de l'économie libanaise," *Le Monde Diplomatique,* January 1985, p. 4.

2. Cl. Dubar and S. Nasr, *Les classes sociales au Liban* (Paris: Presses de la Fondation Nationale des Sciences Politiques, 1976), p. 277.

3. S. Nasr, "Les travailleurs de l'industrie manufacturière au Machrek," *Maghreb-Machrek* 92 (1981): 9.

4. E. Picard, "Liban, guerre civile, conflit regional," *Maghreb-Machrek* 73 (Summer 1976): 69, and *Le Monde Diplomatique,* February 1984, p. 12.

5. Cl. Dubar and S. Nasr, *Les classes sociales au Liban,* p. 332.

6. E. Salem, *Modernization Without Revolution. Lebanon's Experience* (Bloomington, Ind.: Indiana University Press, 1973).

7. Daniel Lerner, *The Passing of Traditional Society: Modernizing in the Middle East* (Glencoe, Ill.: Free Press, 1958), and E. M. Koury, *The Crisis in the Lebanese System* (Washington, D. C.: American Enterprise Institute, 1976).

8. A. Messara, *Le modèle politique libanais et sa survie* (Beirut: Librarie orientale, 1983). p. 284.

9. A. Lijphart, *Democracy in Plural Societies: A Comparative Exploration* (New Haven: Yale University Press, 1977), pp. 147–50.

10. D. Rothchild and V. A. Olorunsola (eds.), *State Versus Ethnic Claims* (Boulder, Colo.: Westview Press, 1983), p. 113.

11. E. Picard, "Science politique orientalisme et sociologie au chevet du Li-

ban," *Revue Française de Science Politique* 27 (August 1977): 630–42.

12. R. Chamussy, *Chronique d'une guerre: Le Liban 1975–1977* (Paris: Desclée, 1978), pp. 45–65.

13. E. Picard, "Liban, guerre civile, conflit regional," p. 69.

14. M. Dhahir, "Jabal 'Amil fî Itar il-Tajzi'at il-Isti'mâriyya îil-Mashriq il-'Arabi [Jabal Amil in the colonial division of the Arab East]," in *Safahât min Târîkh Jabal 'Amil* (Beirut: Dar al-Farâbî, 1979), p. 117.

15. A. Kh. Khalil, "Junûb Lubân bayna l-dawla wal-thawra" [South Lebanon between the state and the revolution], *Dirâsât 'Arabiyya* 4 (February 1975): 63.

16. T. Jaber, *Chi'ites et pouvoir politique au Liban (1967–1974): contribution a une approche socio-religieuse* (Paris: IIIe cycle Thesis multig, 1980), pp. 158–63.

17. J. Aucagne, "L'Imam Moussa Sadr et la communauté chiite," *Travaux et Jours* 53 (October–December 1974): 34.

18. M. Yared, "Le reveil du Chiisme libanais," *L'Orient-le Jour,* 19 March 1974.

19. *Al-Nahar,* 18 March 1974.

20. A. Kh. Khalil, "Junûb Lubnân bayna l-dawla wal-thawra."

21. Th. Sicking and Sh. Khairallah, "The Shî'a Awakening in Lebanon: A Search for Radical Change in a Traditional Way," in *Cemam Report 1974: Vision and Revision in Arab Society* (Beirut: Dar al-Mashriq, 1975), pp. 107–09.

22. Yves Schemeil, *Sociologie du système politique libanais* (Grenoble, France: Université des Science Sociales, 1976), p. 326.

23. T. Jaber, "Le discours chi'ite sur le pouvoir," *Peuples Méditerranéens* 20 (July–September 1982): 77.

24. R. Rizkallah, *Contribution à une approche psychosociologique d'un rite chez les Chi'ites du Liban-Sud* (Paris: University of Paris VII. Thèse de 3e cycle, 1977), p. 193.

25. *al-Hayât,* 12 February 1974.

26. *al-Qadhaya l'Zirâ'iyya Fî Lubnân fi dhaw al-Mârksiyya* [The agricultural question in Lebanon in Marxist light] (Beirut: Matâbi' al-Imak, 1974), pp. 91–121.

27. Speech by Mûsâ Sadr in Yâtir, February 3, 1974.

28. *al-Hayât* (Beirut), 12 February 1974, and *Mithâq Harakat Amal* (Amal Pact), 1975, Art. 7.

29. Elias Khoury, "A Question of Culture and a Question of Occupation," *al-Tarîq* (Spring 1983).

30. T. Mitri, "Interview with T. Mitri," *Afrique-Asie* (15 November 1976).

31. A. Messara, *Le modéle politique libanais et sa survie.*

32. A. Lijphart, *Democracy in Plural Societies,* pp. 25 and 96.

33. A. Cheddadi, "Le système du pouvoir en Islam d'après Ibn Khaldûn," *Annales E. S. C.* 3–4 (May–August 1980): 534–50.

34. A. Perlmutter, "Begin's Rhetoric and Sharon's Tactics," *Foreign Policy* (September 1982): 67–83, and G. Corm, "La balkanisation du Proche-Orient entre le mythe et la realité," *Le Monde Diplomatique* (January 1983).

35. *International Herald Tribune,* 18 May 1982.

36. Cl. Dubar and S. Nasr, *Les classes sociales au Liban,* pp. 332–33.

37. P. Kemp, "La stratégie de Bachir Gamayel," *Herodote* 29–30 (1983): 55–82.

38. M. Ibrahim, *I-Harb wa-Tajribat il-Harakat il-Wataniyya Lubnâniyya* [The war and the national movement experience] (Beirut: Bayrut al-Masa', 1984, and *al Tarîq*, January 1983).

39. J. Stork, "Report from Lebanon," *Merip Report* 118 (October 1983): 3–13.

40. *Le Monde Diplomatique*, February 1984, p. 16.

41. S. Kassir, "L'affirmation des Chi'ites lebanais," *Le Monde Diplomatique*, May 1985.

42. F. Khuri, *From Village to Suburb: Order and Change in Greater Beirut* (Chicago: University of Chicago Press, 1975), p. 234.

43. J. Leca, "Pour une analyse comparative de systèmes politiques méditerranéens," *Revue Française de Science Politique* 28 (August–October 1977): 577–81.

44. P. Kemp, "La stragégie de Bachir Gamayel."

# BIBLIOGRAPHY

Aucagne, J. "L'Imam Moussa Sadr et la communauté chiite." *Travaux et Jours* 53 (October–December 1974).

Borthwick, B. M. "The Islamic Sermon as a Channel of Political Communication." *Middle East Journal* 21 (1967).

Bourgey, A. "Beyrouth, Ville Eclatée." *Herodote* (Winter 1980): 5–31.

Central Committee of the LCP. "Excerpts from the IVth National Congress Resolution." *al-Tarîq* 4 (August 1979): 8.

Chamussy, R. *Chronique d'une guerre: Le Liban 1975–1977.* Paris: Desclée, 1978.

Cheddadi, A. "Le système du pouvoir en Islam d'après Ibn Khaldûn." *Annales E. S. C.* 3–4 (May–August 1980): 534–50.

Chrara, W. *Transformations d'une manifestation religieuse dans un village du Liban-Sud (Ashura).* Beirut: Publication of the Centre de Recherches, Institut des Sciences sociales-Lebanese univ., 1968.

Conclusions of the Meeting of the LCP Central Committee. *Liban; deux années de guerre. Bilan et perspectives.* Paris: n.p., 1977.

"Conference on 'Achourâ." *Cahiers de l'Ecole Superieure des Lettres n.5.* Beirut, 1974.

Corm, G. "La balkanisation du Proche-Orient entre le mythe et la realité." *Le Monde Diplomatique* (January 1983).

Dagher, A. "La grande détresse de l'économie libanaise." *Le Monde Diplomatique* (January 1985): 4.

Dhahir, M. "Jabal 'Amil fî Itâr il-Tajzi'at il-Isti' mâriyya lil-Mashriq il-'Arabî [Jabal Amil in the colonial division of the Arab East]." In *Safahât Min Târikh Jabal 'Amil*, pp. 107–31. Beirut: Dar al-Farâbî, 1979.

Dubar, Cl., and S. Nasr. *Les classes sociales au Liban.* Paris: Presses de la Fondation Nationale des Sciences Politiques, 1976.

Farah, T. "The Modernizing Individual in a Consociational Democracy: Lebanon as a Case Study." *Indian Journal of Political Studies* (January 1979): 24–26.

Faris, W. *At-Ta'dudiyya Fî Lubnan* [Pluralism in Lebanon]. Kaslik: Imprimerie Arabe, 1979.

Frangieh, R. "Sectarianism and Class Division in Lebanon." *Plural Societies* 11 (Fall 1980): 71–80.

Girard, R. *La violence et le sacre.* Paris: Grasset, 1972.

Hawi, G. "Israeli Invasion in Lebanon and its Consequences." *al-Tarîq* (December 1982).

Haydar, A. *Min Jinif ila Luzân* (From Geneva to Lausanne). Publication of Amal Political Bureau, 1984.

Ibrahim, M. *I-Harb wa-Tajribat il-Harakat il-Wataniyya Lubnâniyya* [The war and the national movement experience]. Beirut: Bayrut al-Masâ', 1984.

"Interview with Shaikh Muhammad Mahdî Shams al-Din." *al-Hawâdith*, 23 January 1976, pp. 20–22.

Jaber, T. "Chi'ites et pouvoir politique au Liban (1967–1974): contribution a une approche socio-religieuse." l'Université de Paris III, troisième cycle, thesis, 1980.

_____. "Le discours chi'ite sur le pouvoir." *Peuples Méditerranéens* 20 (July–September 1982).

Kassir, S. "L'affirmation des Chi'ites libanais." *Le Monde Diplomatique* (May 1985).

Kemp, P. "La stratégie de Bachir Gamayel." *Herodote* 29–30 (1983): 55–82.

Khalaf, S. "Primordial Ties and Politics in Lebanon." *Middle East Journal* 4 (April 1968): 243–69.

Khalil, A. Kh. "Junûb Lubnân bayna l-dawla wal-thawra" [South Lebanon between the state and the revolution]. *Dirâsât 'Arabiyya* 4 (February 1975).

Khuri, F. *From Village to Suburb: Order and Change in Greater Beirut.* Chicago: University of Chicago Press, 1975.

Koury, E. M. *The Crisis in the Lebanese System.* Washington, D. C.: American Enterprise Institute for Public Policy Research, 1976.

Leca, J. "Pour une analyse comparative des systèmes politiques méditerranéens." *Revue Française de Science Politique* 28 (August–October 1977): 557–81.

Lerner, Daniel. *The Passing of Traditional Society: Modernizing in the Middle East.* Glencoe, Ill.: Free Press, 1958.

Lijphart, A. *Democracy in Plural Societies: A Comparative Exploration.* New Haven: Yale University Press, 1977.

Messara, A. *Le modèle politique libanais et sa survie.* Beirut: Librarie orientale, 1983.

*Mithâq Harakat Amal* (Amal Pact). 1975.

Nasr, S. "Les travailleurs de l'industrie manufacturière au Machrek." *Maghreb-Machrek* 92 (1981): 7–24.

Norton. A. R. "Political Violence and Shi'a Factionalism in Lebanon." *Middle East Insight* 3 (1983): 9–16.

Perlmutter, A. "Begin's Rhetoric and Sharon's Tactics." *Foreign Policy* (September 1982): 67–83.

Picard, E. "Liban, guerre civile, conflit regional." *Maghreb-Machrek* 73 (Summer 1976): 53–70.

_____. "Science politique orientalisme et sociologie au chevet du Liban." *Revue Française de Science Politique* 27 (August 1977): 630–42.

"Political, Social and Economic Reform." Working paper of the Supreme Shi'i Islamic Council. Translated from *al-Nahâr,* 28 November 1975.

*al-Qadhaya l'Zirâ'iyya Fî Lubnân fi dhaw al-Mârksiyya* [The agricultural question in

Lebanon in Marxist light]. Beirut: Matâbi' al-Imak, 1974.

Rammal, H. *al-nuzûh al-Sukkânî min al-Junûb ilâ Bayrût* [Migration from the south to Beirut]. Beirut: Lebanese University Institut de Sciences Sociales, 1973.

Rizkallah, R. *Contribution à une approache psychosociologique d'un rite chez les Chi'ites du Liban-Sud.* Paris: University of Paris VII. These de 3e cycle, 1977.

Rothchild, D., and V. A. Olorunsola. eds. *State Versus Ethnic Claims.* Boulder, Colo.: Westview Press, 1983.

Rouleau, E. "Les chi'ites veulent devenir des citoyens a part entière." *Le Monde,* 12–13 February 1984.

Salem, E. *Modernization Without Revolution. Lebanon's Experience.* Bloomington, Ind.: Indiana University Press, 1973.

Schemeil, Yves. "La crise libanaise. Du pacte national au pacte laique." *Maghreb-Machrek* 95 (Winter 1982): 30–55.

————. *Sociologie du système politique libanais.* Grenoble, France: Université des Sciences Sociales, 1976.

Sicking, Th., and Sh. Khairallah. "The Shi'a Awakening in Lebanon: A Search for Radical Change in a Traditional Way." In *Cemam Report 1974: Vision and Revision in Arab Society,* pp. 97–130. Beirut: Dar al-Mashrig, 1975.

Stork, J. "Report from Lebanon." *Merip Report* 118 (October 1983): 3–13.

Yared, M. "Le reveil du Chiisme libanais." *L'Orient-le Jour* 19–26 (March 1974).

*L'Orient-le Jour* (Beirut), February 1973, February 1974, February 1975.

*al-Hayât* (Beirut), March 1970, February 1974, February 1975.

*al-Nahâr (Beirut).*

# 9 The Iranian Revolution: A Crisis of Social-Science Theory

Martha Brill Olcott

The departure in flight of Shah Mohammad Reza Pahlavi in January 1979 was a tremendous jolt for those who advocated the development and maintenance of a pro-American Western-style regime in Iran. The Shah's downfall, as well as the consequent assumption of power by Ayatullah S. Ruhollah Musavi Khomeini, who instituted an Islamic Republic as the successor regime in Teheran, stunned and angered American citizens and diplomats. For American scholars it created yet another set of problems, as this largely unpredicted event was not easily explained by Western theories of nationality and nationalism, which are predicated on an assumption that the modern polity will rest on secular foundations, and once instituted, a secular society will not easily revert to clerical rule and a solely religious definition of community and culture.

In many ways the Iranian revolution posed equally troublesome problems for students of Oriental studies in the Soviet Union, long used to viewing religion as a negative social phenomenon and finding the coincidence of conservative religious (and especially Muslim) values with pro-American and anti-Soviet policies so frequently that the exceptional divergences did not threaten the explanatory power of the decades-old commonplace Soviet interpretations of the Marxist theory of religion. For the popularly led revolution in Iran did not surprise Soviet theorists, the demise of a pro-American monarchic regime was to be expected, and the failure of man but a confirmation of the natural laws that are asserted to govern all social events, as first noted and elaborated upon by both Marx and Lenin. What did cause them difficulty was that the culmination of the bourgeois monarchic phase in Iran had not neatly led to the assumption of power by socialist forces. This in itself was not unprecedented or even unusual in the Third World. What did differentiate the revolutionary outcome in Iran from events elsewhere was the takeover of

179

power by a conservative religious leadership who were not only anti-American but who were also antiimperialistic, i.e., vehemently opposed to the leading role played by American business and military interests in the Iranian economy. Moreover, the Iranian revolutionaries were committed to an egalitarian strategy of economic development. Whereas Khomeini and his Provisional Revolutionary Councils were clearly determined to institute a regime that advocated and enforced policies that were predicated on a rather narrow interpretation of Shi'i religious doctrines, they were also strongly committed to running the economy and equally importantly the foreign policy of Iran according to policies similar to those that had earned secular rulers in other developing societies the title "progressive" and the right to receive massive amounts of Soviet economic and military aid.

Although the causes of consternation were quite different for the Soviet and American scholars, what the earlier failures of scholarship led to in both countries was in fact remarkably similar, a thoroughgoing reexamination of the relationship of Islam and nationalism, in Iran in particular and in Muslim countries more generally. Thus, in the wake of the Iranian revolution, while the ability to do fieldwork has been sharply curtailed, there has nonetheless been a marked increase in publication by Iranian experts and students of Islamic political thought, as Americans and Soviets alike struggle to make sense of the events that led to the Shah's downfall and to the subsequent institutionalization of rule by the 85-year-old Khomeini, as well as to try to anticipate the events that his inevitable forthcoming death could bring.

There is more agreement in the writings of the Soviet and American scholarly communities than one might ordinarily expect. This is particularly true of assessments of Khomeini and his supporters' manipulation of events to engineer his takeover rather than that of one of the other major spiritual leaders, such as Ayatullah S. Mohammad-Kazem Shariatmadari, and of how he precluded shared rule with a devout lay figure like Mehdi Bazargan. The Soviets of course see the underlying causes of the revolution in the economic and social injustices of the Shah and his supporters, whereas the Americans place no blame on the Shah's pro-Western philosophy of rule but see the underlying contradictions of prerevolutionary Iranian society as a product of the Shah's faulty understanding and application of Western theories as well as his own personal limitations as a ruler. But although the Soviet and the American scholars differ as to whether the underlying causes of the revolution were economic (in the Soviet writings) or political (in the case of the Americans), both groups of scholars agree that the immediate reason for the Shah's downfall is linked to his underestimation of the potentially political rule of the Shi'i clergy and their ability to enlist mass support through a manipulation of religio-cultural symbols; that despite his best efforts, Mohammad-Reza Shah failed to wrest control of religious symbolism from the *madrasas* and clerical establishment and wed it to the Pahlavi dynasty and Iranian throne. And the Shah's biases in this regard were mirrored in a relative lack of concern for religious questions in both American and Soviet social-science scholarship in the 1970s.

The Iranian revolution marked the end of the intellectual isolation of students of Islamic jurisprudence from their more social-science oriented colleagues. Iranian specialists in both countries have sought to increase their knowledge of the development of Shi'i thought in Iran from the period of the Islamic founding to the present day. American scholars have had two distinct advantages over their Soviet counterparts in the quest to master the subtleties of Iranian religious life. The first advantage is that a large number of Iranian scholars fled to the West after the revolution, whereas few if any Persian scholars relocated in the Soviet Union. Some of these émigré scholars have produced distinguished studies on the nature and practice of Iranian Islam, and others have contributed by translating previously unavailable works of classical and modern religious literature.[1] These Iranian scholars have allowed the non-Muslim Western reader to gain a sense of how the political events of the Shah's final years appear to a believer. Although the Soviet Union has a number of distinguished Islamicists of Muslim extraction, these individuals have either turned from the faith or are definitionally precluded from publishing sympathetic first-person accounts of the relationship between religious belief and political action. However, over the last five years great strides have been made in the quality of scholarship on Iranian religion within both the Soviet Union and the United States.

The studies on the nature of modern Iranian religio-political development have shown that there are several tensions between the assumptions of Western theories of national development and the pattern of development in Iran. Western theorists assume that the process of national consolidation is a slow one, led by secularly educated elites who achieve and then seek to maintain mass support. There is an assumption that this elite has a shared set of values designed to maintain national independence. Their goals are a direct offshoot of Western intellectual and political development and are predicated on a commitment to rights of individual self-expression within a unified nation-state whose government preserves individual liberties while assuring economic autarky and self-sustaining economic growth.[2]

It is assumed that a commitment to these goals can be instilled through education, even if the youth come to their schooling from traditional systems that do not share the Western Judeo-Christian heritage that produced the above-stated political goals.[3] Certainly many of the foreign-educated Iranian elite shared the commitment to a pro-Western model of development that was advocated by the Shah, and when they broke with him it was because of the excesses of the Shah's policies and not because they supported the Islamic model of development advocated by Khomeini and his supporters. But what Western theorists seem to underemphasize is that individuals who come from a traditional society have already been socialized with a distinct, and oftentimes both complex and coherent, alternate set of values, which they may seek to challenge by exposing themselves to a Western education, but which they need not wish to wholly discard.

An Iranian youth who had completed secondary education at home would already have gained a distinct set of political values linked to both Iranian history and Shi'i Islam. His religious education would not have exposed him to the existence of individual political liberties like freedom of speech, press, and assembly, but would have concentrated on the meaning of leadership (*imāmah*), custodianship (*wilāyah*), and infallibility (*'ismah*) of those who are divinely inspired. Moreover he would have been taught that there is no such thing as a distinctly political sphere, but that justice should be dispensed only by those knowledgeable in Quran, Hadith, and Sunnāh.

Western students of nationalism have assumed that there must be a recreation or redefinition of a nation's past to make it supportive of the goals of the modern nation-state, a "transvaluation of values."[4] This entails elaboration of founding legends and a reinterpretation of some primary religious teachings to make the modern state appear the preordained successor to some previous regime whose legitimacy was predicated on religious criteria. However, the view of religion held by most Western (as well as Soviet) social scientists is a cynical one, that religion is instrumental and not inspirational, and they discount the possibility that a modernizing elite could be committed to the preservation of a civil order whose code of morality was inspired by religious thought. Ali Shariati, a French-educated physician and major Teheran countercultural figure until his mysterious death in 1977, was just such an anomalous figure. His goal was to redefine the curriculum at the *Husayniyah Irshad* (the successor to the Monthly Religious Society) to introduce the subjects taught in traditional *madrasas*, but to teach them from an analytic position inspired by Western sociology rather than from the traditional ideological perspective. Shariati sought to achieve the modernization of Iran, while maintaining a popular commitment to Iranian Islamic values, and felt that this could best be accomplished by a secular regime which was under close and direct religious guardianship.

Finally, the Western analysts erred in their analysis of Iranian political history and underestimated the impact of the 1906 Constitutional Revolution. The solution not taken often comes to overshadow the resolution that has been achieved, and in this case an Islamic Republic was called for at the turn of the century and its religiously inspired basis was justified in numerous theological tracts. This made it part of one possible founding myth for a modern Iranian state, and virtually the only myth that was not tarnished by the nearly sixty years of rule by the Pahlavi family. Hence it could be rediscovered and glorified by the generation of youth of the 1970s, who could see in Khomeini a chance to achieve this untried vision of rule and a possibility of fusing religious authority to the rather inchoate ideas of the now martyred Shariati.

Because of all these theoretical contradictions, American scholars have found it difficult to reconcile Western theories of nationalism and national movements with the events that took place in Iran in the late 1970s, and so they have looked to other examples from social-science theory to use in their postmortems of the Shah's downfall. There has been no uniformity of view as to what conceptual framework has the greatest explanatory value in describing the relationship between religion and politics in Iran. R. Hrair Dekmejian presents a good argument for evaluating the Iranian revolution in terms of a failure of the Shah's developmental model. He maintains that the Shah failed to achieve a sufficient institutionalization of authority to sustain and support his economic and social programs, which in turn led to a rise in, and then consequent failure to satisfy, popular expectations. Decreasing popular hopes led eventually to a rejection of the philosophic underpinnings of the Shah's programs, and the Iranian masses sought to replace the Shah's pro-Western and heavily pre-Islamic definition of Iranian nationalism with a political culture and leadership that stressed the fusion of Iranian culture with Islamic teachings, with the latter assured primacy in determining the acceptable elements of the pre-Islamic Iranian culture. Dekmejian thus relegates religion to the role of an also-ran, and depicts a population turning to religion for inspiration when secular values ceased to be a source of gratification.[5]

Michael Fischer, an anthropologist by training, explains Khomeini's successful takeover and institutionalization of authority as a consequence of his unique political style, a form of charismatic leadership that manipulates and accentuates religio-political symbols long associated with Iranian Islam. The first of these, Khomeini's projection as a marginal ethnic, is a rare recognition of the political power that rested with the national minority population of Iran. Fischer asserts that Khomeini often emphasized his own mixed ethnic background. In fact he is pure Persian, but his grandfather lived much of his life in India, and Khomeini himself used the pseudonym Hindi in poetry written in his youth.[6] This projection of ethnic marginality certainly helped broaden Khomeini's appeal, but the large Azeri community remained firmly under the control of rival Ayatullah Shariatmadari. Fischer places great emphasis on Khomeini's manipulation of the imagery of martyrdom, drawing parallels between events in Khomeini's own life, such as the murder of both his father and his eldest son, and the life of the martyr of Karbala. He also credits Khomeini with increasing his popular appeal by dabbling in mysticism and choosing to lead a public life as an ascetic.[7] One is continually presented throughout Fischer's writings with a picture of Khomeini as a political actor who self-consciously manipulates religious imagery, as opposed to the picture which Khomeini has used the state-controlled Iranian media to project at home and abroad, one of a divinely inspired figure, a *wiliyat-i-faqih*, supreme overseer and judge, selflessly responding to a popular call that he spend his old age in guiding his country and inspiring devout Muslims everywhere.[8]

Marvin Zonis blames the Iranian revolution on a failure of political leadership and seeks his theoretical explanation of the events that led to the Shah's downfall in an application of political leadership theory. He criticizes existing Western scholarship for failing to adequately consider the political role played by opposition leaders (especially Khomeini just prior to the revolution). He attacks them for ignoring the actual structure that the opposition organization developed, for minimizing the potential for revolutionary mobilization that was latent among the city dwellers, and for failing to isolate the political actions actually taken by the Shah to combat the mounting opposition, concentrating instead on the manifestations of social protest.[9] Zonis gives little credence to the argument that there was something inherent in either the economic or the social policies that were pursued by the Shah to make the revolution inevitable. He concludes that the Shah could have prevented the revolution had he been more politically astute.[10] Zonis thus tacitly rejects the argument that the Shah's relationship to the Islamic beliefs of his subjects made a religious challenge to his authority preordained.

Jerrold Green is a young American scholar who owes much of his understanding of events in Iran to Zonis's guidance, and this influence is apparent in his recent book. He too does not see the Iranian revolution as inevitable, but attributes it to the weakness of the Shah as a policymaker. He specifically finds fault with the Shah's attempts to reduce the perceived spiritual authority of the clerical establishment by presenting himself as a mystical figure with divinely inspired powers of miraculous recovery.[11] Green too shares Zonis's perception that the Shah's understanding of the latent political power of Iranian Islam was not at fault, but his error was one of political misjudgment, of underestimating how far an aggrieved clerical establishment would go in the attempt to restore their perceived loss of prestige. Moreover, Green argues that the Shah further exacerbated the situation by providing the clerical establishment with a large and receptive audience to sympathize with their grievances, the *bazaari*. The Shah's strategy of encouraging economic development through the use of large businesses and banks made this large and formerly quite powerful economic interest group socially and politically redundant, and hence more likely to take to the streets in protest if some unifying cause could be found. Green sees the Iranian revolution as produced by a crisis of political participation. He describes a popular desire for justice, equity, and economic involvement combined with opportunity, combined with a mass perception that the Shah had not and would not accommodate the desire of Iranians to go from subjects to citizens, a prescription reminiscent of Almond and Verba's *Civic Culture*.[12]

American social scientists may have foresworn theories of nationalism in trying to categorize the events that led to the Iranian revolution, but they have sought to portray the revolution as consistent with social-science theory, often casting around widely in order to find an appropriate theoretical explanation. In most cases such theories have provided a less than perfect fit, which probably explains why no single theoretical perspective has been adopted by

Iranian specialists more generally. However, most scholars[13] have been reluctant to embrace an explanation of the Iranian revolution that is predicated on the dogmatic or doctrinal content of the Islamic faith in general and its particular manifestation in Iran. One exception to this is Daniel Pipes, an historian, who sees the misguided economic and social policies of the Shah as the catalyst of the revolution, but implies that in Muslim societies, once challenged, the Western developmental model is likely to mutate in the direction of a religious response.[14]

The Iranian revolution has proved equally problematic for Soviet scholars and theoreticians, requiring them to reexamine many of their assumptions about political development in Iran and the relationship between Islam and politics more generally. Here too the theoretical literature on nationalism and national consciousness was little help in explaining post-facto the events in Iran, and was absolutely no help in predicting them. Since the late 1960s Soviet scholars, particularly ethnographers and social theorists, have greatly expanded the study of nationality and national consciousness. While most of these studies have focused on the development of national relations within socialist societies in general and the Soviet Union in particular, a broader theoretical framework has been developed which is intended to have universal application. The agenda for most recent discussions on ethnicity and politics has been set by Iulian Bromlei, director of the Institute of Ethnography in Moscow. He offers a theory of *etnos* in lieu of the concept of national identity. Bromlei maintains that ethnic consciousness may exist on one of several levels. An individual may perceive himself as part of a tribe, a nationality (*narodnost'*), a nation (*natsiia*), or all three. An individual considers himself as part of a distinct cultural group, with the criterion for membership being self-selection.[15]

Certainly, as Bromlei's writings make clear, the central focus for Soviet scholars is the question of national self-definition, and with Andropov, Chernenko, and now Gorbachev's most insistent chiding that scholars must ask socially useful questions, they have concentrated on how this national self-identity and cultural consciousness can be changed to introduce an international identity. Their focus is on the process of self-selection and the perception of cultural or national uniqueness with far less attention being given to the content of culture. Culture is malleable, or must be made so, and in such a conceptual framework religion is conceived of as but one manifestation of cultural or ethnic uniqueness, depending upon the context, without any preordained values or eternal right of replication in succeeding generations.

One must remember that the Soviet Union is officially an atheistic state with legal rights to the believer grudgingly but constitutionally granted. However party, state, and the educational-socialization networks are all actively engaged in trying to convince the Soviet citizens that religious doctrines are obsolete and predicated on superstition, having little claim to be positively received by a population that is enjoying the fruits of socialism. Since the celebrations marking the fiftieth anniversary of the formation of the USSR in 1972, a succession of First Secretaries have gone on record as accepting the idea that cultural differences are real and self-perpetuating, and even that national differences are likely to be with us far into the future, long after class distinctions have ceased to exist. It is possible for the party to embrace such ideas without violating Marxist-Leninist precedent, because it then goes on to argue that all cultures have progressive and archaic features and the national minorities of the Soviet Union must strive to preserve and share among themselves the progressive socialist values while actively striving for archaic conservative values to disappear and not be transmitted to the next generation.

Soviet scholars make quite clear that religion must be classed with such archaic values, and the customs and rituals of all the faiths still surviving in the Soviet Union, of which Islam is certainly one, must be shown up to their practitioners as what they are, vestiges of the past. This position is explicitly argued in Soviet theoretical writings on the relationship of Islam to politics. This literature, a good example of which is the work *Islam and Nation* by N. Ashirov, is usually intended for students of the Soviet Islamic community. Ashirov, and his colleagues and disciples, have as their primary function to dispel what they allege is the misinformed idea of some Muslims, that their Islamic faith is a basis of national consciousness. To Ashirov and to virtually all Soviet scholars, national consciousness, itself transient, can only be based on ethnic, cultural, or linguistic bases.[16] Religious identification may be a common bond within a society, but the sense of national community can and will be maintained long after religious self-identification has ceased to be characteristic of the population.

Given these shared value assumptions of the Soviet academic community, the Islamic revolution in Iran must have been perceived as a theoretically interesting yet extremely disturbing event. Here was a bourgeois society that underwent a popular anti-Western revolution and ended up introducing a clerically led economically progressive regime. Soviet scholars could and did study Khomeini and his policies, but his revolution also demanded that they question many of their long-standing assumptions as to the definitionally conservative nature of religion, to look again both at Marx and at Islam as found in Iran, to query whether the Islamic faith could ever manifest progressive features, and if so under what social and political conditions.

Although the Soviet Iranian experts may not have had a sufficient theoretical base for reexamining the events in Iran, they did have a strong factual base from which to work—a nearly century-old tradition of Russian study of Iran. This sound foundation notwithstanding, Soviet scholars of contemporary Iran did little better in forecasting the downfall of the Shah than did their American colleagues. Prior to the late 1970s most scholars failed to see Khomeini as the central religious figure, arguing as did Kliashtorina that

there were a number of competing religious leaders and religious philoso-
phies.[17] She chose to focus her 1978 article on S. Hossein Nasr, a Sufi writer
who was closely associated with the Shah and the Pahlavi family. If there was
an official Soviet scholarly position, it was that religion was an important
legitimator of the bourgeois nationalistic regime of the Shah, and so Iran was
yet another instance of religion being in the service of negative social ideals.
This is certainly the stance taken by Doroshenko in her thorough 1975 study
on *Shiite Clergy in Contemporary Iran*. She admits that the clerics of Qum,
led at the time of writing by Ayatullah Mortaza Motahhari, are philosophi-
cally distinct from those clerics that were grouped around the Shah, but
Doroshenko attacks the Qum group as being insensitive to the moral superiority of the socialist East, seeing it as no better than the morally corrupt
West.[18] Doroshenko does admit that the younger generation in Qum could be
distinguished from their elders by the strength of their convictions, but she
too fails to appreciate their revolutionary potential.[19] In general Soviet
scholars continued up until the eve of the 1979 revolution to counsel their
readers that the most volatile stress points within the Pahlavi regime were
those fallen victim to the Shah's unjust economic policies and the politically
disenfranchised national minorities.

When the Iranian revolution occurred and the Ayatullah seemed firmly in
command, the Soviet academic community appears to have realized that not
only had they failed to anticipate the events of Teheran but that unless they
changed prevailing academic norms Soviet scholars could attribute the Iranian revolution to popular desire for an Islamic society only at professional
risk. But in 1979 and 1980 there was lots of evidence to suggest that a revival
of Islamic fundamentalism was beginning, and the politicization of Islam
more generally seemed in the offing. So much more appeared at stake than
merely writing perceptive histories of the Iranian revolution and accurate
chronicles of Khomeini's rule. Keeping in mind the need for Soviet social
scientists to provide an accurate and adequate analytic basis for Soviet
foreign-policymakers, such intellectual breakthrough was required if the Soviet scholars were to respond to the challenges posed by the changing religio-
political climate in the Middle East.

This breakthrough came in the form of the article titled "Islam and the
Process of Social Development in the Countries of the Foreign East," written
by Evgeny Primakov, Director of the Institute of Oriental Studies From 1977
until late 1985.[20] Primakov established an analytic position which is still in
vogue, having achieved official recognition when incorporated in Brezhnev's
address before the Twenty-Sixth Party Congress. Primakov argued that Islam
can be a progressive social force when it is characterized by a union of
clerics and left-wing forces, when the assumption of rule by Islamic authorities may in fact hasten the development of a socialist society. However, if
Islam is controlled by reactionary anti-Soviet forces, then a takeover by religious authorities will lead to the further entrenchment of conservative forces,

and so must be avoided. According to Primakov, a good example of an attempted conservative Islamic revolution is the guerrilla movement in Afghanistan. Primakov defends his theory as consistent with Marxist teachings. Because of their unusual pattern of economic development, he argues, in most Muslim societies the alienation of the workers from the means of production has been achieved in the absence of a large working class or widespread working-class consciousness. In addition to this, the introduction of capitalism in these societies has often proceeded without an accompanying secularization of society, and so national cadre has had to use the vocabulary of religion to achieve the politicization of the masses.[21] Primakov sees the union of progressive left-wing forces and Muslim clerics as temporary but nonetheless characteristic of the current phase of socio-political development in much of the Middle East.

Primakov's notion of the two sides of Islam, progressive and conservative, was widely disseminated and adopted in Soviet scholarly journals and in outlets of the popular media. It received particularly wide press in the Muslim regions of the Soviet Union. An article entitled "Under the Green Banner of Islam" appeared in several Russian-language Central Asian newspapers on 7 December 1981 and was quickly followed by companion pieces in the local-language press, thus enabling the regime to boast to their Muslim population that despite the fact that the Red Army was bogged down in Afghanistan the Soviet Union should more properly be regarded as the defender of Islam, provided of course that religion was not being used as a shield for conservative or reactionary social and economic interests.[22]

Practical concerns of maintaining public morale aside, Primakov's 1980 article and subsequent pieces eased analytic restrictions which had constrained scholars of Muslim societies. During the first few years following the Iranian revolution literally dozens of articles and books appeared which dealt with the socio-political role of Islam in Iran as well as in other Middle Eastern societies. Many of these pieces strongly endorsed the proposition that the revolution in Iran was clerically inspired, a product of Shi'i dogma and the unusual and prominent position occupied by the clergy in the social structure as an offshoot of Iran's uneven economic development;[23] that Khomeini and his followers were on a firm antiimperialist course, committed to an egalitarian strategy of development, and in search of a third course of development that neither condemns capitalism nor embraces socialism but advocates "Islam is all"; and that this makes him a fitting heir of the antiimperialistic traditions of Shi'i reformism.[24]

However when Khomeini began to sporadically persecute the Tudeh party in 1982 and more vociferously in 1983, when Tudeh members began to be arrested and tried, many Soviet academics who had previously praised the progressive qualities of Khomeini now first began to depict him as having a rational and an irrational side and then to attack him as a representative of the conservative qualities of Islam.[25] Khomeini, it is now again stressed, after

Soviet scholars had temporarily ceased reminding us of this fact, is only one of many religious leaders in Iran, and his assumption of a monopoly of jurisprudential decision-making, by self-declaration as *wilayat-i-faqih,* is subject to dispute among rival ayatullahs on grounds of personal fitness and the doctrinal validity of the institution itself.[26] Probably the most serious criticism was offered by S. Agaev in a recent article in *Aziia i Afrika segnodia.* After a thoroughgoing review of Soviet writings on Iran published since 1979, Agaev concludes that while the February revolution was undoubtedly religiously inspired and a religiously led culmination of popular desire for a progressive path of development, nonetheless many of the goals of the revolution have been compromised by a pattern of institutionalization of clerical rule that is reminiscent of the structure of authority characteristic of the Shah. Thus to Agaev, the Iranian revolution, itself a religiously inspired response to the conditions of class struggle, has not led to a diminution of the class struggle, and so this revolution, like many of its predecessors from the bourgeois stage of history, is destined to be a temporary phenomenon.[27]

Although Khomeini's popularity among Soviet scholars has begun to fade, the impact that his revolution made on the analytic frameworks employed by Soviet scholars is likely to be a more lasting one. Primakov has reiterated that the "double-edged" character of Islam makes it possible for Khomeini to easily go from being a progressive to a conservative figure, because ultimately the alliance between religious and progressive forces must be a temporary one.[28] While Primakov reminds his readers that only internationalist consciousness can be enduring and that while Islam may serve as the foundation of a social or political movement it is not a valid category for individual self-identity, nonetheless he exhorts Soviet scholars to make a more thorough study of the appeal of religion, rather than to simply chronicle the evolution of Islamic movements.[29]

In his criticisms, Primakov has highlighted the primary weakness of Soviet scholarship of postrevolutionary Iran. It is not the politicization of scholarship but its rather one-dimensional quality that is ultimately most objectionable. Soviet scholars have failed to appreciate, or at least to demonstrate that they appreciate, the phenomenal public presence that Khomeini has and why his religiously based regime can obtain such broad support and mass allegiance that adolescent males will march off to battle virtually unarmed to martyr themselves for the faith.

As the current plan of study at the Institute of Oriental Studies begins to be fulfilled, Soviet scholars not only should but will begin to address these questions.[30] However, any sort of meaningful analysis will demand that Primakov, or someone that he delegates, further expand the boundaries of acceptable analysis of the social role of religion through an even more esoteric analysis of the expansive and often inconsistent writings of Marx. Although the credulity of orthodox Marxists may be strained the resulting enhancement of the quality of the social-science analysis and hence its potential policy applicability should be sufficient compensation.

What then are the lessons of the Iranian revolution and the comparison of Soviet and American perceptions and analyses of this event? It is hard to draw conclusions that are not disheartening. Not only were both American and Soviet scholars caught unaware by the events of late 1978 and 1979 but the course of subsequent developments in Iran not only shocked and dismayed them but seems also to have eluded their analytic grasp. The Ayatullah Khomeini and his followers are simply not acting according to the patterns either Americans or Soviets expect from leaders or large, strategically situated states with economic and human resources sufficient to maintain a successful developmental strategy.

Although American and Soviet scholars proceed from very different analytic assumptions and employ conceptual frameworks that are quite distinct, nonetheless the reasons why both the Americans and Soviets have had difficulty working with Khomeini's Iran are quite probably because of perceptions that they share. Western and Soviet theories of nationalism and national consciousness are predicated on the existence of a secular society, and both schools of thought maintain that once introduced secularism should be considered an irreversible phenomenon. Although Western and Soviet analysts alike seem willing to grant the aberration of Khomeini's successfully using religious symbolism to achieve and possibly even briefly maintain political control, neither the mainstream of American nor of Soviet social thought is willing to grant that the Iranians are seeking to achieve a theocratic state as their ultimate or primary goal. Both groups of scholars see religion as a form of false consciousness, or a temporary blind which conceals from the religiously inspired activist his own deeper secular goals. Linked to this is the belief that political actors are rational and hence subject to regular and even predictable patterns.

We assume that all peoples will seek to identify with an ideology like national consciousness, which is time-bound and linked to a uniqueness based on membership in a distinct social group, as opposed to the eternal and universalistic ideology of Islam, where the reward structure is not geared to objective social categories but to the subjective performance of individual confessants striving to achieve the purity of their souls.

In the Iranian case there are some distinct challenges which must be overcome before there can be an easy fusion between religion and nationalism, unlike in the Arab case where they can overlap quite nicely. Islam was an Arab faith first, and many preexisting Arab customary practices were simply incorporated in the new faith. Arabic is the language of the Quran and the Hadith, and the major writings of the classical period. The challenge of state building in many Arab states is to develop a doctrine of nationalism that is comfortable for Muslims and Christians alike. But in the Iranian case, placing the primacy on ethnicity, on being Persian, creates real problems for the devout Muslim. To eliminate foreign loan words from the language is to strip it of the vocabulary of the faith, and many Persian customary practices coincide with Islamic proscription. Moreover, Iran is a multiethnic state with Persians living alongside Arabs and Turks, with both Sunni and Shi'i Muslims. What a complex national message it would take to hold all those disparate elements together. But a charismatic religious leader with a heavily symbolic yet doctrinally simplistic message could allow Persians and Turks, Sunnis and Shi'is, all to feel inspired.

## NOTES

1. Hamid Enayat, *Modern Islamic Political Thought* (Austin: University of Texas Press, 1982).
2. Anthony C. Smith, *Theories of Nationalism*, 2d ed. (New York: Holmes and Meier, 1983), p. 171.
3. Elie Kedourie, *Nationalism in Asia and Africa* (New York: New American Library, 1970), p. 27.
4. Ibid., p. 37.
5. R. Hrair Dekmejian, "The Anatomy of Islamic Revival: Legitimacy Crisis, Ethnic Conflict, and the Search for Islamic Alternatives," in *Religion and Politics in the Middle East,* ed. Michael Curtis (Boulder, Colo.: Westview Press, 1981), p. 38.
6. Michael Fischer, "Imam Khomeini: Four Levels of Understanding," in *Voices of Resurgent Islam,* ed. John Esposito (New York: Oxford University Press, 1983), p. 160.
7. Ibid., p. 161.
8. Ibid., and Michael Fischer, *Iran from Religious Dispute to Revolution* (Cambridge: Harvard University Press, 1980).
9. Marvin Zonis, "Iran: A Theory of Revolution from Accounts of the Revolution," *World Politics* 35 (July 1983): 586–606.
10. Ibid., p. 602.
11. Jerrold Green, *Revolution in Iran* (New York: Praeger, 1982), p. 39.
12. Ibid., p. 138.
13. One Western scholar worthy at least of an aside is Hamid Algar, of UC Berkeley. Algar, a Shi'i Muslim by conversion, was a singular voice in allowing for the possibility of a religiously inspired revolution in Iran, over a half-decade before the event. Writing in 1972 he argued that ". . . it would be harsh to predict the progressive disintegration of the political role of the ulama. Despite all the inroads of the modern age, the Iranian national consciousness still remains wedded to Shi'i Islam, and when the integrity of the nation is held to be threatened by internal autocracy and foreign hegemony protests in religious terms will be continued to be voiced, and appeals of men such as Ayatullah Khymayni to be widely heeded." Algar Hamid, "The Oppositional Role of the Ulama in Twentieth Century Iran," in *Scholars, Saints, and Sufis,* ed. Nikki Keddie (Berkeley: University of California Press, 1972), p. 225.

14. Daniel Pipes, " 'This World is Political': Islamic Revival in the Seventies," *Orbis* 24 (Spring 1980): 9–41, and *In the Path of God* (New York: Basic Books, 1983).

15. Iu. v. Bromlei, *Sovremennye problemy etnografii* (Moscow, 1981), p. 27.

16. N. Ashirov, *Islam i natsii* (Moscow, 19785), p. 6.

17. B. V. Kliashtorina, " 'Kul'tura' i 'kul'turnoe nasledie' v kontseptsiiakh iranskikh burzhuaznykh ideologov" (70e gody xxv), *Narody Azii i Afriki* 2 (1978): 95–107.

18. E. A. Doroshenko, "Nekotorye aspekty shiitsko-sunnitskikh otnoshenii," in *Islam v stranakh Blizhnego i Srednego Vostoka* (Moscow, 1982), pp. 118–19.

19. Ibid., p. 127.

20. E. M. Primakov, "Islam i protsessy obshchestvennogo razvitiia stran zarubezhnogo vostoka," *Voprosy filosofii* 8 (1980): 60–71.

21. Ibid., p. 62.

22. K. Kh. Tazhikova, "Islam and the Contemporary Islamic Struggle," *Qazaqstan ayelderi* 3 (1982): 25–26, translated in *JPRS USSR Political and Social Affairs*, 82087, 26 October 1982, pp. 1–3.

23. E. A. Doroshenko, "Shiitskoe dukhovenstvo v Irane," *Nauka i religiia* 9 (1983): 28.

24. S. W. Aliev, "Problems of Political Development of Iran," *Aziia i Afrika segodnia* 11 (1980): 15–19 trans. in *JPRS USSR Political and Social Affairs* 1092, 8 January 1981, p. 5; S. L. Agaev, *Iran. V proshlom i nastoiaschem* (Moscow, 1981); and E. A. Doroshenko, *Shiitskoe dukhovenstvo i sovremennom Irane* (Moscow, 1975).

25. S. L. Agaev, "Revoliutsionnye dvizheniia i reformy v Irane," in *Revoliutsionnyi protsess na Vostoke* (Moscow, 1982), p. 270–308.

26. E. A. Doroshenko, "Shiitskoe dukhovenstvo v Irane."

27. S. L. Agaev, "O poniatii i sushchnosti 'islamskoi revoliutsii,' " *Aziia i Afrika segodnia* 5 (1984): 29–30.

28. E. M. Primakov, *The East After the Collapse of the Colonial System* (Moscow, 1983).

29. Ibid., p. 61.

30. L. Birchanskaia, "Forum of Orientalists," *Aziia i Afrika segodnia* 10 (1983): 40–41, translated in *JPRS UPS-84-010*, 2 February 1984, p. 25.

# BIBLIOGRAPHY

## U. S. Sources

Abrahamian, Ervand. *Iran Between Two Revolutions.* Princeton: Princeton University Press, 1982.

Akhavi, Shahrough. *Religion and Politics in Contemporary Iran.* Albany, N. Y.: State University of New York Press, 1980.

Akhavi, Shahrough. "Shariati's Social Thought." In *Religion and Politics in Iran,* edited by Nikki Keddie, pp. 125–44. New Haven: Yale University Press, 1983.

Algar, Hamid. "The Oppositional Role of the Ulama in Twentieth Century Iran." In *Scholars, Saints and Sufis,* edited by Nikki Keddie, pp. 231–55. Berkeley: University of California Press, 1972.

Dekmejian, R. Hrair. "The Anatomy of Islamic Revival: Legitimacy Crisis, Ethnic Conflict, and the Search for Islamic Alternatives." In *Religion and Politics in the Middle East,* edited by Michael Curtis, pp. 31–42. Boulder, Colo.: Westview Press, 1981.

Enayat, Hamid. "Iran: Khumayni's Concept of the 'Guardianship of the Jurisconsult.' " In *Islam in the Political Process,* edited by James Piscatori, pp. 160–80. New York: Cambridge University Press, 1983.

————. *Modern Islamic Political Thought.* Austin: University of Texas Press, 1982.

Fischer, Michael. "Imam Khomeini: Four Levels of Understanding." In *Voices of Resurgent Islam,* edited by John Esposito, pp. 150–74. New York: Oxford University Press, 1983.

————. *Iran from Religious Dispute to Revolution.* Cambridge: Harvard University Press, 1980.

Gellner, Ernest. *Nations and Nationalism.* Ithaca, N. Y.: Cornell University Press, 1983.

Green, Jerrold. *Revolution in Iran.* New York: Praeger, 1982.

Keddie, Nikki. *Iran: Religion, Politics and Society.* London: Frank Cass, 1980.

————. *Roots of Revolution.* New Haven: Yale University Press, 1981.

Kedourie, Elie. *Islam in the Modern World.* New York: Holt, Rinehart and Winston, 1980.

————. *Nationalism in Asia and Africa.* New York: New American Library, 1970.

Pipes, Daniel. *In the Path of God.* New York: Basic Books, 1983.

————. " 'This World is Political': Islamic Revival in the Seventies." *Orbis* 24 (Spring 1980): 9–41.

Sachedina, Abdulaziz. "Ali Shariati: Ideologue of the Iranian Revolution." In *Voices of Resurgent Islam,* edited by John Esposito, pp. 191–214. New York: Oxford University Press, 1983.

Said, Edward. *Covering Islam.* New York: Pantheon Books, 1981.

Smith, Anthony C. *Theories of Nationalism.* 2d ed. New York: Holmes and Meier, 1983.

Zabih, Sepehr. *Iran's Revolutionary Upheaval.* San Francisco: Alchemy Books, 1979.

Zonis, Marvin. "Iran: A Theory of Revolution from Accounts of the Revolution." *World Politics* 35 (July 1983): 586–606.

## Soviet Sources

Adveev, G. I. "Prazdnovanie ramazana v sovremennom Irane." In *Iran. Istoriia i sovremennost',* pp. 132–37. Moscow, 1983.

Agaev, S. L. *Iran. V proshlom i nastoiashchem.* Moscow, 1981.

————. "O poniatii i sushchnosti 'islamskoi revoliutsii.' " *Aziia i Afrika segodnia* (1984): 27–31.

————. "Revoliutsionnye dvizheniia i reformy v Irane." In *Revoliutsionnyi protsess na Vostoke*, pp. 270–308. Moscow, 1982.

Aliev, S. W. "Problems of Political Development of Iran." *Aziia i Afrika segodnia* 11 (1980): 15–19. Translated in *JPRS USSR Political and Social Affairs* 1092, 8 January 1981, p. 5.

Arabajan, A. "Signposts of the Socio-political Development of Modern Iran." In *The Near and Middle East Countries: Economy and Policy*, pp. 14–29. Moscow, 1982.

Ashirov, N. *Islam i natsii*. Moscow, 1975.

*Bakinskii rabochii*, pp. 1–2. 7 December 1983.

Birchanskaia, L. "Forum of Orientalists." *Aziia i Afrika segodnia* 10 (1983): 40–41. Translated in *JPRS UPS-84-010*, 2 February 1984, pp. 23–28.

Bromlei, Iu. V. *Sovremennye problemy etnografii*. Moscow, 1981.

Doroshenko, E. A. "Nekotorye aspekty shiitsko-sunnitskikh otnoshenii." In *Islam v stranakh Blizhnego i Srednego Vostoka*, pp. 131–43. Moscow, 1982.

―――――. "Politicheskie traditsii shiizma i antimonarkhicheskoe dvizhenie v Irane" (1978–1979 gg). *Narody Azii i Afriki* 6 (1980): 58–66.

―――――. "Puti i formy vozdeistviia shiitskogo dukhovenstva na obshchestvenno-politicheskuiu zhizm' Irana." In *Islam v istorii narodov Vostoka*, pp. 72–85. Moscow, 1981.

―――――. *Shiitskoe dukhovenstvo i sovremennom Irane*. Moscow, 1975.

―――――. "Shiitskoe dukhovenstvo v Irane." *Nauka i religiia* 9 (1983): 54–56.

*Iran. Istoriia i kul'tura v srednie veka i novoe vremia*. Moscow, 1981.

Iurtaev, V. I. "Politicheskoe dvizhenie Iranskogo studenchestva i 'islamizatsiia' vysshie shkoly." In *Iran. Istoriia i sovremennost'*, pp. 230–43. Moscow, 1983.

Kliashtorina, B. V. " 'Kul'tura' i 'kul'turnoe nasledie' v kontseptsiiakh iranskikh burzhuaznykh ideologov" (70e gody XX v). *Narody Azii i Afriki* 2 (1978): 95–107.

Krutikhin, M. I. "Tegeranskoe vosstanie 9–12 fevralia 1979." In *Iran. Istoriia i sovremenost'*, pp. 152–70. Moscow, 1983.

Moscow in Persian to Iran 1700 GMT. 19 December 1983. *JPRS-UPS-84-005*, 18 January 1984, p. 7.

Primakov, E. M. "Islam i protsessy obshchestvennogo razvitiia stran zarubezhnogo Vostoka." *Voprosy filosofii* 8 (1980): 60–71.

―――――. *The East After the Collapse of the Colonial System*. Moscow, 1983.

Stepanianits, M. T. *Musul'manskie kontseptsii v filosofii i politike XIX–XX vv*. Moscow, 1982.

Tazhikova, K. Kh. "Islam and the Contemporary Islamic Struggle." *Qazaqstan ayelderi* 3 (1982): 25–26. Translated in *JPRS USSR Political and Social Affairs*. 82087. 26 October 1982, pp. 1–3.

*Zarubezhnyi Vostok i sovremennost'*. Vol. 2. Moscow, 1980.

# 10 Ethnic Identity in a Plural Society: A Case Study of System Breakdown in the Punjab

Surendra Chopra

More and more states are facing the struggle between the supporters of politicized ethnicity and those of antiethnic integrationists as various minority groups have started asserting their identity. The ethnic dimension of politics and political dimension of ethnicity is a problem which many states are confronted with today. The problem seems to be equally acute in traditional and in modern states; but it appears to be more acute in transitional or marginal societies. There has been an increasing tendency to "rediscover" or even invent ethnicity "for personal identification, emotional security, and communal anchorage."[1] The entrepreneurs of ethnicity have vigorously mobilized this invented ethnicity for political purpose, i.e., the struggle for power and all the concomitants of power. For this purpose even ethnic militancy is being preached by various kinds of ethnic subelites: for example, by the new middle class in Canada, Wales, Scotland, France, and Assam (India), and the landed aristocrats in Baluchistan (Pakistan) and the Indian Punjab. Socio-psychological-cultural variables, however, strengthen the politicization of ethnicity and give a fillip to its mobilizational efforts. Even those states that have long been regarded as homogenous, like Italy and France, are facing ethnic problems. The elite of the multiethnic and multinational states, their subelites, and their academia are seriously engaged in analyzing the factors contributing to core/periphery conflicts and finding solutions to these problems.

Karl Deutsch[2] is of the view that cultural differences between the core and the peripheral groups of a nation-state are gradually dissolved under the impact of industrialization, mass communication, increasing activities of national government, and, above all, individual and group mobility. There are few supporters of Deutsch's view, even though it seems to be convincing. Herbert J. Gans[3] holds a slightly similar view, while most scholars hold the view that "politicized ethnicity had increased with the increasing pace of modernization and increasing levels of modernity in different countries," as Joseph Rothschild says.[4] Walker Connor points out that "ethnic consciousness is definitely on the ascendency as political force," and that "multiethnic states of all levels of modernization have been afflicted."[5] Modernization makes people conscious of their rights but variables of modernization, such as industrialization, help shed parochialism.

In the socialist countries, such as the USSR, Czechoslovakia, and Yugoslavia, the fact that those polities are multiethnic and multinational has been recognized and institutionalized. There is a large number of other states that have faced and are facing the problem of ethnicized polities: states like Libya, Ethiopia, Nigeria, Burma, Malaysia, Thailand, Sri Lanka, Iran, Iraq, Pakistan, and India have faced demands ranging from autonomist to secessionist. Pakistan, for example, which was carved out as a result of the physical surgery of India on the basis of religion, lost more than half its population and a little less than half its territory in 1971, primarily because its response to autonomist demands was poor. It suffered the process of *atimia* at the altar of ethnicized polities. The creation of Bangladesh has proven that religion cannot serve as a basis of nationhood. Pakistan still faces problems of ethnicized polities in Baluchistan and North West Frontier Province. India, too, has been confronted with similar problems based on ethnicity and religion. On its periphery in the east, the Nagas and Mizos have been struggling for sovereign status, while Sikhs in Punjab have vacillated from carving out a majority Sikh state to autonomy, and from autonomy to secession. This study deals with the problem of the Punjab Sikhs, who are a religious minority in India, but a majority in the Punjab.

Sikhs form 2 percent of the total population of India, with a heavy concentration in Punjab and less heavy in Haryana and Delhi. There is a sprinkling of Sikh population in Jammu, Kashmir, and Himachal. Sikhs are found in small numbers all over the country, and all over the world. (There is a joke that when the first astronaut landed on the moon, he ran into a Sikh gentleman. Obviously flabbergasted, he asked, "When did you come here?" Pat came the reply, "I came here after the partition of the Indian subcontinent in 1947.") In just about three hundred years, i.e., from the beginning of the sixteenth century, when Nanak preached, to the beginning of the nineteenth century, Sikhism spread throughout northern India, and Ranjit Singh set up a powerful kingdom with its seat at Lahore, which crumbled as quickly as it was built.

There are four analytical theories of the present Punjab situation. First, that the whole problem is the handiwork of Congress (I); second, that the Sikhs are deprived politically and economically; third, that the Akalis (members of the Shromani Akali Dal, a political party of Sikhs) have resorted to the agitational approach whenever they have been out of power; and fourth, that the "Green Revolution" has given the Kulaks (landed aristocracy) immense financial power to manipulate politics. The present situation in Punjab is the result of the Green Revolution, and the Sikh demands will be examined with the fourth theory, with slight variation.

As far as the first theory is concerned, it is alleged that the extremists are the creation of the Congress (I) after it was routed in the 1977 general election and that the Congress has deliberately allowed the conditions in Punjab to worsen in order to destabilize the Akali Dal. This has been done, according to Rajni Kothari, with a view to maintaining Congress (I) supremacy in the state.[6] The Dal Khalsa, a Sikh extremist organization, is said to have been blessed by President Zail Singh and is reported to have been supported by many other Congress (I) leaders.[7] Sant Jarnail Singh Bhindranwale was also said to be the creation of Congress (I). Those who subscribe to this analysis point out that during the SGPC (Shrimoni Gurdwara Prabandhak Committee, the religious parliament of Sikhs which controls the Gurdwaras) election in 1978–79, the Congress supported the extremists, including Bhindranwale's nominees. The extremists used confrontational idiom even during those elections but the Sikh masses rejected them. There is no doubt about the Congress's involvement in the early extremist activities with a view to embarrassing the Akali government. It is maintained that when there is tension between various communities in the Punjab, the Congress gains. But to say that the Congress has been behind the extremist activity during the last three years, and that in its narrow political interest the Congress (I) had complicated the Punjab tangle, is a challenge to common sense.

But it is true that the Congress government failed to gauge the situation and arrest the deterioration, to the extent that the system completely broke down in Punjab. For almost two years there was a parallel government being run from Darbar Sahib (the Golden Temple, Amritsar) until the decision to take military action was made in June 1984. The present situation in Punjab seems to have alienated the Sikhs from the Congress and the central government. The assassination of Mrs. Indira Ghandi and the massacre of innocent people in Delhi and various other parts of the country put further strains on the Center-Akali relations. Democratic, secular, and progressive forces have suffered a grievous setback. Some argue that Congress might have lost the sympathy of many Sikhs, but it would bag more Hindu votes. Those who argue on these lines forget that the Congress had already gained the confidence of Hindu voters in 1980.[8] The 1985 elections in Punjab have clearly proved that this line of reasoning was erroneous. The Bhartiya Janta party (BJP), a communal Hindu organization, won just one seat in 1980, while in 1985 the party's tally was six seats. The ideals of secularism have suffered a serious blow, and one fails to understand how Congress gained politically— even short-term benefits. Additionally, this line of reasoning gave cover to the extremists who had been going about their nefarious activities with impunity.

The second theory needs closer examination. The Akalis maintain that there has been discrimination against the Sikhs and Punjabi.[9] They allege that Punjab has received stepmotherly treatment because of the Sikhs. They argue that Punjab's share in public investment has been negligible; that the central government's efforts to industrialize Punjab have been niggardly. Even though Punjab had been the largest contributor to the national food kitty, the conditions of the farmers were far from being enviable and returns are poor in comparison with the inputs.[10]

In this connection, it would be worthwhile to examine the idiom which the Akalis have used during the last few years. During the Punjabi Suba agitation, the word *vitkara* (discrimination) was used, while during the Talwandi agitation another word was added to the Akali agitational lexicon— *Dhaka* (injustice).[11] The present *Dharam Yudh* (holy war or religious war) has further enriched the confrontational vocabulary. Harch and Singh Longowal and Bhindranwale have been freely using the expression *zoolam* (tyranny)[12] on the Sikhs and finally *ghulami* (slavery). Bhindranwale had repeatedly used that expression portraying the position of Sikhs in the country, and the leaders of the *Dharam Yudh* agitation made use of all of these expressions. It is difficult to say what new word might be added when the Akali lose power. The Sarbat Khalsa (representative Sikh congregation), convened by the extremist elements in the Golden Temple, passed a resolution calling upon the Sikh masses to "break the shackles of slavery and strive for the concept of Raj Karega Khalsa" (Sikh World Rule).[13]

It is necessary to grasp the significance of Sikh demands against the backdrop of the idiom they have used. No concrete evidence has so far been given to prove that the Sikhs have been discriminated against. The most important illustration given by the Akalis is the reduction of the number of Sikhs in the armed forces. Some of the recent decisions stipulating area-wide representation in the armed forces seem to have hit the Sikhs, whose number in the armed forces was large in proportion to their population. That situation was the hangover of the British policy of divide and rule. The British had, for the protection of its imperial interests, declared certain sections of the Indian society as "martial" and, at the expense of others, provided various benefits to the so-called martial sections.[14]

With the change in socioeconomic conditions, certain sections of society hitherto ignored demanded a just share in the services, including the armed forces. The spread of education among tribals of northeast India, Bihar, Orissa, and Madhya Pradesh aroused their legitimate aspirations. Since justice had to be done to these sections of the society, "it is not fair to cry discrimination if justice is sought to be done to other sections."[15] The above irritant, however, has been removed by the Rajiv-Longowal Accord.[16] Another example which is usually advanced is that the creation of a Punjabi-speaking state was delayed too long.

The connotation of the second expression, *i.e.*, *"dhaka,"* is that the Sikhs were victims of injustice all around. But no concrete facts are given to support the charge. The killing of fourteen persons on 13 April 1978 in a clash between the followers of Bhindranwale and Akhand Kirtani Jatha with the Nirankari is sometimes cited as proof of discrimination against the Sikhs. But it should not be forgotten who went to the area of the Nirankari congregation, and who attacked whom. Bhindranwale and others have time and again referred to the stopping of Akalis from going to Delhi during the IX Asiad (the Asian Games held in Delhi in 1982). There is no doubt that a number of innocent persons were harrassed, but then the Akalis had declared that they would disrupt the Delhi Asiad. Finally, it is argued that all this will end when the shackles of slavery are broken. Bhindranwale never elaborated upon what he actually meant by this. An obvious explanation is the achievement of sovereign status.

The Akalis have made a number of demands, which include: (1) enactment of the All India Gurdwara Act (passed by the British government in 1925 which transferred control of the Sikh temples to the Shrimoni Gurdwara Prabhandak Committee; earlier the control was vested in hereditary priests); (2) holy city status for Amritsar; (3) installation of a high-powered transmitter at the Golden Temple for the broadcast of Shabad Kirtan (recitation of devotional music); (4) autonomous status for states;[17] (5) inclusion in Punjab, which at present is a Union Territory directly administered by the Union government, of Chandigarh and left-out Punjabi-speaking areas; (6) application of the internationally and nationally recognized principle of riparian rights for the distribution of Punjab river waters; (7) vesting of control of river headworks (which control the discharge of water into the irrigation canals) in the Punjab government; (8) grant of second-language status for Punjabi in neighboring states as provided in the Nehru formula; (9) proper representation for the Sikhs in the central services; (10) ending of forcible eviction of Punjabi peasants from Uttar Pradesh and Haryana; (11) installation of heavy industry in Punjab; and (12) end of "repression of innocent and amritdhari (baptised) Sikhs."[18]

The third analytical theory, that the Akalis have resorted to an agitational approach whenever they have been out of power, is partly true. But this analysis does not explain the reality as it excludes deeper socioeconomic causes of unrest and the factors that cause a kind of crisis of identity. It is necessary to identify causes that are responsible for making a minority or a particular section of society feel alienated.

The fourth theory is that the situation in the Punjab is the result of the "Green Revolution," which tended to make the rich richer and the poor poorer.[19] It has tended to reduce the small farmer to the position of a mere tiller, compelling him to part with his land and swell the ranks of landless farmers. The fruits of this so-called revolution have been enjoyed by barely ten percent of the agricultural communities, who own 37.08 percent of the land and have become capitalist farmers. Incidentally, it is these farmers who have benefitted from the government's policies in Punjab, i.e., subsidy on inputs, credit facilities, support price for the produce and its procurement, and cheap electricity for agricultural purposes.[20] This theory also does not explain the reality of the situation when it is mechanically applied. It does not explain why, for instance, on the call given by a Kulak, a large number of "exploited" tillers are prepared to make sacrifices. This class has been manipulated to believe that their interest lies in intracommunal cohesion rather than transcommunal class solidarity. In India, political phenomena cannot be explained merely in the terms of class conflict. Psychological and sociocultural factors, including caste, religion, and regionalism, are important variables which play a significant role in political mobilization. The basic postulate of this theory, however, continues to be important. If this theory is extended, the concept of "relative deprivations," as defined by Ted Gurr, would perhaps explain the present Punjab situation. The Sikhs are a dynamic community; they are hard-working, intelligent, and ambitious. It is the gap between their expectations and perceived capabilities vis-à-vis their economic situation, political power, and social status in relation to others[21] that is the root cause of the present Punjab imbroglio.

Sikh problems are as much psychological as they are economic and political, and it would be unfair to gloss over the causes of the psychological malaise. The identity crisis is probably the most significant dimension of the problem. The process of modernization has brought about a change in the psyche of the Sikhs: many Sikhs having started trimming their beards, or even shaving them off. Once they shave off their beards, the Sikhs lose their identity. While emphasizing the commonness between the Sikhs and Hindus, some communal Hindu elements insist on saying that "Sikhs are Hindus." The more the emphasis on commonality, the louder is the protest by the Sikh extremists. It deepens the crisis further. Invidious propaganda claims that the Hindus of Punjab "have made every effort to absorb them [Sikhs]." Worse still, it has been pointed out that the Punjabi Hindus, having failed to absorb the Sikhs, are "inciting Hindus [against Sikhs] elsewhere." Such poison is being spread through prestigious media.[22] The Sikh religious leaders had all along been talking of Muslim tyranny over their Gurus and their followers. But recently the wrath is directed against the Hindus. The military action against the extremists who had turned the holiest of the Sikh shrines into an arsenal, with every nook converted into a pillbox and every corner into a bunker, is equated with the desecration of the shrine by Ahmed Shah Abdali. Even what Muslims did to the Sikhs is attributed to the instigation of "Brahamic courtiers." Again reference is made to the "repression" of Sikhs at the hands of "Brahamical Hindus" and to Dewan Lakhpat Rai and the battle of Ghallughara. Is the history of Punjab being rewritten? It seems that the seeds of separateness sown by the British have started bearing fruit now. Before such "historians" are able to do damage beyond repair, let it be made clear that Lakhpat Rai was an employee of the Mughals, and as such he did not represent the "Brahamical Hindus." Such "historians" conveniently forget that Dewan Sawan Mal and his son Mul Raj, both Hindus, did more than any Sikh chieftain to support the Lahore Durbar. Mul Raj was the last to surrender and kept the Sikh flag aloft longer than everybody else did. They have also forgotten the role of Zorawar Singh, a Hindu general in Ranjit Singh's army, who extended the territories of the Sikh kingdom to Kashmir and Ladakh. The contributions of Dewan Mohkam Chand and Raja Dhian Singh and his brothers to the strengthening of Ranjit Singh's empire are being completely ignored.

Some writers, while overemphasizing the crisis-of-identity issue, have pointed out that this dilemma is more predominant among the urban Sikhs, popularly known as Bhapas, and that the present crisis is attributed to the role of the Bhapas.[23] The empirical evidence actually proves the opposite. Again, it is also argued that the Bhapas cannot compete with Hindu businessmen; hence they are frustrated. This again is far from being true. Bhapas are probably the shrewdest businessmen in India. They not only compete favorably with Punjabi Hindu businessmen, they have equalled even shrewder businessmen like Marwaris. Equally untenable is the diametrically opposed argument. Some argue that Bhapas "swamped" the cities of the Indian Punjab and went into business "shopkeeping, trading, seeking their fortunes in a world hitherto dominated by the Hindu community,"[24] which hit the Hindu businessmen. There is no empirical evidence to prove this point either. But the empirical evidence proves that the first argument, that Bhapas are responsible for the present crisis, is a travesty of facts and an attempt on the part of the dominant caste amongst the Sikhs to find a scapegoat. Only a few Bhapas were involved in the formation of Dal Khalsa, an extremist Sikh organization, but most of the leaders who have used confrontational idiom and advocated secessionism are of rural background and are jats (peasant caste), namely Kapur Singh, Gurtej Singh, Bhindranwale, Sukhjinder Singh, Tohra, Talwandi, Ganga Singh Dhillon, etc.; Jagjit Singh Chauhan, however, is a Rajput (warrior caste).[25] Most of the extremists, including ex-army officers, belong to the same caste.

Another reason usually advanced for the present unrest is that a number of predominantly Sikh sects, like Nirankari Mandal and Radhaswamis, have mushroomed over the years, vying with the fundamentalist saints in popularity, and that lots of offerings have been diverted from the traditional places of Sikh worship to the new sects. The cry of Panth (the Sikh community as a whole) in danger, and that the shackles of slavery have to be broken, raised by some "saints" are said to be the result of this psyche.

There may be some truth in the argument that periodic agitation by the Akalis has helped the Sikhs to keep their identity intact. Additionally, the Sikhs have maintained their identity by using three sets of symbols developed by Sikh historians and theologians. These are (a) historical symbols derived from the history of Sikh; (b) symbols which have been used to define the boundaries between Hindus and Sikhs in modern times; and (c) linguistic symbols which have been associated with the particular form of the Punjabi language written in Gurmukhi script.[26]

The Akali Dal's Sikh-are-a-nation theory, which seems to have emerged recently, is actually not new.[27] After the defeat of the Sikhs at the hands of the British, the community was pampered by the new rulers of the country. The British assiduously tried to instill in the minds of the Sikhs the idea of their separate identity. The armed forces were a training ground where an image of separate ancestry and heritage was conjured up and a consciousness created that the Sikhs had a different identity. D. Petrie, a senior officer of the Intelligence Department of the British government in India reported that

> Sikhs in the Indian Army had been studiously nationalized or encouraged to regard themselves as a totally distinct and separate nation. Their national pride had been fostered by every available means.[28]

The British historians, too, did not lag behind in highlighting the distinctiveness of the Sikhs. J. D. Cunningham, for example, points out that the history of the Sikhs is the story of evolution from "a sect to a people" under Guru Gobind Singh and "from a people to a nation" under Maharaja Ranjit Singh.[29] On the face of it the argument is not convincing. There were over 500 independent states in India. Does it mean that there were 500 nations in the country? This idea has been taken up by some Sikh writers who claim that Guru Gobind Singh transformed "a religious community into a sociopolitical nation in the Khalsa form."[30] Cunningham wrote that "in religious faith and worldly aspirations, they are wholly different from other Indians and they are bound together by a community of inward sentiment and of outward object unknown elsewhere."[31]

Contemporary foreign scholars of the Punjab situation have also added a great deal to the creating of this consciousness,[32] they have exaggerated the distinctiveness of the Sikh community with the establishment of the *Singh Sabha* movement in 1873 and the Chief Khalsa Dewan in 1902, and with the Sikhs opening their own schools and colleges the emphasis on Sikh identity continued to grow. The Chief Khalsa Dewan–run college at Amritsar did the same service for the Sikhs as Mohammedan Anglo Oriental College, Aligarh, did for the Muslims. Communalization of politics was complete when all the communities started their own colleges and schools.

The Sikh writings, by and large, tried to emphasize the distinctiveness of the Sikhs, while the Hindus, particularly the Arya Samaj, laid emphasis on the Sikhs being an integral part of the Hindus. By 1900 Sikhs, according to Kenneth W. Jones, were "less and less willing to class themselves automatically with the Hindu community."[33]

The successes achieved by the Sikhs in their fight for a separate electorate, the formation of the SGPC, the Anand Marriage Act, the creation of Punjabi Suba (Punjabi-speaking state), and the formation of an Akali-led government, strengthened the consciousness of the Sikh community and the "Raj Karega" (Sikh would rule, an expression that is part of the Sikh daily prayer) syndrome. The logical conclusion of a Sikh-are-a-nation theory is a homeland for themselves, either within the Indian Union or as a sovereign state. The mainstream of the Sikh community has so far not been in favor of a sovereign state but some of the peripheral groups like Babbar Khalsa, Dal Khalsa, All India Sikh Students Federation, National Council of Khalistan, Akal Federation, Dashmesh Regiment, and some foreigners of Indian origin have been vocalizing the demand for a sovereign Sikh state. A dismissed civil servant turned politician is of the view that Sikhs are *"sui generis* a free and sovereign people,"[34] while G. S. Tohra, formerly president of the SGPC, characterized Sikhs as "a national *sui generis* as well as a national minority."[35]

The Akali leadership has, under the cover of egalitarian democratic aims, fed the regressive instincts and overemphasized the religious and cultural differences which are politically irrelevant. It has also blunted the search for the causes of class inequalities. By overemphasizing group values and solidarity, the Akalis, particularly the extremists among them, have devalued "universalistic norms" and discouraged "a truly open and democratic opportunity system." Moreover, they have encouraged primordial instincts by relegitimating ascription.[36] The politicization of their distinctiveness has enabled the Sikhs to preserve themselves as a communal group by emphasizing their singularity and yet has also engineered and eased their modernization by transforming that communal group into a political conflict group for the modern political arena, where they have deployed "cosmopolitan modern skills and resources."[37]

Given the above psyche, some Sikh leaders have said that Sikhs had been betrayed by the majority community.[38] They point out that in 1929, as a result of protest against the Nehru Report, which did not safeguard the position of the Sikhs, the Lahore Congress Session assured the Sikhs, as well as the Muslims, that the Congress would not accept any solution that did not fully satisfy both Sikhs and Muslims.[39] Gandhi and Nehru, too, are quoted to prove their points.[40] As a result of these assurances, points out Kapur Singh, the Sikhs spurned various attractive offers made by the British and Jinnah. The British, in 1932, suggested that the Sikhs would be considered as the third independent element in India if they disassociated themselves from the Congress. Second, in 1946, the Cabinet Mission proposed that no constitution would be framed that did not have the concurrence of the Sikhs. Third, in April 1947, Jinnah offered a Sikh state, from areas east of Ravi up to Panipat, which would ultimately federate with Pakistan. Fourth, in May 1947, the British offered the Sikhs "political feet of their own."[41] All these proposals were rejected by the Sikhs in order to cast their lot with India.

**Table 10.1   Sikh Membership in Punjab Legislature**

|  | Percentage of Population | 1967 Legislative Assembly Elections | 1969 Legislative Assembly Elections |
|---|---|---|---|
| Sikhs | Variously estimated at 55 to 58% | 67.3% 70 seats including 13 Scheduled Castes | 76.9% 80 seats including 17 Scheduled Castes |
| Hindus | Variously estimated at 41 to 44% | 31.7% 33 seats including 10 Scheduled Castes | 22.1% 23 seats including 6 Scheduled Castes |
| Others | About 1% | About 1% 1 seat Muslim | 1% 1 seat Muslim |

Source:   J. C. Anand, "Mid-Term Poll in Punjab," *Political Science Review,* vol. 10, nos. 1 and 2 (January–June 1971) p. 19.

Even after making such "extreme sacrifice," the Akali leaders claim, the Sikhs were discriminated against. Longowal said in a press conference that all demands contained in the Anandpur Sahib resolution were based on promises made by Congress leaders on the eve of independence.[42] As pointed out earlier, some of the demands seem absolutely flimsy and they can be dismissed outright. The charge of discrimination against Sikhs cannot be proved. The Sikhs had all along been a thriving and privileged community all over the country, especially when one compares their position with other minorities in the country. In politics, the Sikhs have always had a large slice of the power cake in the Punjab, both under the Congress and the Akali regimes. But they want a larger share. Most of the important portfolios in the Cabinet in Punjab have been held by Sikhs. In the state legislature the Sikhs always have had more seats than their population warranted. (See Table 10.1.)

In the 1972 general election, out of a total of 104 seats, 70 were occupied by Sikhs, 28 by Hindus, 6 by others (including one Muslim), while in 1977, out of 117 seats, 82 went to Sikhs, 32 to Hindus and 3 to others (including one Muslim). In 1985 the Sikh members increased to 86 while Hindus fell to 31.[43]

In both the armed forces and civil services, the Sikh share had always been on the heavy side, in terms of population. Since most Sikhs are convinced of the hollowness of the Akali claim of discrimination in the services, it is not very strongly put forward. To debunk this claim one has only to see the civil list of Punjab. The lists recommended by the Public Service Commission for various jobs will also demonstrate the flimsy nature of the argument. Even though the Sikhs have a larger share in the services than their number would warrant, there seems to be dissatisfaction. They feel that they neither get return for their efforts in the fields of agriculture nor have enough scope for employment.

Regarding the religious demands, there are some which could be accepted without difficulty and there are others on which some thought has to be given. The question of an All India Gurdwara Act is an important matter. It has to be decided in the context of other religious minorities. With the desire to bring all the important Gurdwaras in the country under the SGPC, the Akalis have been making this demand. This proposal, however, is stoutly opposed by Sikhs controlling Gurdwaras outside Punjab. Whenever Akali Dal feels threatened about its control over Gurdwaras, even if the threat is imaginary, it reacts strongly. The Akali Dal passed a resolution on 2 August 1983 in which it called upon the Sikhs to "line up and foil the move" of Congress (I) to control the Gurdwaras. Longowal called upon the Sikhs to be prepared to protect the "democratic system of the SGPC." This angry outburst was in response to a petition filed by two persons, both Sikhs, Vikram Singh of Kothapura and Barjinder Singh of Ropar, challenging the validity of the Sikh Gurdwara Act of 1925. Longowal said that the Congress (I) "clique" had been making efforts to take over control of Gurdwaras but its "nefarious" designs had failed, and pointed out that now it wanted to "circumvent the democratic system."[44] To this the Congress MPs from Punjab reacted equally strongly, repudiating the charge.[45] The government of India has, however, agreed to consider the formulation of an All India Gurdwara Bill.[46]

Installation of a high-powered transmitter in the Golden Temple for the broadcast of *shabad kirtan* (devotional music) also needs closer scrutiny. If it has to be controlled by the All India Radio (AIR), the matter can be considered in the context of the demands of other religions. Though the broadcast of *shabad kirtan* by the AIR Jullundur had been accepted by the government, the Akalis were not satisfied. After the military action, the AIR started relaying the recitation of the holy scriptures and devotional music from Darbar Sahib. The extension of holy city status to Amritsar can also be conceded.

As far as inclusion of Chandigarh and other Punjabi-speaking areas of Himachal Pradesh and Haryana in Punjab is concerned, Chandigarh will go to Punjab, while the question of other Punjabi-speaking areas has been referred to a commission.[47] The demand to stop eviction of Sikhs from areas in Uttar Pradesh and Haryana is justified, for Sikh peasants have worked hard to improve those lands. Since these lands have started producing "gold," the greed of local farmers has been whetted and they are pressuring their government to evict the Sikh peasants.

The economic demands, however, need to be more closely examined. The Akalis have been demanding the setting up of heavy industry in Punjab. They are probably justified, for Punjab cannot for long live on agricultural prosperity. Agricultural output seems to have come very near to the optimum limit. The intersectoral linkages are probably the weakest in Punjab. Punjab produces 19 percent of the cotton grown in India but most of it is processed, spun, and woven in Maharashtra and sold back in Punjab at huge profit. This the Akalis in "their naivete call colonialism."[48] The Punjab produces 32 percent of the sugar cane, but has only six sugar mills. Most of the sugar cane is used for less remunerative purposes, like production of jaggery and inferior sugar. K. S. Gill, however, is optimistic about the increase in farm output. He is of the view that the scope for further improvement in cropping intensity, and thus yields per hectare, and cropping pattern does provide room for continued increases in agricultural production.[49] Others believe that in the respect of agricultural growth rate Punjab has reached the "plateau." Cropping intensity, in terms of percentage of net area sown to total geographical area and of yield level already achieved, points to a growth rate of no more than 2 to 3 percent. Industrialization is desired in the interest of expanding employment opportunities. Industrialization encompassing coordinated growth of large, medium, and small-scale industries can be an important element in the state's employment policy.[50] It is suggested that agro-based industries should be financed and encouraged in the rural areas, which could use agricultural waste for raw material. Apart from providing jobs to the rural unemployed, these industries could pay farmers for their agricultural produce.

Another important grievance of the Akali Dal is that Punjab's water resources are being transferred to Haryana and Rajasthan. The canal system built during the last 60 years has been more in the interest of Haryana and Rajasthan. The Akali Dal feels that the small quantity of water that is yet to be harnessed should not be allowed to be transferred to these two states because of the present and projected needs of Punjab.

The water level is falling so rapidly, and the tubewells are becoming so expensive, that the only hope lies in harnessing the river waters. According to the Indus Water Treaty which was signed on 19 September 1960, Pakistan could use the waters of the western rivers, while to India's share fell Ravi, Beas, and Sutlej.[51] Under Section 78 of the Punjab Reorganization Act, which created the present Punjab, it was stipulated that the rights and liabilities of the successor states in the Bhakra Nangal and Beas Project would be as agreed to by them. But in the absence of any such agreement within two years, they would be determined by the Union government. Since Punjab and Haryana could not agree on the question, the Union government allocated Ravi-Beas Waters as follows:

| | |
|---|---|
| Rajasthan | 8.00 MAF (million acre-feet) |
| Haryana | 3.00 MAF |
| Punjab | 3.50 MAF |
| Delhi drinking water supply | 0.20 MAF |

When the Akali government came to power in Punjab, it filed a case in the Supreme Court on 11 July 1979 challenging the validity of the central government order and Sections 78 to 80 of the Punjab Reorganization Act of 1976, which empowered the central government to make such allocations. While the case was *sub-judice,* an agreement between Punjab, Haryana, and Rajasthan was concluded, after the Congress government came to power in Punjab in 1980, which reallocated the waters and increased Punjab's share from 3.50 to 4.22 MAF.

| | |
|---|---|
| Share of Punjab | 4.22 MAF |
| Share of Haryana | 3.50 MAF |
| Share of Rajasthan | 8.60 MAF |
| Quantity earmarked for Delhi Water Supply | 0.20 MAF |
| Share of Jammu & Kashmir | 0.65 MAF |

Later the Punjab government withdrew the case.

The Akalis have subjected even the revised allocation of waters to scathing criticism, for it claims that more than 75 percent of Punjab's waters have been allocated to states that have absolutely no right to the waters. The Akalis have borrowed the principle of riparian states from international law and tried to prop up their claim on this principle. A former irrigation expert of the Punjab government points out:

> In legal terminology the "riparian rights" denote the rights of a person owning land containing or bordering on a water course or other body of water in or to its banks, bed or waters. At the common law a person owning land bordering a navigable stream owns the bed of the stream . . . and may make reasonable use of it. In relation to states this denotes identical rights of the states through or alongside the territory of the water way passes.[52]

According to the Akali stand, neither Haryana nor Rajasthan has any claim to Punjab water. Moreover, they claim that Punjab faces deficits of 6.71, 9.39, and 31.07 MAF if it wants to achieve 100 percent, 150 percent, and 200 percent irrigation intensity. The Akali claim, which has been articulated by Paul Singh Dhillon, is that even if all the water is restored to it, it would still need 15.0 MAF more to meet its minimum requirement.[53]

To prove their point the Akalis refer to the award of the Narmda Water Tribunal, which rejected Rajasthan's claim to a share in Narmda water because it was not a co-riparian state. The whole question of water has been complicated because of the absence of any compromise on allocation and the fact that water for all these years flowed to Pakistan. The Akali demand does not seem to be fully justified, for the interest of Haryana, which is a successor state, cannot be completely ignored. The intensity of irrigation of Punjab is 73 percent as against 27 percent in Haryana. The Punjab's share needs to be increased, and after meeting the legitimate demands for water in Punjab, the neighboring states of Haryana and Rajasthan could be given some water. Need it be added that the flow of some water to Haryana and Rajasthan would ultimately be in the interest of Punjab, for that would check the march of desert to the Punjab. In accordance with the Rajiv Longowal Accord, the Eradi Water Tribunal has been formed, which would verify the claims of the Punjab and Haryana.[54]

The program known as Operation Blue Star brought in its wake new problems. A large number of Sikh soldiers revolted and attacked their officers. According to the law, they were court-martialled and punished. Many extremists were rounded up and tried on charges ranging from murder, arson, and looting to waging war against the Indian government. The extremists, as expected, carried out a vigorous hate–Indira Gandhi campaign all over the world. Threats of assassination were made against Gandhi and her family and other leaders, including the Sikh President of India and various Akali leaders. Indira Gandhi's assassination, and the consequent retaliation in Delhi and other parts of the country, left many scars on the Indian body-politic. It was a most unfortunate development, for the acts of a few hundred persons and some foreign-inspired individuals stigmatized the entire Sikh community and the Delhi pogrom left many women widowed and others homeless. These developments added the following to the list of Akali demands: (1) rehabilitation of the army deserters; (2) release of Sikh detainees; (3) punishment to the persons guilty of organizing, leading, and abetting the massacre of innocent Sikhs; and (4) rehabilitation of the families that suffered in the Delhi carnage.

The Rajiv-Longowal Accord, which was the result of vigorous parleys between the Akalis and the Union government, promised to redress almost all of the major grievances of the Akalis. The Memorandum of Settlement is a very significant step in the field of ethnic crisis management in India. No other crisis has been given such importance as the Punjab crises. The Accord was formally signed by Rajiv Gandhi. Never before had a prime minister signed a document with a group of the people, although during the last thirty-five years, three such important agreements had been concluded with portions of the population. In 1951, the chief executive of the then-Hyderabad state came to an understanding with the underground communists. Nehru supported the initiative but did not permit any official to sign a formal truce. On another occasion an important confidante of Indira Gandhi formally signed an agreement with Sheikh Abdullah on behalf of the Prime Minister, which brought the Kashmir leader back into the mainstream of politics.[55]

A three-pronged strategy seems to have motivated Rajiv Gandhi to take this unprecedented step. First, he wanted to assuage the hurt feelings of the Sikhs; secondly, since the people of Punjab were fed up with the terrorist activities, he sought to isolate the terrorists, and finally he wanted to put the system back on the rails. Longowal found the Prime Minister well-intentioned and agreed to a settlement on 24 July 1985. By agreeing to this settlement, both Rajiv Gandhi and Longowal have shown immense courage and imagination. The accord paved the way for holding elections in Punjab, which could not be held along with the rest of the country. The extremists, however, characterized the accord as a "sell-out" and called on the Sikhs to boycott the elections. The purpose of the extremists presumably was to keep tension in Punjab alive and the issue internationalized. Candidates for the elections and voters were threatened. One of the authors of the accord, Longowal, was assassinated, and it appeared at that point that not many candidates would come forward and the voters would stay away. The unprecedented response of the voters, however, belied all fears. Never before did the Punjab electorate go to the polls in such large numbers, and the moderate Akalis swept the polls.

## CONCLUSION

The problem in the Punjab has been the result of a deprivation syndrome, carefully nursed by the landed aristocrats, who have enough money to maneuver the masses. They have been able to convince even the expolited members of the community that intracommunal solidarity is more important than intercommunal class consciousness. The Sikhs are hard-working, dynamic, intelligent, and ambitious. They have a sense of adventure and enterprise. The peasant class particularly is very ambitious and wants to dominate political, economic, and social life, of the state of Punjab at least. They do not seem to be satisfied with consociational democracy based on power-sharing between Sikhs and Hindus. The gap between their perception and their achievement has created a deprivation syndrome. The landed aristocracy has successfully manipulated the "Raj Karega Khalsa" syndrome of the Sikhs. The idiom of militant leaders, like Bhindranwale and some peripheral groups, had been confrontational and raucously expressed. The rhetoric had been replete with images of irreconcilability, arousing of religious fundamentalism and primordial foci of consciousness and solidarity that result in catastrophic violence and the breakdown of the system in Punjab. Bhindranwale wanted to take the Sikh community to the brave new world of Khalistan; his followers, particularly the Sikh Students Federation, continue raising the same slogan. Being too close to the scene of holocaust, it would not be wise for the present author to be dogmatic, but it is obvious that by and large the Sikhs stand alienated from the system. Faithful implementation of the Rajiv-Longowal Accord is likely to go a long way in assuaging the Sikh feelings.

Even though most of the demands of the Akalis have been conceded, and a few more are in the process of being conceded, a handful of extremists have continued to keep the crisis alive. Punjab has suffered immensely from the tension and uncertainty. In five years, business has suffered 30 percent and production (nonagricultural) 40 percent. After the 1985 elections, business and industrial activity have, however, shown some recovery.

## NOTES

1. Joseph Rothschild, *Ethnopolitics: A Conceptual Framework* (New York: Columbia University Press, 1981), p. 247.

2. Karl W. Deutsch, *Nationalism and Its Alternatives* (New York: Knopf, 1969). Also see his essay in *Nation Building,* ed. Karl W. Deutsch and William J. Foltz (New York: 1966).

3. Herbert J. Gans, "Symbolic Ethnicity: The Future of Ethnic Groups and Cultures in America," in *On the Making of Americans: Essays in Honor of Davis Riesman,* ed. Herbert J. Gans et al. (Philadelphia: University of Pennsylvania Press, 1979), pp. 193–220.

4. Rothschild, *Ethnopolitics,* p. 3.

5. Walker Connor, "Nation-Building or Nation-Destroying?" *World Politics* 24 (1971): 327. Other distinguished scholars who support this contention are Dale C. Nelson, "Ethnicity and Socioeconomic Status as Sources of Participation: The Case for Ethnic Political Culture," *American Political Science Review* 73 (1979): 1024–38; Taroslav Krejci, "Ethnic Problems in Europe," in *Contemporary Europe,* 2d ed., ed. Salvador Giner and Margaret S. Archer (London: Routledge & Kegan Paul, 1978), pp. 124–71; Malcolm Anderson, "The Renaissance of Territorial Minorities in Western Europe," *West European Politics* 1 (1978): 483–99; Milton J. Esman, "The Management of Communal Conflict," *Public Policy* 21 (1973): 49–78; and "Perspectives on Ethnic Conflict in Industrialized Societies," in *Ethnic Conflict in the Western World* (New York: Cornell University, Press, 1977), pp. 251–86.

6. See for example, Rajni Kothari and Giri Deshingkar, "Punjab: The Longer View," in *The Punjab Crisis,* Abida Saminddin, ed. (Delhi: 1985), pp. 622–626; and Rajni Kothar, "The New Face of Democracy, in *Punjab in Indian Politics: Issues and Trends,* Amarik Singh, ed. (1985), pp. 447–468. Kotharis's analysis shows complete lack of understanding of the complex Punjab situation.

7. The Dal Khalsa activists called the Akalis "impotent" and even presented glass bangles to them. Membership of Dal Khalsa is very small but it kept closely in touch with Sant Bhindranwale ("Dal Khalsa: An Organization with Little Support," *Link,* 9 May 1982, p. 10). Much of the extremist activity, including murders, hijacking, and cow slaughter, were attributed to the Dal Khalsa. After a hijacking incident, Harsimran Singh, an activist, said: "The Dal will step up its struggle against Hindu imperialism to achieve the aims of Khalistan." Cited in *Onlooker,* 1–15 May 1982.

8. Equally erroneous is the view that it was Mrs. Gandhi's gamble, referring to the swing of voters from the BJP to the Congress Party in Jammu. ("Pran Chopra, Punjab: Will Mrs. Gandhi's Gamble Pay Off?" *Sunday,* 31 July–6 August 1983.) A careful study of the voting pattern of 1980 would be rewarding.

9. Kapur, Sing, *Sachi Sakhi* (Delhi: 1979); Ajit Singh Sarhadi, *Punjabi Suba* (Delhi: 1985), and Pritam Singh Gill, *Heritage of Sikh Culture* (Jalandhar: 1975).

10. Of every 100 kg. of rice and wheat, Punjab's contribution to the Union government is 56 kg. and 63 Kg. respectively. For details, see M. V. Kamath, "Myth

and Reality," in *The Punjab Story,* Amarjit Kaur, et al. (Delhi: 1984), p. 138.

11. See Jagdev Singh Talwandi's presidential address at the Ludhiana Akali Conference held in October 1978.

12. Sant Bhindranwale had popularized this idiom. In interviews with a large number of newspapermen, he has been using this idiom. He told a journalist that Sikhs had been victims of "Hindu Zoolam." He said, "Our patience is nearly exhausted and our struggle may not be peaceful: the Gurus exhorted us to take up arms against injustice." K. C. Khanna, "Whither Punjab?" *Illustrated Weekly,* 14 April 1983.

13. *The Tribune,* 14 April 1986.

14. This also encouraged Sikh separateness. For details see Khushwant Singh, *A History of the Sikhs,* 2 vols. (Princeton: Princeton University Press, 1966), p. 119; and Teja Singh, *Gurdwara Reform Movement and the Sikh Awakening* (Jullundur: 1922), p. 21.

15. Satyapal Dang, "Sikh: Is There Discrimination," *Mainstream,* 6 (March 1982), p. 32.

16. The Triumph of Peace: Memorandum of Settlement (Chandigarh: 1985), Art. 2.1, hereafter cited as "Memorandum."

17. In order to examine this question *de novo,* the government of India appointed a former judge of the Supreme Court of India to give a report on the whole question. The commission, called the Sarkaria Commission after the name of the judge, has invited the opinions of political parties, intellectuals, academicians, and laymen.

18. *The Tribune,* 5 August 1983. In a 58-page document released on 4 August 1983 to mark the first anniversary of the Dharsmyndh Morcha Righteous War. These demands have been spelled out in details by Harchand Singh Longowal, called the Morcha Dictator.

19. For details see T. R. Sharma, "Political Implications of Green Revolution," in *Political Dynamics of Punjab,* ed. Paul Wallace and Surendra Chopra (Amritsar: 1981), pp. 264–91; Francine R. Frankel, *India's Green Revolution: Economic Gains and Political Costs* (Princeton: Princeton University Press, 1971); Jasbir Singh, *The Green Revolution in India: How Green Is It?* (Kurakshetra: 1974); M. S. Randhawa et al., *Green Revolution: A Case Study of Punjab* (Delhi: 1974); Bi lab Dasgupta, "India's Green Revolution," *Economic and Political Weekly* 12 (1977); and G. S. Bhalla, "The Impact of Green Revolution on Rural Structural Changes" (New Delhi, 1977, mimeograph).

20. *Indian Express,* 22 July 1984. See also Pritam Singh, Emerging Patterns of Punjab Economy (Bombay: 1975); Sucha Singh Gill and K. C. Singhal, "The Punjab Problem: Its Histrical Roots," *Economic and Political Weekly,* 19, no. 14, 1984.

21. Ted Gurr, *Why Rebel.*

22. Inderjit Singh, "Sikh Dilemmas," *Seminar,* April 1983, p. 34.

23. M. S. Dhami, "Changing Support Basis of Congress Politics: Analysis of Policy Strategy and Ideology, 1974–62," *Punjab Journal of Politics* 8 (1984): 98–117.

24. Anil Sari, "The Punjab Riots," *Sunday,* 16–22 May 1982, p. 35.

25. Foreign hands behind the secessionist activities, i.e., Sikhs living in the U.K., U.S. and Canada, cannot be ruled out. Though the government of India in its *White Paper* has not spelled out those and other powers instigating the secessionist activities, lest the relations with those powers be further spoiled, the links of the

foreign-based protagonists of Khalistan do give a hint.

26. Paul R. Brass, *Language, Religion and Politics in North India* (New York: Cambridge University Press, 1975), p. 171.

27. See for example, Kushwant Singh, "Genesis of the Hindu-Sikh Divide," in *The Punjab Story,* Amarjit Kaur, et al.

28. D. Petrie, *Developments in Sikh Politics 1901-1911: A Report* (Amritsar, n.d.), p. 11.

29. J. D. Cunningham, *A History of the Sikhs from the Origin of the Nation to the Battles of the Sutlej* (Delhi: 1966), p. 120.

30. J. S. Ahluwalia, "The Nirankari Mandal's Challenge to Sikhism," in *The Sikhs and Nirankari Mandal,* ed. Taran Singh and Harbans Singh (Chandigarh, n.d.), p. 25. Also see Khushwant Singh, *The Fall of the Kingdom of the Punjab* (Bombay: 1962), and *A History of the Sikhs,* 2 vols. (Bombay: 1977).

31. Cunningham, *A History,* p. 63.

32. Brass, *Language, Religion and Politics;* London Sarsfied, *Betrayal of the Sikhs* (Lahore: 1946); N. J. Barrier, "The Punjab Government on a Communal Politics, 1870-1908," *Journal of Asian Studies* 27 (1968).

33. Kenneth W. Jones, "Communalism in the Punjab: The Arya Samaj Contribution," *Journal of Asian Studies* 27 (1968): 528.

34. Kapur Singh, cited in K. R. Bombwall, "The Nation State and Ethno-Nationalism" *Punjab Journal of Politics* 7 (1983): 177.

35. Gurcharan Singh Tohra, *Federal Polity* (Amritsar, 1978), p. 6. A very forcefully argued case for the distinctiveness of the Sikh community is found in a booklet written by the first Akali Chief Minister of Punjab, Gurnam Singh, *A Unilingual Punjabi Suba and the Sikh Unrest* (New Delhi, 1960).

36. For a theoretical analysis of the role played by ethnic groups see Orlando Patterson, *Ethnic Chauvinism: The Reactionary Impulse* (New York, 1977), pp. 288-304; and "Hidden Dangers in the Ethnic Revival," *New York Times,* 20 February 1978.

37. Joseph Rothschild's views relating to the politicization of ethnicity and the dialectical process it undergoes have been used to explain the role of the Sikh leadership. Rothschild, *Ethnopolitics,* p. 3.

38. See for details Kapur Singh, *Sachi Sakhi* (Delhi: 1979).

39. *Congress Bulletin,* 9 January 1930. For details, see K. L. Tuteja, "The Sikhs and the Nehru Report," and "Sikhs and the Congress: 1930-1940," in *Political Dynamics of Punjab,* Surendra Chopra and Paulk Wallace, eds. (Amritsar: 1981), pp. 82-94.

40. See Kapur Singh, *Sachisakhi* p. 109. Also see J. S. Bhullar et al., *The Betrayal of the Sikhs* (Chandigarh, n.d.), pp. 5-12.

41. Kapur Singh, pp. 172-244.

42. *The Tribune,* 5 August 1983. Also see *White Paper on Punjab* (Delhi, 1984). The Anandpur Sahib Resolution of 1973, wanted, *inter alia,* the curtailment of the center's jurisdiction to a few subjects (like defense, foreign affairs and communications) and the preeminence of Sikhs in Punjab.

43. For details, see M. S. Dhomi. "The Punjab Assembly Elections, June 1977: An Enquiry into the Sociopolitical Dimensions of the Electoral Process," (Amritsari: 1979). Mimeograph.

44. *The Tribune,* 3 August 1983.

45. *The Tribune,* 4 August 1983.

46. *Memorandum,* Article 5.

47. *Memorandum,* Article 7.

48. M. V. Kamath, "Myth and Reality," in *The Punjab Story,* Amarjit Kaur, et al.

49. K. S. Gill, "Agricultural Development in Punjab," in *Studies in Punjab Economy,* ed. R. S. Johar and J. S. Khanna (Amritsar, 1983), pp. 1–10.

50. R. S. Johar et al., "Industrial Development of Punjab," *Studies in Punjab Economy,* pp. 171–72.

51. For details see F. J. Fowlers, "The Indo-Pakistan Water Dispute," *Yearbook of World Affairs* (1955), pp. 101–25; F. J. Berber, "The Indus Water Dispute," *Indian Yearbook of International Affairs* (1957), pp. 46–62; Hafeez-ur-Rehman Khan, "Indo-Pakistan Water Dispute," *Pakistan Horizon* 12 (December 1959): 323–36; A. N. Khosla, "Development of the Indus River System: An Engineering Approach," *India Quarterly* 14 (July–September 1958): 234–53.

52. For details see Paul Singh Dhillon, *A Tale of Two Rivers* (Chandigarh, 1982).

53. Ibid.

54. *Memorandum,* Art. 9.

55. For further details, see *Mainstream,* "The Akali Accord," 27 July 1985; A. G. Noorani, "The Punjab Accord: The Balance Sheet," in *Punjab in Indian Politics,* Amnk Singh, ed., pp. 383–389; and Pran Chopra, "The Accord," in *Punjab: The Fatal Miscalculation,* Patwant Singh and Araji Malik, eds. (Delhi: 1986), pp. 230–235.

# Contributors

John A. A. Ayoade, Professor of Political Science, University of Ibadan, Nigeria

Michael Banton, Professor of Sociology, University of Bristol, Bristol, England

Naomi Chazan, Truman Research Institute for the Advancement of Peace, Hebrew University of Jerusalem, Jerusalem, Israel

Surendra Chopra, Professor of Political Science, Guru Nanak Dev University, Amritsar, India

Marth Brill Olcott, Associate Professor of Political Science, Colgate University, Hamilton, New York

Omo Omoruyi, Professor of Political Science and Public Administration, University of Benin, Benin City, Nigeria

Elizabeth Picard, Attachée de Recherche at the Centre des Etudes et des Recherches Internationales, the Fondation Nationale des Sciences Politiques, Paris, France

Dov Ronen, Director, Africa Research Program, Center for International Affairs, Harvard University, Cambridge, Massachusetts

Donald Rothchild, Professor of Political Science, University of California, Davis, California

Joseph J. Rudolph, Professor of Political Science, University of Tulsa, Oklahoma

Dennis L Thompson, Professor of Political Science, Brigham Young University, Provo, Utah

Robert J. Thompson, Assistant Professor of Political Science, East Carolina University, Greenville, North Carolina

# Index

217